CATHERINE OF SIENA

CATHERINE OF SIENA

A Life of Passion and Purpose

ANDRÉ VAUCHEZ

TRANSLATED BY MICHAEL F. CUSATO, OFM

Paulist Press
New York / Mahwah, NJ

Cover image by Fr. Lawrence Lew, OP
Cover design by Joe Gallagher
Book design by Lynn Else

Library of Congress Cataloging-in-Publication Data

Names: Vauchez, André, author.
Title: Catherine of Siena : a life of passion and purpose / André Vauchez ; translated by Michael F. Cusato.
Other titles: Catherine de Sienne. English
Description: New York : Paulist Press, 2018. | Includes bibliographical references.
Identifiers: LCCN 2017052758 (print) | LCCN 2018004822 (ebook) | ISBN 9781587687099 (Ebook) | ISBN 9780809153411 (pbk. : alk. paper)
Subjects: LCSH: Catherine, of Siena, Saint, 1347-1380.
Classification: LCC BX4700.C4 (ebook) | LCC BX4700.C4 V3813 2018 (print) | DDC 282.092 [B] —dc23
LC record available at https://lccn.loc.gov/2017052758

ISBN 978-0-8091-5341-1 (paperback)
ISBN 978-1-58768-709-9 (e-book)

Published by Paulist Press
997 Macarthur Boulevard
Mahwah, New Jersey 07430

www.paulistpress.com

Printed and bound in the
United States of America

To Odile Redon (†),
Sofia Boesch Gajano, Alessandra Bartolomei Romagnoli,
and Gabriella Zarri
whose studies on Catherine of Siena have been extremely helpful to me;
and with heartfelt thanks
to Nicole Bériou and Sonia Porzi
for having read through this manuscript
and for having given me their advice

CONTENTS

FOREWORD

This is a book I would love to have written! André Vauchez brings to his task a remarkable comprehension of the life and thought of Catherine of Siena, weaving together the strands of content and context to present a vivid portrait of this complex woman. I know of no other published commentary that so effectively taps into the multiple sources of our knowledge of her.

Vauchez begins with a review of Catherine's life, and then proceeds with an account of her journey to canonization and the depiction of her through the Middle Ages. The heart of the work, however, is to be found in chapter 4, which deals with her personality and her mission within the Church and the Dominican order both during and after her lifetime.

One of the strengths of this study is that the author does not evade the problematic aspects of his subject, such as her sometimes naive understanding of ecclesiastical politics or her often abrasive manner. Yet he manages to show, above all, her genuine greatness as a woman, as a believer, and as an active participant in the life of her Church and her world.

This work will be enlightening to those who already know Catherine quite intimately as well as to those who are meeting her for the first time.

Suzanne Noffke, OP
author of *Catherine of Siena: The Dialogue*

CHRONOLOGY OF CATHERINE'S LIFE

1347	Probable date of the birth of Catherine Benincasa.
1348	Black Death in Italy and the West.
1352–1362	Catherine sees Christ appearing to her above the church of San Domenico in Siena.
1362	Urban V, pope in Avignon.
1364 (ca.)	Catherine joins a group of *Mantellate*, that is, of lay penitents attached to the Dominican convent in Siena. She becomes noted for her piety and her care of the sick.
1367	Urban V returns to Rome.
1368	Mystical marriage of Catherine and Christ.
1370	Urban V returns to Avignon, where he dies on December 10.
1371–1378	Gregory XI, pope in Avignon. First letters from Catherine to papal legates in Italy and to other ecclesiastical dignitaries on behalf of the reform of the Church and the crusade. Birth and development of the *famiglia*, a group of devout laity and clerics who accompany Catherine until the end of her life.
1373	Death of Saint Birgitta of Sweden (July 25). Her spiritual director, Alphonse Pecha, takes an interest in Catherine and seeks to make her the spokesperson of the reform movement in Italy.

1374	Catherine is called to the general chapter of the Dominican order in Florence, where her orthodoxy is acknowledged. Raymond of Capua is charged with becoming her spiritual director and accompanying her on her journeys. Beginning of the preaching of the crusade in Tuscany.
1375	The papacy turns to Catherine and Raymond of Capua to oppose the uprising in Florence, which established a Tuscan League in political opposition to the papacy. Missions to Pisa (during which time she received the stigmata) and to Lucca. In Siena, she is present at the execution of Niccolò di Toldo and becomes aware of the salvific mission that God has entrusted to her. First known letter (of the fifteen that are extant) to Gregory XI.
1376	Sojourn of Catherine in Avignon, where she pleads for peace between the Holy See and the Florentines; but her efforts are disavowed by the latter. She exhorts the pope to return to Rome as quickly as possible and to organize a crusade against the Turks. Gregory XI issues an interdict against Florence and, on September 13, leaves for Rome.
1377	Gregory XI enters Rome on January 17; Catherine is not present, being occupied with the foundation of the monastery of Saint Mary of the Angels in Belcaro, near Siena. Massacre in Cesena by papal troops. Catherine writes letters pleading with the pope to work for peace and love within his Papal States and to administer them better. Raymond of Capua leaves her, having been named prior of Santa Maria sopra Minerva, the Dominican convent in Rome.
1378	Catherine is commissioned by Gregory XI as his legate to the government of Florence, but negotiations drag on. Gregory dies on March 24. His successor, the Italian Urban VI (1378–89), is elected in April and makes peace with Florence in the Treaty of Tivoli on July 28. In the fall, Catherine finishes *The Dialogue*, her great spiritual and mystical treatise. In September

1378, the cardinals who were engaged in a struggle against Urban VI elect a new pope, Clement VII, during a conclave at Fondi. Catherine runs to the support of Urban VI, goes to Rome, and undertakes a flurry of correspondence with the sovereigns and political authorities of Europe and Italy to demand that they support the one whom she considers to be the only legitimate pope.

1379 Urban VI takes control of Rome and Clement sets up his court in Avignon; the beginning of the Great Western Schism. Catherine tries to organize a "council of holy ones" in Rome, a gathering of the most respected personalities on spiritual matters in the Church; but it founders, despite the support of Urban VI.

1380 Catherine's health deteriorates and she becomes more and more disappointed in Urban VI, who continues to delay in engaging in the reform of the Church that he had been recommending. Having completely ceased eating, she dies in terrible pain on April 29; and she is buried in Rome in the cemetery of Santa Maria sopra Minerva.

INTRODUCTION

Catherine of Siena (1347–80) is one of the great figures of religious history in the Middle Ages—and surely, one of the most astonishing. Indeed, this laywoman, born into rather modest circumstances, who had not had the benefit of a formal education, was proclaimed a saint by the Catholic Church in 1461 and a Doctor of the Church in 1970! During her lifetime, her contemporaries had especially been struck by her severe asceticism and by the zeal she deployed to get the papacy to return from Avignon to Rome and to persuade its leaders of the urgency to reform the Church and its religious orders. After her death, her disciples collected her letters—383 of them have come down to us that she had written, in Italian, to the most varied of recipients, from popes and kings to simple artisans—and they circulated the treatise, titled *The Dialogue*, in which she had noted the conversations that she had had with God during her visions. Catherine of Siena's chief originality rests in the fact that she was a mystic who did not hesitate to engage in politics and that she exercised an authority of the prophetic type in Church and society at a time when women were generally restricted to domestic spaces and excluded from power. And if her interventions in the unfolding of historical events in which she became involved were hardly crowned with success, she nevertheless exerted a profound influence upon the spiritual life of her time and contributed to the elaboration of a new model of female spirituality that would know a greater success in the centuries that followed.

We can, therefore, wonder why Catherine of Siena is not better known today, outside of the Dominican order, with which she was closely associated, and the circle of specialists in the religious history of the Middle Ages. The reason for this is probably because her personality can appear, at first glance, unattractive to modern sensibilities.

In the preface of the first historical biography devoted to her, which appeared in France in 1919, its author, the Danish Catholic writer Johannes Jørgensen, wrote, "To be honest, I have to admit that I had much less of an attraction for Catherine of Siena than I did for Francis of Assisi. There is, in the boisterous nature of the Sienese, a kind of overpowering spirit, an element of tyranny that put me off."[1] Similarly, in 1948, as fine a scholar of medieval mysticism as was the Frenchman Louis Canet, he began his study of the spiritual experience of the saint with the following comment: "Catherine of Siena is not particularly pleasant. The spirit, the imagination, the grace which gives Theresa of Avila so much of her charm are not to be found in Catherine. It's not that she lacks spirit but that her spirit is acerbic."[2] I subscribe all the more to these reactions since I, too, have shared them. Although the testimony of her disciples shows us to what degree they were beholden to her influence, the way in which Catherine always put herself forward ends up getting tiresome, whereas her lack of understanding with respect to certain realities of her day and her naiveté in the realm of politics and religion stir up within the most sympathetic of readers stupefaction and sometimes unease.

One must, nevertheless, move beyond this first impression and not let oneself get sidetracked by her personality, as impulsive as it was imperious. Catherine of Siena deserves, first of all, to hold our attention because she is the first woman in the Middle Ages on whom we possess a rather abundant documentation, starting with her own writings. Then, she has been the victim, throughout the centuries, of misunderstandings and hasty judgments that often impede us from understanding her. Thus, one attributes to her the merit—or the demerit, depending on one's perspective—of having persuaded the pope in Avignon to return to Rome: something that is debatable, as we will see. Or else, one has even focused—almost with a kind of voyeurism—on her "mystical states" (ecstasies, stigmatization, levitations), which she herself rarely spoke about in her writings and which constituted only the most dramatic part of her private religious experience. Today, these aspects of her life are not those that are the most interesting; and they sometimes impede us from grasping what really was the true grandeur of this exceptional woman.

This book is not the first to attempt this. It fits into a stream of studies since the 1970s and 1980s that have restored some respectability to Catherine of Siena beyond the realm of spirituality, especially in

Italy and in the Anglo-Saxon countries. Historians like Odile Redon, Sofia Boesch Gajano, Caroline Walker Bynum, Rudolph Bell, Antonio Volpato, and Gabriella Zarri; philosophers like Dominique de Courcelles; and female theologians like Giuliana Cavallini have all been interested in her from the perspective of the history of women and of female religiosity. Psychoanalysts as well, such as Ginette Raimbault and Caroline Eliacheff, have studied her.[3] Their works—and those more recently of Alessandra Bartolomei Romagnoli, Thomas Luongo, and Sonia Porzi—have profoundly renewed the way we approach this thoroughly original personality whose influence has not ceased to make itself felt, and continues to do so. Moreover, the publication of new English translations of her works now makes them more readily available.[4] All this scholarly activity—which is finally giving back to Catherine of Siena the place she deserves—is what the present volume would like to synthesize, by placing her life and her work within the history of holiness and the religious culture of the last centuries of the Middle Ages.

CHAPTER 1

A BIOGRAPHICAL SKETCH

CATHERINE—FROM SIENA TO ROME, 1347–1380

The woman known to us as Catherine of Siena was indeed born in this city. But her actual name—as it appears in the register of admissions into the *Mantellate*—is, in Latin, "Katarina Jacobi Benincasa." Her father was Jacopo di Benincasa, and her mother, Lapa di Puccio di Piagente (also called "Monna Lapa"), was the daughter of an amateur poet. In 1347, Lapa gave birth to twins who were her twenty-third and twenty-fourth children; but, of the two, only Catherine survived. Her mother devoted all her attention to Catherine, feeding her at the breast, which she had not done for her brothers and sisters, since Monna Lapa always found herself pregnant again before they were able to reach the typical age for weaning. Her date of birth is not attested to in any contemporary document since no apparatus for a civil state existed at that time and the parish registers, in which her name would have been recorded at the time of her baptism, have not come down to us. Certain historians have indeed noted that, since Catherine died on April 29, 1380, the span of her earthly existence would have been thirty-three years—a number that recalls that of the life of Christ and thus could have been the result of wanting to emphasize the saint's conformity to the one whom she calls in her writings "God-and-man." Reasonable doubt is thus in order. But perhaps we are being overly suspicious. Overall, serious criticism considers as probable, if not certain, that the date of 1347 was the year of her coming into the world. Her family lived on the Via dei Tintori, in the neighborhood of Camollia, in the Contrada dell'Oca, where numerous textile manufacturers lived. Her paternal home was in an outlying zone of the city, dominated by the convent of San Domenico, which had been built on the bluff of Camporeggi.

SIENA AT THE TIME OF CATHERINE BENINCASA

By the middle of the fourteenth century, Siena, along with Florence and Pisa, was one of the principal cities of central Italy. It had experienced real growth and expansion during the thirteenth century and, by that time, was an important commercial and banking center. Active since the end of the twelfth century at the fairs in Champagne, the Sienese, who had invented the bill of exchange, were for a long time the chief bankers of the papacy, especially after the suppression of the Templars in 1312. This flourishing city-state controlled the Via Cassia (or *Francigena*), which was used by pilgrims and travelers who were going to Rome. The city controlled a territory—its *contado*—that extended to the south all the way to the port of Talamone and to the Maremma and bordered the Papal States as far as Massa Marittima and Grosseto, which it had seized control of in the 1330s.[1] Its prosperity occurred thanks to some remarkable achievements in the field of urban planning. Built upon three hills with steep inclines that dominate the famous Piazza del Campo, with the Communal Palace flanked by a tall campanile, the Torre del Mangia, the city contained numerous seigneurial palaces in which the members of the great aristocratic families resided who possessed seigneuries out in the *contado*. Excluded from power by the communal regime, these families, however, did play a significant role in the political life of the city thanks to the abilities of their members and their prestige. The town was divided into three *terzieri*: the Città to the southwest, which corresponded to the old city; that of San Martino between the center and the southeast; and that of Camollia to the north—each of them with socially distinct neighborhoods, like that of Ovile, populated mostly with members of the working class.

Politically, Siena was a city in the Ghibelline tradition, that is to say, favorable to the empire, having defeated the Guelfs—the partisans of the Church—at the Battle of Montaperti in 1266. But this great victory was never capitalized on. Three years later, the Sienese forces were crushed by those of Florence at Colle Val d'Elsa, and the city was struck with an interdict by the papacy, with which it had maintained close financial relations and upon which the prosperity of Siena depended. After these events, the Guelf party took power in 1287 and kept it until 1355. Under this regime, government was exercised in a collegial manner by the Nine—a group of "priors" (leaders) who were members of the upper levels of the bourgeoisie, that is, the urban patricians whom the sources of the time refer to as the *Popolo grasso*—as well as by the general council of the commune. Significantly, the coat of arms of the city, which is found on the walls of the Communal Palace, consisted of a black and white shield (the commune) superimposed by a prowling lion (the *Popolo*).

In the fourteenth century, Siena was one of the greatest centers for art in Tuscany, with painters like Duccio († ca. 1320), Simone Martini († 1334 in Avignon), and the brothers Ambrogio and Pietro Lorenzetti († ca. 1348). The symbolic high point of this sumptuous period is symbolized by the Salla della Pace in the Palazzo Pubblico, where Ambrogio depicted the biblical theme of *Diligite iustitiam* (Love justice) by representing the effects of good and bad government in the city and its *contado*.[2] The increasing prosperity of the city gave the Sienese the idea of building a grandiose monument: a gigantic cathedral. The one already in existence would but serve as its transept; the main part of the new edifice would then stretch southward, forming an immense nave. Considerable work to make this a reality was begun in 1339, but it was halted in 1355 and never taken up again. Today, there remains only a forest of enormous pillars—witnesses to the aborted ambitions of the city that, by this time, was contending with Florence for predominance over Tuscany.

In fact, beginning around the middle of the fourteenth century, Siena had entered a crisis that would last until the first third of the fifteenth century. Its population, estimated at between fifty thousand and sixty thousand inhabitants around 1330, found itself reduced to less than twenty thousand after the plague of 1348—an occurrence interpreted by many contemporaries as a divine punishment. Less spectacular, though with graver consequences, was the periodic return of an epidemic that swept away entire families in the space of but a few years. One such person—a father of seven children and friend of Catherine's—lost several brothers and sisters due to this recurring disease. The Sienese chronicler Agnolo di Tura has left us a very concrete and striking account of the consequences that the epidemic had had upon the life of the city:

> No bell tolls anymore; there is no one left to mourn the dead because the survivors fear the same fate.... The father was not present at the death of his son, brother fled from brother, wife abandoned her spouse for fear of contagion because survivors feared the same fate, since this horrible sickness could be communicated just by the breath of someone who had already been stricken. The dead are buried as quickly as possible, without any solemnity; and many are simply devoured by dogs in the middle of the city streets.... And as for me, Agnolo di Tura, nicknamed "the Fat": I myself have buried five of my sons with my own hands in a single tomb.[3]

The presence of sickness and death everywhere underscored the critical role of hospitals—particularly that of Santa Maria della Scala—the control over which was the object of conflicts between the ecclesiastical and civil authorities. The same could be said about charitable institutions such as the *Misericordia*, managed at first by a confraternity that had been created in the middle of the thirteenth century by a pious layman, Andrea Gallerani, which then fell under the control of the commune in the fourteenth century. The economic crisis aggravated the social tensions and political conflicts, due to the agitation maintained by the two social groups that were excluded from power: the nobles—against whom the *Popolo grasso* had been formed and established—and the manual laborers (the *Popolo minuto*), which consisted of commoners despised by the entrepreneurs and who were liable to violent outbursts.

In 1355, the regime of the Nine and their supporters (the *Noveschi*)—the political party of the urban patricians—was overturned and replaced by that of the Twelve, which gave a significant place to the manufacturing bourgeoisie of the masters of corporations, especially those of the *Arte della Lana* (economic group that oversaw the work with and trading of wool and woolen goods, with which Catherine's family was associated).[4] Two of her brothers, Bartolo and Stefano, entered the government of the city at this time. But this new regime was soon going to face worse difficulties. It had to raise taxes to ward off, at a steep price, the great armed "companies"—those bands of mercenaries who were ravaging Tuscany at that time; and it also had to confront the food shortages that had become more frequent by organizing distributions of grain on the Campo to provide for the needs of the poorest part of the population.

At the time of these food crises, the workers in the wool sector (the *lanaioli*), whose wages were already very low, now became aware of the handicap that their exclusion from the governance of the city was causing, and they began organizing themselves in order to become involved in it through the initiative of the *Compagnia del Bruco*, which was composed of wool combers. In 1368, the government of the Twelve was overthrown, and consequently there was both a redistribution of public offices favoring the popular party and the arrival in power of a new government, called the "Reformers," which was made up of a coalition of representatives of the *Popolo grasso* and some elements of the seigneurial aristocracy. In 1371, the lower levels of the working class rose up again against the coalition in power, and the Twelve, as well as their supporters still present in the city, were now condemned to exile.

After these events, Catherine's two brothers, whom she had been able to hide in the basement of the hospital of La Scala to prevent them from being executed, definitively left for Florence, where the oldest, Bartolo, died of the plague in 1374. The same year, the decapitation of the nobleman Niccolò Salimbeni, who was accused of having plotted against the current government, triggered a veritable civil war within the city that ended in 1375 with a humiliating peace for the communal authorities. We can better understand in this context the distrustful attitude of the communal authorities vis-à-vis Catherine when, in 1376, she passed an extended period of time in the Val d'Orcia on the lands of the Salimbeni, one of the most powerful aristocratic families of the *contado* with whom she was closely associated. As to the communal regime, Catherine could in fact see nothing but its negative aspects: great political instability, violent acts against goods and persons, struggles between factions incapable of reaching a stable compromise, banishment outside the city of adversaries of the clan or the coalition currently in power (which would only incite a desire for vengeance among those who had been banned), and absence of irreproachable leaders and towering political figures. In Catherine's eyes, the meaning of the common good and of "Good Government," conceived and painted a few decades earlier in the frescoes of the Palazzo Pubblico, tended to get lost and the government of the city suffered from a great dysfunction that she never ceased deploring in her letters. Weakened by the demographic and economic crisis, torn apart by internal troubles during the years 1355–85, Siena declined in relation to her rivals—Pisa and especially Florence, into whose orbit Siena had entered by the end of the fourteenth century, before being annexed by her in the middle of the sixteenth century.

As to religious matters, in the middle of the fourteenth century, Siena—a city dedicated to the Virgin Mary ever since the victory at Montaperti with the slogan *Sena vetus civitas Virginis* (Siena, ancient city of the Virgin)—was strongly marked by the influence of the mendicant orders, exerted through their four great convents: San Francesco for the Friars Minor, San Domenico for the Friars Preacher, Sant'Agostino for the Augustinian Friars, and San Niccolò for the Carmelites. The convent of San Domenico in Camporegio, founded in 1226, towered over the birthplace of Catherine, which was located a few steps from the great fountain of Fonte Branda, constructed in the middle of the thirteenth century near one of the city gates.[5] The influence of the Dominicans was based in large measure on the success of their preaching, at least since the time of Ambrogio Sansedoni († 1287).

Sometime later the Franciscan Bernardine of Siena, born in 1380 (the year of Catherine's death), would emerge as the most prestigious personage of the town. But the religious context of the city was equally marked by the role played there by the great monasteries out in the *contado*. Some of them were centers of a reformed Benedictine monasticism: San Galgano to the west, whose Cistercian monks were involved in the activities of the *Biccherna*, that is, in the administration of municipal finances; Sant'Antimo to the east; and especially the monastery of Monte Oliveto Maggiore, founded in 1319 by Ambrogio Piccolomini, Bernardo Tolomei, and two of their companions—all descendants of the great families of the Sienese aristocracy. To this we can add the convents of the Augustinian Friars: that of Lecceto and the hermitage of San Leonardo, located in the forest a short distance from Siena called the Silva del Lago. Here, in this latter place, William Flete resided during Catherine's lifetime. Flete was an English hermit known as "the Bachelor" because he had studied theology at Oxford before going off to Italy. This religious, renowned for his holiness of life and the quality of his spiritual direction, had an enormous influence upon Catherine and on the ruling classes of Sienese society. Indeed, most of the convents and monasteries were associated with noble families (such as the Tolomei, Malavolta, Salimbeni, and Piccolomini), who supported them financially but often ended up drawing them into their circles of clientele and power.

From the thirteenth century on, Siena had become noteworthy through an important current of lay religiosity, demonstrated through the figures of Andrea Gallerani († 1250), founder of the *Misericordia*, and Pietro Pettinaio († 1289), a skilled maker of combs who during his lifetime exerted a strong spiritual influence and preached to his fellow citizens—something that earned him a mention by Dante in the *Divine Comedy*. Beginning in 1329, his feast was celebrated every year by the commune.

But the vast majority of these devout laypeople were female "penitents" and recluses who lived on the edges of the city, near the city gates or along its walls, surviving thanks to alms distributed to them by the commune and other individuals. Most of these women were widows, but a few single women could also be found among them who were too poor to be admitted into a religious community, to which a dowry was required for entry. After 1350, however, there was a marked decline in this urban reclusion as the Church showed itself increasingly hostile to these unattached—and difficult to control—penitents; and the commune no longer had the resources to support them. From having 230 penitents in 1347, their number declined to less than 50 by 1372. In Siena as elsewhere in Tuscany, the mendicant orders strove to draw in the lay penitents who, while remaining out in the world and in their families, aspired to lead a more intense religious life than simply attending Mass on Sundays. The presence of the Franciscan Third Order has been attested to in Siena since 1289, and we know of the existence of a Margaret of Siena, disciple of Saint Margaret of Cortona († 1309) and of Bonizella dei Cacciaconti, who seems to have been associated with the Sienese convent of Humiliati. In addition, a certain Bartolomea (or simply, Mea) and a Catherine († ca. 1340)—

not to be confused with our Catherine—circulated within the orbit of the Servants of Mary (or Servites), an order of converts to a life of poverty that was founded in the middle of the thirteenth century by a group of Florentine merchants. Information on these women is scarce, and it remains difficult to ascertain accurately their membership in a given religious network. However, we do know rather well the female penitents who lived within the circle of the Dominicans, known as *Mantellate*, from the fact that Catherine Benincasa—the future Saint Catherine of Siena—entered this group at the age of sixteen and kept their habit until death, as the register of their confraternity attests.

But the principal form of communal religious life for laity consisted of the penitential and charitable confraternities.[6] Quite a number of these existed and of various kinds; but those of the *Disciplinati* were the most numerous. One of the most important of these in Siena was that of the *Disciplinati di Santa Maria della Scala*, of which Catherine was a member; but there were others that were often associated with the convents of the mendicant orders. These men and women gave themselves over to the "discipline," that is, on certain occasions they flagellated themselves to atone for their sins and devoted most of their time to charitable activities (assistance to the poor and sick, to those condemned to death, and so forth) and to prayers and spiritual conversations. In some of these religious groups known as *laudesi*, poetry and songs in the vernacular were composed that were sung during processions and feasts. These confraternities were made up especially of members of the middle class (such as artisans, skilled professionals, and notaries) who found in them an environment favorable to the public expression of their devotion to Christ, the Virgin Mary, and the saints.

During the 1360s, the aspiration of these groups to a more intense religiosity was translated into a movement launched by two lay Sienese men, Giovanni Colombini († 1367) and Francesco di Mino Vincenti; they called themselves the Poor of Christ (*Poveri di Cristo*) who had renounced their wealth and worldly honors to devote themselves to penance and prayer. There was nothing new in this since, from the end of the twelfth century, Peter Valdès, the merchant from Lyons, and his disciples, the Waldensians—and then, a few decades later, Francis of Assisi—had made voluntary poverty the foundation of a life in conformity with the gospel. But such an important word had lost none of its fascination in the fourteenth century, which it continued to exert upon the most religious of the ruling classes. The purpose of this noncanonical group, referred to as *Brigata*, was to announce the word of God in a manner both ascetical and joyous, in such a way as to inspire in its hearers a renewal of religious fervor and a love for Christ the Savior. It soon attracted to itself women, beginning with the cousin of Giovanni Colombini, and then Catherine, who left her house to follow his example. It was also the inspiration for the Poor Jesuati Sisters, whose house was located near the gate of San Sano, not far from the home of Catherine of Siena. And finally, we should also mention the abbess of Santa Bonda, Pavola di Foresi, with whom Colombini had exchanged many letters. Their principal reference, other than Francis of Assisi, was Saint Jerome, the renowned sacred author and penitent who would be particularly honored in Italy during the Renaissance.

Banished from Siena in 1363 because of the ties of many among them to the aristocratic families who had supported the Nine, and after the emotion prompted by this conversion to poverty of certain noteworthy Sienese, members of the *Brigata* organized various campaigns of evangelization across Tuscany and Umbria. They cared for the sick and suffering and accompanied the remains of the dead to the cemetery while singing the praises of Jesus, especially of the Crucified ("*Viva Cristo crocifisso!*"), to whom they had a devotion. But it was not long before they attracted the suspicions of the Inquisition, which, due to their announced attachment to the poverty of Christ, tended to associate them with the Fraticelli, that is, those Franciscans or Beghini who had cut their ties with the ecclesiastical hierarchy since the pontificate of John XXII († 1334) and were denouncing the wealth and bad behavior of the clergy. At the time of Urban V's return to Italy at the end of 1367, Colombini and his followers barely escaped condemnation, and their movement only survived by agreeing to transform themselves into a structured religious order, known under the name of the Jesuates (*Ingesuati*). Catherine of Siena certainly had some kind of relationship with them during her youth, if only through the person of her sister-in-law, Lisa, a niece of Giovanni Colombini, with whom she lived when the latter had become a widow. But she never refers explicitly to him in her writings, probably out of prudence.[7] After Colombini's death, however, some members of his *Brigata* came to join her *famiglia*, that is, the group of disciples around Catherine who would soon be called the *Caterinati*.

Through Catherine's letters, we know about the existence of other religious communities in Siena to whom she seems to have been connected, especially the Benedictines of Santa Bonda, to whom

Giovanni Colombini had been very close and where he is buried, and the Augustinian "Ladies" of Santa Marta, a monastery founded in 1328 by Camilla Pannocchieschi. Catherine calls these women "truly perfect servants of God." But in the absence of adequate studies on the religious history of Siena during the fourteenth century, the nature and influence of these groups and establishments remain difficult to grasp. We are even less well informed about the secular clergy. The parish to which Catherine belonged seems to have played only a secondary role in her life, since she never refers to it. And she is similarly silent on the various bishops who succeeded each other in the episcopal see of Siena, except when denouncing their inadequacies and their vices in her *Dialogue* and letters. The religious orders themselves seem to have experienced a crisis after 1348 and especially during the 1360s and 1370s, if we can believe the Sienese chronicler Neri di Donato, who mentions the crimes committed by them at this time:

> [The religious] of Saint Augustine stabbed to death their provincial in the monastery of San Antonio and had great difficulties in Siena....In the same city, a young monk of [the monastery of] Camporeggi killed a confrère, son of the lord Cino de Montanini...and the brothers of the monastery of the Rose battled with six confrères and chased them out [of the monastery]. A violent dispute broke out among the Carthusians who were then, as a result, transferred by their general. In sum, it appears that serious conflicts have broken out everywhere and among all the religious. It followed that, no matter the order, the religious were all persecuted and reviled throughout the world.[8]

In reading the writings of Catherine, one really does have the impression that, during her time, the mendicant orders—and not even all of them—as well as the lay devotional confraternities were the chief actors in the realm of the spiritual life of the city. The link between these two groups was as strong as that of the most zealous religious among them, like the fourteenth-century Augustinian hermit friar William Flete. They were, at the same time, the spiritual directors of a lay elite who shared with them the fruits of their own spiritual experience and formed around them groups of disciples and friends who were very much engaged in the social and political life of the city.

THE YEARS OF HER CHILDHOOD AND ADOLESCENCE

Catherine's parents, Jacopo and Lapa, belonged to a circle of rather comfortable artisans and thus were members of the upper middle class. In 1362, Jacopo Benincasa and his son Bartolomeo became the owners of a workshop of dyers subcontracted by the merchants of woolen goods, the *Arte della Lana*. After the fall of the Nine in 1355, the social group to which the Benincasa family belonged ascended to power within the new regime of the Twelve and, as noted earlier, two of Catherine's brothers became responsible for some important public functions during this time. The young child, therefore, grew up in a large family very much respected and certainly not poor, even if, after the father's death in 1368 and during the grave economic and political crisis that Siena went through during the 1360s and 1370s, its situation would have rapidly declined.

We would know very little about Catherine's early years were it not for the hagiographical texts that, by definition, spend little time on this insignificant and wholly worldly period in the lives of male and female saints. She seems, nevertheless, to have been the favorite of her mother, who, she believed, had saved her from death by breastfeeding her, whereas her twin sister, Giovanna, entrusted to a nurse, did not survive for very long. And it was not long before Catherine began to distinguish herself by the keenness of her intelligence. According to her first biographer, Raymond of Capua, around the age of six or seven, while going to visit her sister Bonaventura, who lived in Vallepiatta, she claimed to have seen, on the roof of the convent of San Domenico, Christ seated upon a throne, dressed in liturgical vestments like a pope, according to a then rather current model used for representing God in the iconography of the day. Moved by this apparition, the young child hid herself in a grotto, where she spent the whole day; but one of her brothers brought her home the very same evening. It is worth noting in passing that, in the area where this vision supposedly took place, there were numerous hermitages in which recluses were living, which could have strengthened her precocious desire to flee the world and live a solitary life. In any event, there was no immediate follow-up to this episode.

We are, however, better informed on Catherine's adolescence, a period of time considered in the Middle Ages as the beginning of adulthood.[9] Having reached the age of twelve, like all daughters of high estate she was no longer permitted to leave the family home alone. She went through a period of "vanity"—of infatuation—perfectly normal for a young girl of her age, seeking to dress up in finery and attaching a lot of importance to her physical appearance, with the encouragement of her mother. She must have been pretty, since, in the collection of *Miracles* composed by one of her admirers while she was yet living, there was a male religious who, a few years later, fell in love with Catherine and, after being rebuffed, left religious life and ended up hanging himself, after trying to kill her.[10]

But in August of 1362, when she was fifteen years old, the death of her sister Bonaventura in childbirth caused her real sorrow and was the beginning of a complete conversion of life. After going to confession to Tommaso dalla Fonte, a young Dominican related to her family who, being close to her, played a key role during her youth, she then supposedly made a vow to remain a virgin. Her parents wanted to marry her off to her recently widowed brother-in-law, but she strenuously opposed this idea. Refusing the role of spouse and mother as well as a worldly life that her family wanted for her, she threw herself wholeheartedly into asceticism and devotion and cut her own hair as a sign of penance to demonstrate unmistakably her decision, which was thenceforth irrevocable, to vow her virginity to Christ. To make her change her mind, she was shut up in a tiny room located under the staircase of the house, where she lived in great solitude while taking bread and water as her only nourishment. Considered to be a crazy woman and reduced to the status of a Cinderella by her own family, she held firm and closed herself up in total silence, withdrawing into what she would call her "interior cell," that is, a place of encounter between her conscience and the presence of God. This was the first time—but not the last, because this became her usual ploy—that she would use blackmail by threatening to let herself die if she did not get her own way, as she had seen her sister Bonaventura do successfully when she had stopped eating for some time to force her unfaithful husband to lead a more correct life and to treat her better. Her obstinacy ended up forcing her father, who understood her better than her mother, to give in, and a compromise solution was found: she would be given her own room in which she could devote herself to meditation and prayer—an exceptional privilege in a bourgeois house at this time. To mend her broken health, Lapa took her for a thermal cure in Vignone in the Val d'Orcia; but she could not convince Catherine to abandon her austere life and envision the possibility of marriage.

As a result, her relationship with her mother remained very strained, even if the two women had to live together all the way up to Catherine's death, after which Lapa, an energetic and enterprising woman, lived on for a rather long time. Contrary to the hagiographical tradition that made a saint's father the chief obstacle to the religious vocation of his child—as noted, for example, in the thirteenth-century *vitae* of Francis of Assisi—in Catherine's case, it is her mother who is presented as the problem. Indeed, it is her daughter, in her letters, who never stopped reprimanding her mother for her overly possessive and materialistic love.

For the moment, the problem of Catherine's future remained uncertain. According to the social norms of the time, there was no place within the family for a young unmarried woman unless she was preparing to enter a monastery. Did Catherine entertain this possibility? We do not know for sure, but one can imagine that her aspiration to perfection could not have been satisfied by the often-lax lives of most of the nuns of her own day, even assuming that her extended family—which does not seem to have been particularly devout, since it boasted of no priest or religious other than Tommaso dalla Fonte—could have and would have given her the often considerable dowry required of postulants for a religious life in community. As for reclusion, it was henceforth considered both by the Church and by urban society as a sort of dangerous life for a woman. And if Catherine loved to withdraw into her "little cell of self-knowledge" (her favorite expression), she could not envision living alone in a grotto or a cave. We remember most about this period her rejection of her earthy family, which constituted, in her eyes, the chief obstacle to her encounter with God, as well as her rejection of the roles of spouse and mother that the society around her assigned to her.

These years of domestic enclosure and withdrawal within herself were not, however, wasted time. She spoke of learning miraculously to read and wanting to be able to pray the Divine Office. Very quickly, she attracted the attention of the neighboring Dominican convent, and she received visits from some of them, among whom was Tommaso dalla Fonte, who was the first to understand her spiritual genius and who taught her how to read from the breviary. Another was Bartolomeo Dominici, who introduced her to theology, at least at an elementary level. Other than the Bible, she probably read other works such as the *Vitae patrum*, translated into Tuscan at the beginning of the fourteenth century by the Dominican Domenico Cavalca, in which were recounted the ascetical exploits of the hermits of the deserts of Egypt and Syria and their female counterparts, such as Thaïs or Euphrosyne of Alexandria—the latter of whom disguised herself as a man in order to lead the cenobitical life with other monks.[11] This latter figure seems to have had a certain fascination for Catherine, for later on, one of her disciples, Neri di Landoccio, who had a talent for poetry, composed for her an *Istoria di santa Eufrosina* in the vernacular. Ever since the end of the thirteenth century, religious painting in Tuscany had also loved the theme of the Thebaid—this "desert garden" frequented by monks during the first centuries after Christ, the object of contemplation and a veritable "paradise for the soul."

Consistent with a model of education that would be common up to the middle of the nineteenth century in Scholastic establishments for young women directed by female religious, Catherine had not learned how to read at that time but only managed to do so later; indeed, it was believed that it was enough for a woman simply to know how to read her missal and eventually a few works of devotion or on moral conduct. Destined for the duration of her life to be subjected to the authority of a man—her father or husband—who himself had mastered writing, in the eyes of society she did not need to know or learn how to read.

To go outside into the world by herself without causing scandal—even if that world was, in the beginning, very much restricted to her neighborhood—Catherine needed to have social status. On the advice of her Dominican confessors, she found it by joining, at some time in 1364 or 1365, the female confraternity of penitents known as the *Mantellate*, which existed in the area near the Dominican convent.[12] Contrary to what had been claimed for a very long time, it was not, strictly speaking, a matter of a Third Order, such as existed among the Friars Minor since the time of the bull *Supra montem* of 1289. Among the Friars Preacher, there was, in fact, a text drawn up in 1286 by the master general, Munio de Zamora, for a group of penitents in Orvieto, in which Munio stated that he was approving their way of life, but nothing more. Beginning in 1321, this statement, in a later, more precise and revised form, served as a rule for laywomen in Siena who were affiliated with the Dominican convent of Camporeggi. This updated version of the text strengthened the link of the penitents with the Friars Preacher but did not confer upon them any institutional status within the order. One of the desired aims was to establish strict boundaries between the recluses, who were suspected of instability and sometimes of heretical deviations, and the Dominican penitents (the *vestitae*, in Latin, or the *Mantellate*, in Italian) in order to protect their reputation. It was thus, at that time, forbidden for the former (the recluses) to enter the confraternity and, for the latter (the penitents), to become recluses. Indeed, since the end of the thirteenth century, the Church had condemned the domestic monasticism (that is, a monastic life lived within one's home) that had been so important in the previous century. Nevertheless, women who wanted to live a religious life without leaving the world continued, for some time, to pay no attention to the canonical norms set out in the decretal *Periculoso* (1298), which imposed on them the cloister as well as the vows of poverty, chastity, and obedience. These consecrated laywomen had to wear a distinctive habit consisting of a white robe covered with a black mantle—hence, their name—and always to have their heads covered with a white veil.

After having endured a crisis during the 1330s, the Sienese community of *Mantellate* witnessed a certain flourishing beginning in 1352, as attested to by its register of admissions, which has survived and in which the name of Catherine Benincasa can indeed be found. When they were received into the confraternity, the *vestitae* or *pinzochere* (penitents) of Saint Dominic promised to wear the habit to the end of their lives but did not, strictly speaking, pronounce any religious vows. A married woman could not enter into the confraternity without the agreement of her husband; and if she was a widow, which was the case with most of them, she had to agree not to remarry. For a young woman like Catherine, who was less than twenty years old when she entered, the simple fact of agreeing to this constituted a public commitment to the renunciation of marriage, while the veil was meant to guarantee her physical integrity. But each of these women lived in her own home or that of her family, and they did not gather as a group but once or twice a month at the convent of San Domenico, in the *Capella delle Volte*, to listen to a sermon and to devote themselves to prayer. The rest of the time they devoted themselves to works of charity, especially the visitation of the sick and imprisoned. The community was directed by a "mistress" named by the prior of the Dominican convent and subject to the correction of the hierarchy of the order. It really seems that, in its early days, Catherine may not have been all that welcome into this confraternity—which was composed primarily of elderly widows—because of her young age, but perhaps also because her fervor surpassed by a wide measure that of her companions. She and her mother expended a great deal of effort to have her admitted there. This status of consecrated laywoman, which she maintained throughout her entire life, allowed her to develop her religious education, thanks to the sermons that she heard at the time of the gatherings and to a reading of the biblical texts that her spiritual directors translated and commented upon for her. After the death of her father in 1368, she assured her brothers that she would not claim any right over her inheritance and that she would not cost them anything in the future; but she asked them to look after the needs of her mother, with whom she remained in the family home of Fonte Branda, accompanied by Lisa—her "sister-in-law according to the flesh but her sister in Jesus Christ," as she referred to her in her letters—who had become a widow after the death of Catherine's brother Bartolo. They both became *Mantellate* afterward and thus formed a kind of small *béguinage* where daily life was apportioned among domestic activities, prayer, and reading, as well as works of mercy.

We might wonder why the Friars Preacher who were close to Catherine urged her to take the habit of the *Mantellate*, rather than to enter the Dominican nuns of Santa Caterina in Siena. Perhaps this represented a strategy aimed at reforming their female monasteries, which were experiencing a crisis at that time. Paradoxically, it was indeed easier to achieve such reform through a laywoman, like Catherine, capable of acting from the outside, rather than by urging her to enter a convent in which her desire for perfection risked provoking negative reactions among the less zealous religious. Besides, the very flexible status of the *Mantellate* gave Catherine the possibility of moving about and intervening in public life by using, for the benefit of the Church, the relationships that she had not hesitated to establish among the Tuscan aristocracy.

THE ORIGINS AND DEVELOPMENT OF HER REPUTATION FOR HOLINESS

As short as the life of Catherine of Siena may have been, it was marked by a series of events that enabled her to pass, in just a few years, from the status of a simple penitent in a neighborhood of Siena to that of a prophetess who intervened with authority in the affairs of the Church and Christianity. We see her gradually exerting herself, not in an egotistical or narcissistic way, but through an anxious quest for the truth about herself and about God. We can only understand the results of this search to the extent that this process occurred during the years of her "hidden" life—that is, during a period of seven or eight years that she spent as a recluse in her home in meditation and prayer. Since childhood, she had been gifted with visions of Christ, and from very early on, she was aware of being called to establish an intimate union with him; this had led her to make a vow of virginity and to consider herself as his "spouse." Though but a teenager, Catherine renounced the world as it was and threw herself into an interiority—her "interior cell," as she called it—that led her to experience her own nothingness and to become aware that only God could fill this emptiness and heal the evil that she discerned within her own depths—what she would refer to in her writings as her "self-worth." It is during this time that her desire arose to build within herself a "spiritual body" and to go beyond gendered identities that assigned to women in society and the Church of her day a secondary role and a status of perpetual inferiority.

Such a transformation, which occurred over a relatively short period of time and was accompanied by the healings of several illnesses that were assumed to be miraculous, earned the Sienese *Mantellata* the reputation for possessing a kind of charismatic power and to be known for her holiness of life, all of which would confer upon her actions a legitimacy of the supernatural order. In the beginning, before she was twenty years old, the young girl had distinguished herself within her own family and among her close associates, who had not failed to be struck by the rigor of the penances she was inflicting on herself. From the time of her adolescence, she had, of her own volition, pursued an eremitical version of asceticism, pushed to the extreme: the search for solitude and silence within a hostile family environment, prolonged fasts and vigils, flagellations, renunciation of every kind of comfort, and so forth.[13] These penitential practices were nothing exceptional among religious and laity smitten with the idea of perfection; they are mentioned in the *vitae* of many holy women (*mulieres religiosae*) in the thirteenth and fourteenth centuries, from Marie d'Oignies († 1213) to Margaret of Cortona († 1297) and Clare of Montefalco († 1309). In Catherine's case, perhaps the length of these practices has been exaggerated by her biographer, Raymond of Capua, so that she corresponds to the then-fashionable stereotype of female sanctity. Indeed, for men of this time, a woman was perceived first through her outward appearance, according to whether she was beautiful; and her holiness, when she achieved it, had to have a physical component to her interior piety. Thus, the female saints are almost always presented in the *Lives* of the period as ascetics, as if they had to compensate for their educational and social inferiority by an emphasis on rigor toward their bodies. It is important, however, not to reduce Catherine's asceticism to a series of hagiographical stereotypes, for even while she was still living, numerous witnesses had been struck by her strange dietary regime, which would have constituted a form of silent protest against the gluttony and excessive comfort into which many clerics and prelates of her day had fallen. From the time of her adolescence, her taste for food had already disappeared, and she soon lost the capacity to eat anything at all except for a few "herbs," that is, uncooked vegetables and a little water. We will return to this question in more depth while considering the origin and meaning of these practices.[14] But it is certain that the excesses in this regard into which she threw herself appeared improbable from a natural point of view, as it did in the eyes of her contemporaries; but they gave witness to the presence of God in her life, and her survival seemed almost to be a miracle.

In fact, during her canonization process, which took place in Venice between 1411 and 1416 and aimed to promote her cult, her closest disciples had much to say about her alimentary regime because, within the expectations of mystical experience, abstaining from food was very often mentioned as an incontestable sign of the presence of grace that was being expressed in the language of the body. Her first confessor, the Dominican Tommaso dalla Fonte, believing at first that the privations that she was imposing on herself were but caprice and fantasy on her part, reports that he had commanded her to eat normally. She obeyed but fell so seriously ill that he had to allow her to vomit up her meal, as she had had the custom of doing. Catherine confessed to the Dominican that, ever since childhood, because she had the habit of craving too much fruit, God was now punishing her for her self-pampering.

Francesco Malavolti added to this theme with respect to the last years of her life:

> All during the time I spent with this virgin, she lived only on the Holy Eucharist. But, in order to not cause any scandal,

> she sometimes took a little salad and a few other cooked vegetables and fruits and she chewed on them, but then turned away to spit them out. And if she came to swallow the least morsel, her stomach would not allow her any rest until she had vomited it back up.... Similarly, she would withdraw at a distance with one of her friends and tickle her throat with a small piece of fennel or with a goose feather, until she got rid of what she had just ingested. She called this "doing justice." As she had the custom of saying: "Let's go put this miserable sinner on trial!"[15]

In addition, she deprived herself of sleep through vigils and mortifications. She wore a rough hair shirt against her skin and an iron chain as a belt, and used a plank of wood or a bundle of straw as a pillow. She allowed herself only one or two hours of sleep each night and, at dawn, she rose to go and attend the first Mass, at which she took communion every day "with real boldness," says the author of her *Miracles*, in that laypeople were not normally permitted communion except on Sundays and the great feasts of the liturgical calendar.

For Catherine, however, asceticism was not an end in itself; indeed, she wrote about this subject several times to the female penitent Daniella da Orvieto, who was going overboard with her privations, in order to warn her against the temptation of punishing herself too cruelly:

> You should not beat down the body without discernment, but with the soft light of discretion....If I use bodily penance as a foundation [for my spiritual life], I am building the city of my soul on sand because no edifice can be built upon it. But if I build it on virtue, if I establish my foundation upon living stone—Christ, the gentle Jesus—no matter how great the edifice that I build upon Him, it will be solid and no storm will ever be able to sweep it away....Because of all the bad effects that result from it, penance therefore has to be thought of as a means.[16]

Catherine did not do penance to punish or destroy herself, but to arrive at real intimacy with God. The mastery that did not take her long to acquire with respect to physical and material realities, and the renown that her ascetical exploits earned her in wider and wider circles, allowed her to throw herself passionately and wholeheartedly into active life and into politics. That did not happen overnight, nor without difficulties. But she had the good fortune in her youth to be able to rely upon wise confessors and spiritual directors, like the Dominicans Tommaso dalla Fonte and Bartolomeo Dominici—regardless of what Raymond of Capua might have said, who took her on as a spiritual directee in 1374 and who spoke about his predecessors with a somewhat dismissive tone—and especially William Flete, an English Augustinian hermit who lived at San Leonardo al Lago near Lecceto. William, who had been the spiritual counselor of Giovanni Colombini at the end of his life and who had a real influence on the Sienese society of his time, followed Catherine's spiritual progress beginning in 1367, while she was working among the sick in the hospital of Santa Maria della Scala. She was in contact with him at a time when she was beset with temptations, and he helped her to overcome them by convincing her that sin was not an actual thing but rather a lack of love, and that it consisted of—as she would write later—a nothingness (*quella cosa che non è*), whereas God is defined as the fullness of the One who is. These Augustinian themes would have a profound influence upon her, and we find traces of them in the twenty-one letters she wrote between 1367 and 1374 to the pious women of Sienese high society and to communities of female religious in the city.

This process of spiritual growth was crowned by an event that seems to have played a determinative role in her life: her mystical marriage with Christ. According to Raymond of Capua's account of it, on Mardi Gras in either 1367 or 1368, Catherine, who was about twenty years old at the time, was in her room when she heard the voice of the Lord saying to her,

> Since you have renounced all vanity for my sake and despised the pleasures of the flesh in order to fix the pleasure of your heart in me alone, in this very moment when the people who live in your house are feasting and pampering their bodies, I have decided to celebrate with you the solemn feast of the espousal of your soul; and as I have promised it, I now want to espouse you in faith.[17]

Then she saw the Virgin Mary appear—no marriage at this time was conceivable without the agreement of parents!—accompanied by

Saint Paul and Saint Dominic, while King David played a musical accompaniment on the harp. Christ is then supposed to have handed to the maiden from his right hand a wedding ring invisible to all except to her, which the hagiographer describes as "a ring of gold studded with four pearls and topped with a diamond of indescribable beauty." However, what she saw there was a ring of flesh consisting of "the holy foreskin" that had been detached from the body of Christ at the time of his circumcision, adorned with a trickle of blood that foreshadowed the sufferings of his Passion.

This vision can seem to us to be in poor taste or even to scandalize us. It must, however, be placed within the context of the images and texts with which Catherine could have been familiar. In many churches of her day, there could indeed be seen visual representations of the mystical marriage of Saint Catherine of Alexandria. She was a young Christian woman of the early fourth century AD who, with her eloquence, held her own alongside pagan philosophers who wanted to persuade her to renounce her faith and to whom Christ, according to the *Golden Legend*, had given a ring, before she was martyred, which made her his fiancée or bride. The same scenario is found in the legend of Saint Agnes, a Roman martyr who was a victim of imperial persecutions and one for whom Catherine had a great devotion. Furthermore, as Nicole Bériou has rightly noticed, this reference to a ring figures in the ritual for the consecration of virgins when the celebrant says to the candidate, who is called to live in the hope of the consummation of her marriage on the day of her death, "Accept this ring of faith in order that you may deserve to be called the bride of Christ." There were thus, in the tradition and in Christian iconography, precedents that must have influenced Catherine when her desire to be mystically united to her Creator and Savior could be fulfilled.

This mystical marriage also carried with it another dimension, no less important. We read in the *Life* of Saint Bona († 1207)—a laywoman from Pisa who went on pilgrimage to the Holy Land and to Saint James of Compostela and who founded a monastery upon her return—that, when she visited Calvary, Christ had said to her, "You must generate sons—you, who are both my daughter and my bride." The same invitation to action in the world for the salvation of souls is found in the words that, according to Raymond of Capua, Christ had addressed to Catherine:

> My daughter, do now, with manly force and without hesitation, all that my Divine Providence will lead you to do; the arm of faith which you now possess will have you conquer by faith every adversary.[18]

From that moment forward, Catherine felt competent to leave her isolation and to mingle in the world of men and women in order to save them. In doing this, she was only following the example of Mary Magdalene, whose legend, illustrated by some Italian painters in the fourteenth century, told of how, upon her arrival in Provence, she had consecrated herself until the end of her life to an apostolate among the inhabitants of this region whom she had converted to Christianity. But Catherine also had other affinities with this same saint, whom she considered as an adopted mother and whom she proposed to the recipients of her letters as a model of love, humility, and patience:

> It is thanks to this weapon [of patience] that the gentle Magdalene no longer thought about herself; she put on Christ Crucified and never looked back towards wealth, honors, and the vanities of the world. She lost all interest and all love for the world and no longer thought about anything except how she could follow Christ. As soon as she had placed all her affection in Him and when she came to know herself, she embraced and then took the road of abnegation; she despised herself because she saw no other means of following Him and pleasing Him. She accepted to look upon herself as the vilest of creatures that exist....This is the companion that I am giving to you and whom I want you to follow, for she knows only too well the way that she can teach us.[19]

Catherine was all the more encouraged to commit herself in this way as she was receiving more and more frequent and intimate visions of Christ, to such an extent that one day, probably in 1370, she had the sensation that Jesus had pulled out of his own chest his very heart to place it within her, after which she remained as if dead for several hours, before coming back to consciousness and retaining the scarring from this event. Whether one takes this account literally or figuratively, the episode marks a decisive step in the process of union with Christ in which she had been engaged since the time of her youth, and that was impelling her to throw herself into activity of even wider breadth in the world. Indeed, for her, the graces that she had received both validated and confirmed the role—extraordinary for a laywoman of modest station—that she felt herself being called to play. Available for every kind of apostolic action, Catherine was now going to change the direction of her life. Accepting to "leave God for God"—as Saint Vincent de Paul would later write to devout women whom he was inviting to place themselves at the service of the forgotten—she decided to leave her voluntary isolation and to go back into the realm of men and women.

Catherine and William Flete, first of all, collaborated in an apostolate among the population of the city and succeeded in converting two libertine gentlemen, as well as a wealthy citizen, Nanni di Ser Vanni, who was accused of many misdeeds and murders and whom they both persuaded to go in front of the civil authorities to be judged. In addition, Catherine threw herself into action that aimed to reconcile individuals who hated each other or family clans engaged in a vendetta over several generations. This role of peacemaker was often played in the Italian cities by religious, clerics as well as laymen and -women, especially by tertiaries and penitents who used their influence over people's hearts to try to reestablish peace among leading adversaries to conclude peace accords, which were then recorded in the presence of a notary. Catherine had the gift of moving souls, and she succeeded in having spectacular results among old men hardened in their anticlericalism and their refusal to reconcile with their enemies, such as Niccolò Saracini and Giacomo Tolomei, both of whom belonged to important families of the Sienese aristocracy.[20] Nor did she hesitate similarly to reprimand the members of the clergy whose dissensions were scandalizing her, such as the pastor of Semignano, a small town of the Sienese Montagnuola, who was in open conflict with one of his confrères and to whom she wrote in the following terms:

> I am really bewildered that a man of your condition can live in such hate. God has taken you out of the world and made you an earthly angel in this life by virtue of the sacrament. And here you are concerned about what is happening in the world. I do not understand how you dare to say the holy mass; and I predict that if you persist in this hatred and in other crimes, the justice of God will come down upon

> you....I implore you to root out of your soul these vile sentiments and especially hatred. I want you to make peace! It is shameful that two such priests live as enemies. It is truly a miracle that God does not command the earth to be split open and swallow both of you up![21]

Between 1367 and 1374, while she was engaged in this peacemaking activity, Catherine, following the works of mercy that the Church was then proposing to the laity as an instrument of their sanctification, devoted herself to the sick and incarcerated of the city. Siena had experienced some terrible years, marked especially by recurring epidemics of plague and by acts of violence connected to political and social troubles. Catherine's charity toward the poor and sick, especially at the Hospital of Santa Maria della Scala, where families were abandoning their dying; at the leprosarium of San Lazzaro; and in the neighborhood in which she was living: these activities became known to all. In this way, she emerged from the obscurity that had enveloped her up to then and acquired, both locally and regionally, such renown that, in Siena and throughout Tuscany, she began to be called a *santa donna*, a holy woman. It is difficult to follow in any detail the birth and development of this *fama sanctitatis* (reputation for holiness) because of which Catherine became the spiritual counselor of a certain number of families, especially young women of the great Sienese families.

The miracles that she accomplished also helped to bring her to the attention of her fellow citizens. The news quickly spread well beyond Siena that a certain number of people whom she had been taking care of had been miraculously healed. As her first biographer, Raymond of Capua, emphasizes, Catherine had acquired from Christ a strong power of intercession that she used, initially, on behalf of her family. Thus, by her insistent prayers she had restored her mother, Monna Lapa, who had been in danger of death without having received the sacraments, and one of her brothers who was the father of eleven children. Believing her prayers had been heard, she regarded the cure of her mother from near death and her rescue from damnation a victory of spiritual love over the purely carnal love that her mother had had for her since her childhood.

In addition, by a simple touch she cured a religious sister living near her home who had been crushed by the collapse of her balcony, as well as a hermit, Santi de Rocca d'Orcia, who had been struck with the plague. He then entered her *famiglia* and later helped her to drive a demon out of the soul of someone who was possessed.[22] Some of the miracles she performed at that time had more importance than others during her lifetime. Thus, when Andrea, a *Mantellata* of Siena, had been struck by a purulent illness, so horrible and nauseating that no one wanted to go near her, Catherine devoted herself to her service and cared for her with great devotion, despite the nausea that the stench of her body stirred up in her. But the sick person, who seems to have experienced a veritable repulsion toward her caregiver, spread the rumor that Catherine had committed the sin of fornication and had lost her virginity. She continued, despite everything, to care for her with gentleness, so that Andrea ended up repenting of her gossip and proclaiming Catherine's holiness. When the devil, however, reminded Catherine of the vomiting she had experienced while caring for her, she ingested in one swallow the fouled water filled with pus that she had been using to cleanse the wounds. The next night, Christ appeared to her and said,

> "I will give you a drink which surpasses all nature and every human custom." Then, posing his right hand on the neck of the virgin and bringing her close to his side wound, he said: "Drink, my daughter, the drink from my side which will fill your soul with such sweetness that it will flow miraculously all throughout your body which you have sacrificed for me." She then saw herself placed at the conch of the fountain of life, placing the mouth of her body on the most holy wound, but even more intensely the mouth of her spirit; she sated herself with the ineffable and inexhaustible drink for a very long time, eagerly and abundantly. However, at a sign from the Lord, she pulled back from the source, both sated and yet still parched. But the satiation did not disturb her in her soul, nor the thirst make her suffer.[23]

We can wonder about the nature of the "apparitions" and "revelations" that we find throughout the *Lives* of Catherine, which were written by religious who had known her very well. Is it simply a literary device used by a hagiographer to render more explicit an interior exchange or a lived reality associated with a divine inspiration? It is not easy for the historian to present such things and to comment—but on what basis?—about their authenticity. In any case, let us note that the presence of these dialogues between a saint and Christ or the Virgin Mary is not novel and that we find them in a certain number of *Lives* from the end of the thirteenth and beginning of the fourteenth centuries, such as those of Margaret of Cortona and Clare of Montefalco. Catherine, for her part, remained very discreet about this, although, a few years earlier, the visionary and prophetess Birgitta of Sweden († 1373) had tried to give an account of the state in which she found herself when she was receiving these revelations:

> "O Most Good God," she said, "how marvelous is the way that you deal with me, for you put my body to sleep, while you awaken my soul so as to make it see, hear, and feel the things of above.... You put me to sleep whenever it pleases you: not a bodily sleep but a spiritual rest; and you awaken my soul as if from torpor so as to make it see, hear, and feel spiritually."[24]

Johannes Jørgensen, a biographer of Catherine of Siena known for his saints' *Lives* in the first half of the twentieth century, has rightly likened this text to the passage from *Ecce homo* in which Nietzsche analyzes his own experience after his visions at Sils-Maria:

> Suddenly, with a delicacy, an ineffable purity, a thing comes to be seen, comes to be heard, shakes and overcomes you to the core. One listens; one no longer seeks; one accepts without asking who is the gift-giver; a thought takes flame in a flash of lightning, imposes itself as a necessity, without allowing you the least hesitation about the form that is appropriate to express it. It is an ecstasy whose wonderful tension is relieved intermittently by waves of tears, while the step unknowingly slows down or speeds up. One feels oneself ravished beyond oneself; one is aware only of an infinity of subtle shivers and shudders which run through you down to the toes. It is a profundity of beatitude such that pain and sadness no longer seem like hostile forces but seem to be a required condition, a nuance necessarily called for by this profusion of light. One instinctively feels the great rhythms which embrace the immense spaces where forms live; the amplitude and oscillation, the need for such a broad

> rhythm seems to be the measure of such an inspiration, a kind of counterweight to its pressure, its tension. All of this, unwittingly at first, seems carried away by a gust of freedom, of power, of divinity.[25]

Later Catherine must have known many other ecstasies of this kind, sometimes accompanied by levitations in which her body, detached from the ground, seemed to float suspended in the air. After having drunk the pus of the sick woman and having drunk of the blood of Christ, she knew that she had won a definitive victory over her body, which was henceforth docile to the demands of her soul. After having gone beyond the human use of the senses and identifying herself all the more with Christ, she acquired a real power not only over the bodies of others but over their souls as well. This awareness was probably not immediate, but soon Catherine found herself confronted with a dilemma: she would have probably preferred to remain in the shadows and to enjoy the spiritual consolations that God was granting her. In the end, she was unable to resist the call that was impelling her to leave her retreat. Raymond of Capua, in his *Legenda maior*, sums up her hesitations and her final decision as a dialogue with Christ, who, even if it is a later reconstruction, summarizes well the interior debates within the Sienese *Mantellata*. Invited by Christ to go out even more from her house and to invest herself in the world, she said to him,

> I am stripped of all temporal concerns; must I now, therefore, put them on once again? I have purified my feet of earthly dust; must I now dirty them all over again?

To which Christ replies,

> Have you forgotten your ardent zeal for the salvation of souls? Do you not remember that you once wanted to put on the clothing of men to become a Friar Preacher in a foreign land? Why are you complaining? I am only thinking about having you realize the vocation to which you have been called since your childhood.

And as Catherine objected to him that she was merely an unlearned woman, he retorted,

> For me, there are neither men nor women, learned nor unlearned. Know that in these last days, the pride of the so-called learned has risen so high that I am resolved to humble them. This is why I will raise up unlearned men and women, filled with divine wisdom, who will confound their imaginary learning and, therefore, behold I have decided to send you—yes, you—out into the world.[26]

From this point forward, Catherine engaged fully in the social and religious life of her city with her great capacity for persuasion. It did not take her long to gather around herself a circle of friends and soon disciples: men and women, who aspired to share her life within the *famiglia* of which she was its *mamma*. This name, which the members of her entourage informally gave to her, really demonstrates her new role as mother, having as vocation to gather her "children" around her into an affective community united by the fascination that she exerted upon them. It should be noted that almost all these individuals belonged to a certain social elite and even, in some cases, to the urban patriciate. Unlike Giovanni Colombini, who was strongly marked by Franciscanism and whose *brigata* included not only formerly wealthy people now converted to poverty but also people of modest bearing, Catherine never went in search of the company of the poor—even if she showed them a very great devotedness—or of those on the margins of society. Daughter of an entrepreneur whom we have characterized as middle class, she shared the unfavorable prejudices of her upbringing regarding manual laborers and peasants; indeed, the majority of those who entered her circle were hostile to the "popular" regime that had assumed power in Siena between 1368 and 1371.

In gathering the *Caterinati* around her, she sought above all to create a spiritual family—the antithesis of the carnal family that had rejected her. Those who were a part of it were not breaking the bonds that tied them to their biological families, and most of them did not, in fact, share her daily life. But when they were separated from her by family or professional obligations, this did not stop them from writing to her to ask her for advice and to express their affection. More than just a community, it was more of an informal grouping whose unity was grounded in the bond of a charismatic nature that united its members to the person of Catherine and her message. In addition to former disciples of Giovanni Colombini († 1367) such as Tommaso di Guelfaccio and Santi de Terano, we also find there such nobles as Neri di Landoccio Pagliaresi, Gabriele di Davino Piccolomini, Giacomo de'Tolomei, and Francesco di Vanni Malavolta (a notary in the service of the commune and the hospital Santa Maria della Scala), Ser Vanni Savini (who had been imprisoned and stripped of all his possessions by the regime of the Reformers), as well as Cristofano di Gano Guidini (who served as her secretary). This latter individual, a notary in the neighborhood of Ovile who was one of her first disciples, is really indicative of Catherine's circle: part-time poet, he wrote *laude* in honor of the Virgin Mary and the saints, but also his *Memorie* in which he mentions Catherine with admiration. After the death of the saint, he made a Latin translation, intended for clerics, of *The Dialogue*, which she had written between 1377 and 1378, "without adding a single word," he notes in his *Memorie*; and he gave a bound copy of it to a French bishop who was passing through Siena so that he might make her work known in that country.[27]

We should also mention Stefano Maconi, a married layman and father of a family who, after having lost his entire family, entered the Carthusians upon the advice of Catherine. Maconi played an extremely key role in the collection and diffusion of Catherine's letters between the end of the fourteenth and beginning of the fifteenth centuries.

The *famiglia* also included women: in addition to her mother, Monna Lapa (who took care of the domestic needs and, in the early years, paid for the economic necessities of the little community), and her sister-in-law, Lisa (who had served as her daily secretary), Catherine had also attracted women from high society, such as Francesca, widow of Clemente di Gero, Alessia Saraceni, and Giovanna Pazzi, to whom she wrote several letters. A goodly number of her disciples joined her in a confraternity of Flagellants (*Disciplinati*) under the auspices of Christ Crucified and the Virgin Mary (*Compagnia del Crocifisso e della Vergine Maria*). They met in the basement of the hospital of Santa Maria della Scala; all were convinced, as Guidini writes, that God was renewing in her the gifts of the Holy Spirit. Thanks to the assistance given to her by the Dominicans of Siena—especially Tommaso dalla Fonte and Bartolomeo Dominici—the Augustinians William Flete and Giovanni Tantucci, and the laity of her *famiglia*, Catherine could count on networks that brought her crucial social and economic support and contributed to taking care of her needs and extending her influence.

Robert Fawtier has rightly pointed out that this first group of Catherine's was hardly clerical at all and that one could find there neither secular priests nor any nuns or female religious. This is a characteristic trait of the movement that formed around Catherine: if she preached detachment from the world, she did not counsel its abandonment.[28] In this, she is right in line with those female religious women (*mulieres religiosae*) such as Margaret of Cortona († 1297) who had distinguished themselves before her by their charitable actions and their commitment to peacemaking within their cities. Catherine, however, was noteworthy by the fact that she had very little positive feeling toward the communal regime that, almost everywhere throughout Tuscany but especially in Siena, had entered into a period of crisis after 1350 and had drifted toward a political system in which power remained in the hands of a party, a family clan, or just one man. In a letter from 1378 addressed to the priors and the gonfalonier (standard bearer) of justice in Florence, she deplored this evolution and its effects upon civic life:

> The lords become tyrants and, within the commune, their subjects nourish neither justice nor fraternal charity. Each one cheats and lies with the sole aim of serving his own interest, forgetful of the common good. Everybody is seeking power for themselves and not for the good of the city. Such are the blind: they do not see their misery because, at the same time that they believe they are getting rich, they are impoverishing themselves. And what they *think* they own slips away from them when they are expecting less. We have all seen and lived through this many times over.[29]

In fact, Catherine, who often clashed with the communal authorities of Siena and never tired of heaping reproaches upon its rulers and citizens, was not trying to become a local or civic saint. Her ambition was broader and her fate was going to be quite different. But by what right and by what title was she allowed, in this manner, to reprimand her fellow citizens and, soon, the Church authorities and other rulers? The authority on which her interventions were grounded owed nothing at all to her social position or to any mission entrusted to her by any ecclesiastical authority. Even if she maintained close relationships with male and female religious all throughout her life, she remained in the lay state to the very end. Thus, she was innovative with respect to the female saints who had lived before her time, by announcing and by witnessing through her example that access to contemplation and divine inspiration is separate from every social condition or any form of religious life. It might well be asked why Catherine had chosen not to enter a monastery. Certainly, most monasteries in Tuscany at this time held no attraction for a woman who had spiritual and moral demands as high as hers. Nonetheless, there were a few fervent communities that did exist, such as that of the Dominican sisters of Montepulciano, reformed by blessed Agnes († 1317), where Catherine had gone to visit with Raymond of Capua in 1374 and where she had managed to get her niece Eugenia admitted; or even the Augustinian convent of Santa Marta in Siena, with which she maintained very close ties. Convinced that what was essential was to encounter God—and that this is possible in every context—she remained within the logic of the Incarnation, revealed to her by Christ, by believing that real life is located in history and that it is precisely there where the supernatural destiny of human beings is being played out.

Catherine's position, however, remained fragile; and she was not immune from criticisms and suspicions. Even in Siena the young *Mantellata* was a long way from being unanimously welcomed—and some clerics believed her to be crazy. A Franciscan theologian, Lazzarino da Pisa, did not hold back from denigrating her publicly. On the suggestion of her Dominican confessors, a conversation took place between Lazzarino and Catherine; and he emerged from these talks edified by her responses, after which he repented of the bad things he had said about her—and indeed became one of her disciples.[30] Another influential person in Tuscany at the time, Giovanni dalle Celle of the abbey of Vallombrosa near Florence, wrote a letter in 1376 to a religious, Sister Domitilla, to dissuade her from following Catherine's counsel urging the nuns to leave their convent so as to participate in the crusade. But he, too, was soon charmed by her and also entered into her *famiglia*. Even among the Friars Preacher, not everyone shared the enthusiasm of her first confessors; and some of them reproached her for taking some unusual initiatives in the religious realm on her own authority instead of just limiting herself to silent withdrawal and prayer. Raymond of Capua, who was soon going to become her spiritual director and biographer, realized that before he had met her, he was rather suspicious of her because he feared that she was a phony: "I thought," he admitted in his

Legenda maior, "that we had arrived at the time of the Third Beast [of the Apocalypse] and that she was marked with the sign of the leopard who represented hypocrisy."[31]

Beginning in the years 1372–73, however, Catherine's reputation began to spread well beyond the confines of Siena; and thanks to the Dominicans in her entourage, news about her sanctity reached the highest levels of the Church. In March 1374, she received a visit from Alfonso Pecha de Vadaterra, a Spanish bishop who had resigned his office to become a hermit in Italy. He had known Birgitta of Sweden († July 23, 1373), whose confidant and protector he had become during her Roman sojourn; he was also a supporter of the reformist currents within the Church.[32] He probably came in search of Catherine to check whether she was capable of taking over the reins of that great visionary and to play, in her turn, the role of goad that had been played by the Swedish saint for the ecclesiastical hierarchy and the Christian people. He asked her to pray a "special prayer" for Gregory XI and granted her, on his part, the plenary indulgence in *articulo mortis*. Everything seems to have occurred as if the papacy, which had just lost in the person of Birgitta of Sweden a critical but unfailing support, was now experiencing the need to find a substitute for her in the person of Catherine as one who could reveal the will of God amid the vagaries of history. For the moment, it was still just a matter of a simple exploratory mission, but the report that Alfonso de Vadaterra made regarding her to Gregory XI must have been positive since she was, from this time forward, in contact with the chief representatives of the pope in Italy through epistolary exchanges relative to the crusade that the Holy See was thinking about organizing in the near future against the Turks.

However, before being able to throw herself fully into public life, it was still imperative for her to submit to an examination on the part of the Dominican order, at the time of their chapter, which was taking place in Florence in 1374. The only testimony that we have on this subject is the one transmitted to us in a collection of Catherine's miracles composed that same year by a resident of Florence, perhaps Niccolò Soderini, who was one of her most ardent supporters in this city:

> In the month of May 1374, when the general chapter of the Friars Preacher was being held, a woman wearing the habit of the penitents of Saint Dominic, whose name was Catherine,

> daughter of Jacopo of Siena, came to Florence on the command of the master general. She was twenty-seven years old and had the reputation of being a servant of God; and she was accompanied by three other female penitents of the same habit. Aware of her renown, I sought to see her and gain her friendship, with the result that she came to see me several times. Concerned with [examining] her life, I sought to learn from her the most that I could. I report here, to her honor and for my own consolation, the recollection of what little I was able to learn about her.[33]

Catherine would thus have been subject of an interrogation on the part of several theologians. She came out of it looking fine, but was placed under the direction of a Dominican, Raymond of Capua, who was henceforth going to accompany her everywhere and to serve her as spiritual director before becoming, after her death, her first biographer. It is significant that he does not tell us about her appearance before the general chapter of Florence in his *Legenda maior*. In a hagiographical text like this, whose purpose was to obtain her canonization, the mention of such an event would have made people think that the ecclesiastical hierarchy at that time had doubts about the orthodoxy of the Sienese saint. Thus, it was better not to mention it at all.

Raymond played an essential role in Catherine's life and, after her death, in the construction and diffusion of her reputation for holiness. Born into a great family of Capua, which descended from Pier della Vigna, Frederick II's chancellor, Raymond studied law in Bologna before entering the Dominicans. From 1363 to 1366, he was the spiritual director of the Dominican nuns of Montepulciano in the south of Tuscany, where he wrote the *Life* of Agnes, the reformer of this convent, who had died in 1317. He had apparently heard Catherine speak at the beginning of the 1370s, but it does not appear that he had ever met her before being assigned to her by the master general of the Dominicans in 1374, to examine her and to assist her in her actions concerning the return of the papacy to Rome, the pacification of Italy, and the crusade.

Raymond was not slow to appreciate Catherine's lively intelligence, her ability to express herself clearly, her popularity among the lay elites of the cities of Tuscany, and her talent for conciliation, which could be usefully employed in the service of the Church. In fact, these two exceptional personalities, who were complementary to each other, mutually influenced each other. Raymond was a cautionary influence on Catherine with respect to the pope and Curia as well as the pontifical legates who were the administrators of the Papal State, which extended from Bologna to the border of the Kingdom of Naples by way of Perugia, Viterbo, and Rome. In addition, he helped to broaden the horizons of the *Mantellata* from Siena by opening her eyes to the wider problems of the Church and by supporting her political-religious action. Catherine, who was, from the start, in a situation of inferiority and subordination with respect to Raymond's qualifications as theologian and jurist, speaks of him in her letters as "the father of my soul." And yet she does not hesitate to break free from his tutelage and, because of her strong personality and the intensity of her mystical life, to turn to her own benefit her dependent relationship with him in the spiritual realm. Fascinated by his spiritual daughter, the Dominican became her chief disciple; but several times, we will see her lecture her director of conscience by reproaching him for his own inertia or cowardice.

Raymond of Capua, despite some absences due to missions that the papacy had entrusted to him, was at her side until 1377, the year in which he was named prior of the Dominican convent in Rome, Santa Maria sopra Minerva. Still, he remained in touch with her through letters until her death. When the Great Schism occurred, he supported the Roman pope, Urban VI, who entrusted him with various diplomatic missions and got him elected as master general of the Order of Preachers of the Roman obedience in May 1380. After Catherine's death (at which he was not present), he devoted himself to the promotion of her sanctity by writing her *Life*, the *Legenda maior*, beginning in 1385, while he was engaged in the reform of his order, where he supported the Dominican Observant movement, both in the women's and the men's convents. He died in Nuremberg in 1399 without having been able to obtain the canonization of his spiritual daughter, which occurred only in 1461.

Armed with the approval of the ecclesiastical authorities, the Sienese *Mantellata* threw herself into an itinerant lifestyle and political-religious activity that was something new for her. She was certainly convinced that she had been called by God, like Saint Paul at the beginning of the Church, to fulfill a specific mission; but she still experienced doubts and asked Christ in her prayers for a sign, "not from unbelief but to have a more certain proof." Jesus appeared to her one day and told her to put out her hand. "I showed it to him and he took a nail, put it into the palm of my hand and he pushed against the nail with such force that my hand was pierced through."[34] A little after this vision, on April 1, 1375, Palm Sunday, in the church of Santa Cristina in the city of Pisa, Catherine received on her body the stigmata, that is, the five wounds of Christ in her two hands, both feet, and her side. Raymond of Capua was the witness of this event, and he has given us a detailed account of it:

> Suddenly, we saw her poor little body which, till then, had been prostrate, lift itself up little by little. While she was kneeling upright on her knees, she extended her arms and hands, her face glowing; after remaining really stiff for a long time, with her eyes closed, she bent over as if she had been mortally wounded. A little bit later, she came back to herself...and spoke to me very freely: "You know, Father, that by the mercy of the Lord, I now bear in my body the stigmata of Jesus."[35]

She added that she had asked the Lord for the grace—which he granted her—to ensure that the scars that luminous rays had cut into her body would not be apparent to others and instead would remain invisible. After this, she fell into a deep sleep to such a degree that her disciples feared that she might be dead. A few days later, she regained her strength and responded to Raymond, who had been asking her about her sufferings: "These wounds no longer give me any pain; on the contrary, they give me strength and give consolation to my body: I know this because from the pain now comes consolation."[36]

These invisible stigmata have been the cause of a great deal of ink to be spilled; and in the fifteenth century, they were the occasion of endless controversies and conflicts between the Dominicans and Franciscans—the latter believing that their founder, Francis of Assisi, was the first stigmatic in history and that this phenomenon could not be repeated.[37] I will not get into this debate here; but it is significant that Catherine did not make her stigmata known in any of her writings, something that tends to support their authenticity. Without seeking to say anything more categorically on the reality of these events, we will note, along with Chiara Frugoni, that the suffering that Catherine talks about in the *Legenda maior* was of an exclusively spiritual nature: it was a matter of interior pain that attests to her interior adhesion—"in her heart"—to the Passion of Christ. Moreover, in the same account Catherine really emphasizes that the fact that having shared in the sufferings of Christ has made her stronger and more robust.[38] For her, the stigmata—or, if one believes them to be scarcely plausible, an identification with Christ through the experience of pain—constitutes the supernatural seal that authenticates her historic mission. There was no contradiction in her eyes between her action and her contemplation; the intensity of her relationship with Christ goes hand in hand with the depth of her temporal activities. Far from taking pleasure in the search for mystical states that enabled her to taste the joy of union with God, she felt herself impelled to become more deeply involved in the world and no longer experienced any doubt about it. Fully conscious of being able to and having to exercise a ministry in society and in the Church, she would now engage in an impassioned action aiming to inaugurate—or rather, restore—an order that was in conformity with the will of God for the human race. Indeed, after the general chapter of Florence, Catherine returned to Siena, which was then being struck with a violent epidemic. She devoted herself, without counting the cost, to those afflicted with the plague, and she did indeed fall ill herself. She nonetheless survived and was encouraged to throw herself into an itinerant ministry thanks to a vision of the Virgin Mary, who revealed to her that she would yet save many people in the future. From that time on, Catherine's actions revolved around three principal concerns: the return of the papacy to Rome, the crusade, and the reform of the Church.

CATHERINE'S TRIPARTITE PROGRAM: ROME, CRUSADE, REFORM

During the years before her entrance into public life beyond Siena, Catherine had had the time to develop within her Dominican entourage the main themes of what was going to become her program of action: namely, to get the papacy to return to Rome; to prepare a new crusade for converting the unbelievers (by first restoring peace within Christianity); and to inspire a reform of the Church, which had to begin with the ecclesiastical hierarchy and clergy. None of these ideas was original. Since her arrival in Rome for the Jubilee of 1350, Birgitta of Sweden—a prophetess who carried the hopes of certain devout circles and who would be canonized in 1391—had never ceased reminding the popes of her day, in particular Urban V (1362–70), that it was urgent for them, and for the good of the Church, to leave Avignon.[39] The work of bringing peace to the Papal States—achieved through military means since 1350 by Cardinal Albornoz, who had brought the towns and feudal lands of the Patrimony of Saint Peter into submission—now allowed the pope to return to Rome in 1367. The Romans, for whom the prolonged absence of the Curia had had negative economic consequences, and the Italians, who were increasingly disenchanted with the overweening presence of the French within the papal administration, were really delighted with this news. However, Urban V soon ran into unexpected resistance, in Rome itself as well as in the Papal States. And since, in the meantime, the war between France and England had started up again with renewed vigor, he decided in 1370 to return once again to Avignon in the hope of being able to tamp down the conflict. Birgitta did not hold back her reproaches, even warning him of deadly consequences should he leave Italian soil. Urban V did in fact die less than three months after he had returned to the banks of the Rhone. On January 15, 1371, the Sacred College chose as pope his nephew, Cardinal Pierre-Roger de Beaufort, who took the name of Gregory XI and would reign until March 1378. This succession of events had important repercussions in Italy, where the renewed departure of the papacy had been perceived as a betrayal and incited very strong reactions. Since that time, Catherine—who had sent him at least fifteen letters—and her Dominican entourage began to pressure the new pope—who, it was assumed, had the intention of organizing a crusade—to lead it himself in order to make good on his laudable intentions.

For Catherine of Siena as for Birgitta of Sweden before her, the return of the papacy to Rome was the sine qua non condition for restoring peace to Italy and for reforming the Church. This could only come from the pope, the Vicar of Christ and even "Christ-on-earth," to use her favorite expression. But she was convinced the pope could only play the primary role, which was his alone in the Church, if he actually resided in the city of which he was the bishop. On this point, Catherine did not hesitate to oppose the canonists who had been repeating for over a century that "Rome is wherever the pope is" (*ubi papa, ibi Roma*) and who were emphasizing the universalistic dimension of the successor of Peter, whose power was not tied to the place of his residence. In fact, over the course of the thirteenth century, six popes, especially those who were French, had never come to Rome during their pontificates and nineteen of them had passed most of their reigns far away from the Eternal City.[40] Reacting against this tendency, Boniface VIII (1294–1303) had reasserted the centrality of Rome within the Church by instituting, in the year 1300, the Jubilee or Holy Year, during which time all those who came to Rome on pilgrimage and visited its major basilicas could obtain the plenary indulgence reserved up to that time to pilgrims and crusaders who had gone to Jerusalem. But after the violent conflict that pitted him against Philip IV the Fair, the chief problem for the papacy became its relations with France; and a whole series of practical and political considerations led him to settle in the Rhone Valley, which then constituted the center of gravity for Christianity and, beginning with John XXII (1316–34), to settle within Avignon itself. The war between France and England, called the Hundred Years War, necessitated the prolonged stay of the papacy north of the Alps even more, to the extent that from that time on it dedicated all its efforts toward reestablishing peace between the two principal kingdoms of Christianity.

Until around 1340, Italians in general were not particularly bothered by this situation, since they considered it to be temporary. But once it became obvious that the sojourn in Avignon risked being prolonged indefinitely, recriminations began to increase. They were expressed with such vehemence because the Papal States themselves were being administered by French or Spanish rectors who often maintained deplorable relations with those being served. People accused them of demonstrating arrogance and greed in the exercise of their functions. Catherine of Siena became the spokesperson for this discontent and for their hopes in the new pope, Gregory XI, who was elected in 1370 at the age of forty-one. Gregory's intellectual and moral abilities were unquestionable. For Catherine as for many Christians in Italy, it went without saying that the papacy had to return to Rome as soon as possible so as to free itself from the political clutches of France, to regain its authority, and to restore order once again within its domains. In the end, the "exile" in Avignon, so eloquently denounced by Dante, Ptolemy of Lucca, and Petrarch, had effectively idealized the role of the pope and engendered hopes that his return to the Eternal City would be followed by a time of peace and religious renewal.[41]

From the beginning of his pontificate, Gregory XI understood that he would have to leave Avignon with the Curia. Impeded by the war between France and England, however, and then by the threats of war with Florence emerging in 1374, he kept postponing his return to Italy, which was already being opposed by most of the cardinals. At the end of the day, however, the status quo turned out to be increasingly more dangerous for the Holy See, since Florence was being tempted to take advantage of the void that was widening in central Italy because of the pope's absence. Moreover, with the collapse of the authority of the Holy Roman Emperor during the 1330s and 1340s and the proliferation of conflicts both between and within the Italian cities, the myth of Rome began exercising a renewed fascination on people's minds. Cola di Rienzo had felt it when, between 1347 and 1354, he tried to make of the Eternal City an indisputable political point of reference by gathering into the city a kind of assembly of all the cities and states in Italy. The whole enterprise eventually collapsed, and the fall of this orator severely discredited the plausibility of the idea. But, whether moved by faith, as were Birgitta and Catherine, or by a feeling that we might call "prehumanist," by the year 1370, the conviction that Rome was the center of the Christian world was widespread in Italian civic circles; and it was becoming imperative for the papacy to respond to their expectations.

The other major theme found in Catherine's letters is that of the crusade. This might seem surprising given the failure and death of Saint Louis IX near Tunis in 1270. Indeed, the time of the great overseas expeditions seemed to be a thing of the past. However, this concern had remained in people's minds; and, perhaps, never were so many projects for crusades undertaken as in the fourteenth and fifteenth centuries, even if most of them were never realized. In her writings, Catherine of Siena fell back on the traditional justifications to justify the urgency of this "Great Passage" that was going to open the way for the liberation of the Holy Places in Palestine that were unjustly being held by the Muslims. Christians, she writes, have to avenge the honor of God, which has been mocked by the Saracens, to recover "what belongs to us" (*cio che è nostro*) and to agree to spill their own blood for Christ, who had sacrificed himself for them on the cross. For this is what was key for her: in her letters, Catherine never mentions the military operations that will be necessary to reach this goal, nor does she propose any plan for conquest. In her eyes, as Alphonse Dupront writes concerning the participants in the First Crusade,

> Holy war, whatever the result, ends in glory. But what is surely its true measure is that it is a battle for peace in the final war of wars. Its paroxysmal power has its virtue only in God and for the peace of God. It is lived as the dramatic unfolding of the final combat, after which God will appear: his order and the fullness of this order, where evil and war will no longer exist.[42]

By way of the crusade, Catherine was pursuing a double aim: to reestablish peace in a West that was torn asunder by fratricidal conflicts and to provide unbelievers with the possibility of salvation. She underscores several times that Jesus on the cross has poured out his blood for all people, who are also all called to "enter into his open side," to use an expression she was particularly fond of. For her, the crusade represented, above all, a grand missionary endeavor whose principal aim was the conversion of unbelievers. But it would also have beneficial repercussions for Christians as well, to the extent that the reestablishment of peace constituted an indispensable preliminary to any overseas expedition. For Catherine, the crusade was indeed going to deliver the West from the violence to which the great mercenary bands were contributing. Thus, she wrote to John Hawkwood—an English warrior who, along with his troops, was sowing violence and chaos throughout Tuscany—a letter that she had Raymond of Capua deliver directly into his own hands, in which she urged him to transfer his military activities to the East for the greater good of Christianity. Only the pope, "the Vicar of the Crucified Lamb," had the power to organize this crusade, which Catherine characterizes as a "Holy and Sweet Passage," for he alone personified on this earth the suffering Christ, and every good Christian should be responding to his call by accepting to bear witness to his faith, even unto martyrdom if necessary.

As Claudio Leonardi has rightly emphasized, Catherine believed that, given the generalized corruption that existed in the clergy—and at a time when national churches subject to the authority of monarchical powers were beginning to emerge—the papacy remained the sole historical figure in the Church, and the only entity through which it could continue to exist as a social body.[43] In this, she was not in agreement with the distinction that a number of her contemporaries, from Marsilius of Padua to Wycliffe, established between an institutional Church, carnal and corrupt, and a spiritual Church (the only true Church) that consisted of a small number of the just whose names were known only to God, even if her writings do contain an echo of this same dualistic conception when she opposes the "true servants of God"—on whom the pope should be relying—to the clergy and laity who were Christian in name only. From this perspective, the return of the papacy to Rome and the consequent organization of a crusade were the only means of safeguarding the universality of the ecclesial body, which is not tied to any one country or people—the criticism obviously aimed at France, which was suspected of wanting to place the papacy under its authority—but to one episcopal and apostolic see alone: that of Rome. Having accomplished this, the first obligation of the pope would be to address, without any further delay, the reform of the Church, which had become urgent. Catherine was indeed well aware of the egregious abuses that had been developing within the Church, particularly among the clergy. But she also disapproved of the civil authorities who wanted to do violence to the clergy to force them to change their behavior. In her eyes, only a papacy become Roman once again and renewed by a spirit of love and peace (which would be expressed in a universal crusade) could save the Church and the world from damnation.

These ideas—in particular, the connection made by Catherine between crusade and reform—were nothing new. We find it already among popes at the beginning of the thirteenth century (Innocent III and Honorius III) who had tried to reinvigorate Christianity by uniting diverse components around a project that would allow Christians to reconquer the Holy Land and convert the Muslims. The religion of Islam indeed forbade, under pain of death, to question the Qur'an and Mohammed, thus rendering impossible any kind of debate around religious issues. Therefore, it was imperative firstly to break by force the military power of the Islamic world in order to compel the unbelievers to listen to the message of Christian preachers. However, the crusade, contrary to what we often imagine, did not consist only in the taking up of arms and using them, if necessary, against the enemies of the faith. Christians who engaged in this venture were considered penitents and had to lead an austere life to merit the plenary indulgence promised to the crusaders. The "Overseas Passage" took on its meaning only if it was also accompanied, among those who were making the journey, by a more moral and pious life. During the last centuries of the Middle Ages, this theoretical bond between crusade and reform slipped into the background in the sermons of the clergy. But it did remain deeply anchored in hearts and minds; and we find it at the root of all religious movements that aspired to an individual and collective renewal of Christianity.

It is really along these lines that we need to position Catherine of Siena when she was urging her contemporaries not to remain spiritually asleep, but to engage in the battle for the love of Christ the Savior by first accepting to spill their blood for him, as he himself had done for the salvation of the human race.

Just after his election, Catherine had written to Gregory XI to place herself at his service and to promote the cause of the crusade she held so dearly in her heart. Her letter probably received a favorable welcome, for, in September 1370, she wrote to Cardinal Pierre d'Estaing, pontifical legate in Italy, in intimate terms, urging him to preach the crusade there. She reiterated her plan in October of the same year, asking him to try to bring peace to Perugia, which was refusing to submit to papal authority.[44]

Sometime later, she wrote to Bérenger, abbot of Lezat and papal envoy in Tuscany, who had asked her what needed to be done in order to heal the ills of the Church and to question her about his own sins.[45] In 1376, responding to a series of questions that the abbot had posed to her in a previous letter, she sent an important missive in which she specifically itemized the evils that, she believed, it was imperative to attack in order to promote the reform of the Church:

> I believe and I think before God that it would be good to reform two things which are corrupting the Church of God. The first is a too great affection and concern (of prelates) for their own relatives. It is necessary, once and for all, that these abuses end. The second is too much softness based on too much mercy. Unfortunately, it is due to not having corrected its members that these have become corrupted. But there are three detestable vices which Christ abhors the most: the impurity, the avarice, and the pride which holds sway in the Bride of Christ, that is to say among the prelates, who care

> for nothing but seeking after delights, honors, and riches. They are ensuring that the demons of Hell carry away souls and they pay no heed because they themselves have become wolves and sellers of the divine grace.

And Catherine concludes this brutal analysis with the following statement:

> It seems to me that, in order to rebuild the Church from top to bottom, it would be necessary for us to raze it to its foundations. Yes, I want you to really do everything that is in your power to destroy it; there is no other way.[46]

Was it really, in her eyes, a matter of destroying it? Certainly not the Church itself, which she talks about as "a flower which will never die," but rather a political-religious system that ended up smothering spiritual life under the weight of legalism and the administration of temporal goods.

Such exchanges of letters assume that Catherine was by this time well known at the Curia and benefited from a positive image in the eyes of high ecclesiastical dignitaries, since they did not hesitate to ask her for advice, even if they were nevertheless going to be frightened by its radicalism.

For their part, political leaders, at least in Italy, were often quite mesmerized by Catherine. We know of a letter written in Latin that Elizabeth of Bavaria, spouse of Marco Visconti, son of the Duke of Milan, sent to her in order to recommend to her prayers their daughter, the little four-year-old Anne, who was gravely ill.[47] Many other epistolary exchanges with the Visconti family followed, as witnessed by the letter that Catherine gave in person to Duke Bernabò, who had sent her a message through his ambassadors.[48] Soon, Catherine was in relationship—most often through the mediation of women—with the great families of the Italian communal and seigneurial aristocracy: the Salimbeni, Tolomei, Gambacorta, Soderini, Strozzi, Belforte, Trinci, and many others as well; with the court of Naples (Queen Joanna I, the Caracciolo, and the Mileto); as well as with other jurists, doctors, and notaries from whom she recruited several of her secretaries. To each one she gave spiritual and moral counsel as well as encouragement when they found themselves in difficulties, such as the noblewoman

Pentella of Naples, who complained to her that she was being mistreated by her husband, who had taken her slave as his mistress; or the monk from Rome who wanted to leave his hermit's cell in order to go and visit the Purgatory of Saint Patrick in Ireland—which she strongly counseled against.[49] By all accounts, Catherine's reputation for holiness was by this time widespread, and the great of this world, lay as well as ecclesiastical, were not shy about writing to her.

CATHERINE'S INVOLVEMENT IN THE POLITICS OF ITALY: HER SOJOURN IN AVIGNON

Raymond of Capua had been named lector in the Dominican convent of Siena and was delegated by the pope to check on Catherine's "activities on behalf of peace, the crusade and other affairs of the Roman Church," according to the mission laid out for him by the pope.[50] Thus, accompanied by Raymond, Catherine now threw herself into active politics. We see her writing to Italian princes such as Bernabò Visconti, master of Lombardy, or influential men of state like the Florentine Niccolò Soderini, gonfalonier of justice in 1371 and Prior of the Arts in 1375, in order to convince them to suspend hostilities between their fellow Christians and to stop fighting against the papal policy with this in mind.

Her interventions in the realm of diplomacy were motivated most of all by the desire to gather adherents to the crusade that Gregory XI had officially launched in 1373, which had no chance of being realized unless the main political leaders in Italy agreed to participate in it. Soon, Gregory XI also charged Catherine and Raymond of Capua to turn the leaders of the great Tuscan cities away from an alliance with Florence, which, since 1370, had adopted a political posture hostile to the papacy and seemed to want to challenge the territorial integrity of the Papal States. From this time forward, Catherine totally engaged in Italian politics to defend the Church's cause while, at the same time, she warned the pope about the abuses of his local representatives with respect to governance and the administration of justice and reprimanded certain prelates and rectors about their bad conduct. For her, the papacy had every right to possess towns and territories and to wield a kind of political power there, in addition to its spiritual authority. Nevertheless, the successor of Peter ought not to conduct himself within these states like any mere territorial prince, since the Church was established by vocation to be a place in which peace, gentleness, and love had to reign. With Gregory XI being by temperament hesitant and timid, Catherine had to urge him firmly several times not to hesitate to shed his own blood, in the manner of his Divine Master, by coming to Rome without an entourage or military protection to resume his rightful place there once again and to win over the hearts of his subjects. Thus, one thing led to another to lead her to play a growing role in the peacemaking efforts in Italy that were intended to facilitate the return of the papacy to Rome and to organize a crusade.

To this end, she increased her contacts with the political authorities in the Tuscan cities in order to be certain of their good intentions toward the Holy See and to pressure them to support its overseas expedition. Her first important act in this regard was to go to Pisa in 1375, accompanied by Raymond and her *famiglia*. She had already gone there in 1372 or 1373 in order to establish direct contact with the leader of the city, Pietro Gambacorta, whom she tried to persuade to support the crusade, and with his spouse and daughter, Tora. This latter figure, with whom she maintained contact by letter, took the name of Clare after entering religious life. Catherine took advantage of her sojourn in this port city to visit the abbey of La Gorgona, a charterhouse located on an island of the Tuscan archipelago, whose abbot, Bartolomeo Serafini, was a man of notable spirituality who had become her friend as well as one of her most fervent supporters. In March–April 1375, she returned to Pisa with the aim of trying to dissuade Pietro Gambacorta (the Elder) from joining the Tuscan League, which Florence was in the process of establishing in order to counter papal policy in the region. It was during this second sojourn to Pisa that she received the stigmata.

A little later in the same year, although we cannot really date it for certain, something happened, many elements of which remain a mystery to us but that undoubtedly had great importance in Catherine's life. The event was the decapitation of Niccolò Toldo (or di Toldi), which she vividly described in a letter to Raymond of Capua.[51] The name of this person, which Catherine does not indicate with any precision, is known to us only through the testimony of the Dominican Tommaso Caffarini, who was with her at the time. It seems that this Niccolò was a young nobleman from Perugia sent to Siena by the papal legate, Gérard du Puy, to secure the support of one of the senators, Pietro Marchese, a political personality close to Catherine and favorable to the Church at a moment when Florence was increasing its pressure on the city to obtain its alliance against the pope. The exact circumstances of the matter remain obscure; but be that as it may, Niccolò was condemned to death by the authorities in Siena. Catherine went to find him in his prison cell, in conformity with the custom according to which the members of confraternities frequently went to provide solace to prisoners and then accompanied such individuals to the scaffold, in the hope of leading them to remorse and contrition. What is remarkable here, on the other hand, is that a kind of romantic relationship seems to have been established between both of them on this occasion. Not only did Catherine calm the anxiety of this young man, but she even seems to have converted him in such a way that she presented his execution as a kind of marriage between them that was going to be consummated in the spilling of his blood. This is, at any rate, what she recounts in a text marked by a passionate exaltation in which it is not easy to untangle what comes from an objective account, a vision, or even a dream, even if—despite some cautions expressed by Robert Fawtier on this matter—the reality of the event is not in doubt, since Tommaso Caffarini affirmed, during the canonization process in Castello, that he had been an eyewitness of it:

> Then, he [Niccolò] arrived, meek as a lamb. As soon as he saw me, he began to smile. He wanted me to make the sign of the cross over him. After I did so, I said to him: "Kneel down here: this is the marriage rite, my beloved friend; soon you will taste the life that never ends." He lowered himself with great meekness. I extended his neck on the block, I leaned in towards him and reminded him of the blood of the Lamb. His mouth never stopped murmuring: "Jesus! Catherine!" It was while he was saying these names that I received his head in my hands. And then, fixing my attention on the divine goodness, I said: "I do." Immediately, I saw the God-and-man [Christ] as one sees the brightness of the sun. In this blood, there was the fire of holy desire given and hidden in his soul by grace. He [Christ] received it [that holy desire] in His divine charity. Once He had received the

> blood and the desire, He received the soul which He had placed in this refuge which is His side, open and full of mercy....While the hands of the Holy Spirit pushed him to make it further, he [Niccolò] made a small gesture, capable of delighting a thousand hearts, and I was not surprised since he was already tasting the divine sweetness. He turned like one newly married who, having arrived at the threshold of the spouse, turns around to look and bows her head towards those who accompanied her in order to show them her gratitude. He died. Then my soul rested in peace in the quiet, in such an odor of blood which I could not bring myself to get rid of his that had sprayed onto me.[52]

Catherine understood from this moment forward—and never stopped saying it—that her special mission was to "lead men and women into the open wound of Christ's side" and that her role as "the meek spouse" of the Son of God had placed her above all earthly authority. Indeed, she presents herself in her letter as the instrument of the conversion of the young man through the love she had inspired in him. And she recounts that, with the assent of the Virgin Mary, she had given him her blessing in the place of a priest, just before his head was cut off. In the first paragraphs, she had firmly invited Raymond of Capua and his Dominican companions to enter, in their turn, into union with Christ and to entrust themselves fully to him:

> It seems to me that the first stone has already been laid. This is why you should not be surprised if I impose nothing else on you except that you see yourselves drowned in the blood and in the fire which flows from the side of the Son of God. Now, no more negligence, my very dear sons, since the blood begins to pour out and to receive life![53]

Now, the relationship that bound them and would bind them together until her death had reversed direction and the spiritual director was henceforth the directee. Raymond of Capua does not mention this episode in his *Legenda maior*, however, because, as Thomas Luongo has appropriately observed, "such an auto-hagiographical affirmation of her [Catherine's] identity and her authority," could have scandalized his readers.[54]

Near the end of 1375, the brewing conflict that was pitting Florence against the papacy worsened and things entered a very turbulent period that was called by some contemporaries "the War of the Eight Saints," based on the name "the Eight of War," an executive committee (a *balia*) that had received full power to conduct hostilities as well as diplomatic activity. Indeed, they acquitted themselves so well in the eyes of most of the citizens of Florence that the members were at first characterized as being saints. The basic goal of the conflict was control over central Italy. Florence had followed with unease the seizing of control over the Papal States by Cardinal Albornoz beginning in 1353, as well as the encroachments of the papal legates in the border zones, which Florence perceived as a threat to its sovereignty. In addition, in the eyes of the Florentine government, which espoused a decidedly anticlerical ideology, the papal legates and governors—all either French or *Limousins* (that is, from Limoges), such as Pierre d'Estaing, Guillaume Noëllet, and Gérard du Puy—all hung over the city as a threat, since they were also in league with the Albizzi and a few other aristocratic families who were seeking to destabilize the regime in power and to reestablish the hegemony of the Guelf party. On the other hand, in the eyes of the popes, the pacification and reconstitution of the Patrimony of Saint Peter as it had been were priorities that conditioned their return to Rome, especially after the Italian misadventures of Urban V.

When they learned that Gregory XI had reached a truce with his worst enemy, Bernabò Visconti, duke of Milan, the Florentines, fearing that they were going to be encircled by hostile forces, appealed to the cities of Tuscany to join them in an alliance centered on the defense of communal liberties and the struggle against papal despotism. When revolts erupted at the start of November 1375 in several cities of the Papal States and especially in Bologna, Gregory accused the Florentines of having fomented them and placed an interdict upon the chief city of Tuscany, which meant that the clerics were forbidden from celebrating religious services in the presence of the faithful and from giving them the sacraments. Additionally, the pope excommunicated their political leaders and authorized other Christian powers to confiscate the goods of their merchants. To assure the defense of the city and its territory, the *Signoria* engaged the services of the English mercenary John Hawkwood and his soldiers and, to finance these heavy expenses, decided to seize the goods of the clerics and put them up for sale. Sanctions were then levied against clerics and religious who did not submit to this law and against those whose moral behavior left much to be desired.[55] This was an initiative without precedent on the part of lay authorities, challenging the traditional relationship between the Church and temporal power while taking their inspiration from the ideas of Marsilius of Padua and William of Ockham, which the papacy already deemed profoundly subversive. The stakes in this conflict were not minor: Should the Roman Church have territorial possessions? Should temporal power have the authority to tax the clergy and to dispose of their properties according to its own needs? One can assume that Gregory XI was disturbed by such developments and that he did not want to back down in the face of these unprecedented claims.

Catherine strongly condemned this rebellion against the authority of the Church as well as the measures taken by Florence. In her letters to the authorities and notables of the city, she asserted that one cannot attack the Church without also attacking Christ himself and that the punishment of unworthy priests—which was serving as justification to the Florentines for seizing the goods of the clergy—fell under the authority of the Church alone. But parallel to these stands taken on behalf of the pope, she strove to divert him from punishing the rebellious cities and urged him to reform, as quickly as possible, the administration of his States. Fighting on two fronts, Catherine soon found herself on the razor's edge. The enemies of the papacy saw in her a mere tool of papal policy and thus mistrusted her interventions. But the pope and Curia hardly appreciated her calls to indulgence with respect to the ongoing rebellion, which she was attributing to the abuses of bad governors and the avarice of certain prelates. During her second journey to Pisa, in 1375, Catherine endeavored, successfully (if at least temporarily) to forestall Pietro Gambacorta as well as the government of Lucca from entering into an alliance with Florence. But she had scarcely left these cities in which she had been well received when they caved to Florentine pressure and cut their ties with the papacy, and were followed in this by Siena not long afterward. In March 1376, Catherine went to Florence for a second time to try to reach an agreement between the two camps. Here she had interviews with the leaders of the Guelf party (the *Parte Guelfa*, which favored an accord with the papacy), on whom she was counting for their support; the group then entrusted her with a message for the pope, assuring him of their good intentions in his behalf. But aristocratic friends of Catherine, such as Niccolò Soderini and Buonacorso di Lapo, were not in power; instead, the power was now in the hands of another social group—the *gente nuova*—who were much less favorable to the Church. Its chief representative was the chancellor, Coluccio Salutati, who, in his proclamations, exalted republican liberty while simultaneously seeking to reunite the cities of central Italy into a league directed "against the bad clerics." After having been received by the priors in the palace of the *Signoria*, Catherine now believed herself, rightly or wrongly, invested with a mission between the Florentine Republic and the papacy.

First, she sent Raymond of Capua to Avignon to prepare the groundwork. Then, in June of 1376, she went there herself, accompanied by her *famiglia* (in total, around twenty people who were funded by the Curia, as the registers of the Apostolic Chamber attest), in order to meet with the pope, who had invited her to come to see him. After having submitted herself on his order to an examination by three theologians who judged her fully orthodox, she was received by Gregory XI, who up to now had known her only through the vehement letters she had addressed to him, all of which, except the first, have come down to us. Raymond of Capua has reported this meeting, during which he served as translator between the *Mantellata* of Siena (who spoke the vernacular of Tuscany) and the pope (who addressed her in Latin). For a long time, this exchange has been accorded a great deal of importance, and it has been claimed that during this time Catherine had convinced Gregory XI to return to Rome. But the truth is more complex. The pope had understood for a long time already that if he did not return to the banks of the Tiber, his temporal power in Italy and his authority in Rome risked being definitively called into question. But, in addition, the principal objective of papal diplomacy was to put an end to the Hundred Years War between France and England in order to be able to organize the crusade to which Gregory XI summoned all the faithful. To this end, it was preferable not to stray too far from the theater of military operations and negotiations, which played in Avignon's favor. Thus, he remained especially hesitant, since most of his entourage was composed of people from "over the mountains" who were putting pressure on him in order that the papacy and Curia might remain on the banks of the Rhône.

However, Gregory did not hesitate to make inquiries about Catherine's viability as an intermediary between the Church and the cities in rebellion. During their first interview, she had transmitted to him a message of peace and a request for pardon on the part of the Florentine authorities. But not long after this, a delegation of the *Signoria* arrived in Avignon, carrying official instructions that were in no way conciliatory to the pope. Did Catherine confuse her desires with realities, or had she been used by the Florentine government? She hints at this in a letter full of bitterness that she sent later to Buonaccorso di Lapo:

> When your ambassadors arrived here [in Avignon], they did not conduct themselves as befitted servants of God. They went their own way and I was never able to meet or speak with them; whereas when I asked you for their letter of credentials, you had promised me that you would speak to them and that we could all confer together. You told me: "We do not think that it [peace] will be possible without the intervention of the servants of God"—and yet you have done just the opposite![56]

Bc that as it may, this incident certainly did not play well in her favor in the presence of the pope and Curia.

In fact, today it is well established that it was not Catherine's intervention that prompted Gregory XI to leave Avignon for Rome on September 13, 1376. The pope indeed seems to have made the decision in his heart not long after his election. At most, the *Mantellata* of Siena acted as a catalyzer in conveying to him the forcefulness that he lacked, something that she never stopped criticizing in the letters she sent him.[57] During their meeting in the Palace of Popes, Gregory also seems to have been disappointed that she did not transmit to him any sort of revelation given to her by God concerning his return. He would probably have wanted to learn from her that he would not die shortly afterward, as had happened to Urban V in 1370, or that he would not be poisoned by the Romans, as some members of his entourage were causing him to dread. But Catherine refused to play the "court prophet"—those inspired women and men whom sovereigns sometimes consulted before entering into battle or taking an important decision in order to know whether heaven would be favorable to them—and she referred him to his conscience and to the vow he had made in secret to return to

Rome with the Curia. As Robert Fawtier has said, by way of an understatement: "It is not at all certain that he really knew her will about this."[58] Moreover, if, during the diocesan inquiry that took place in Venice at the beginning of the fifteenth century in the course of the canonization process, the Dominican Bartolomeo Dominici attributed to Catherine the merit of having convinced the pope to return to Rome, Stefano Maconi more discreetly limited himself to saying that she had strengthened the pope in his decision—which seems more consistent with what really happened.

In any case, despite the numerous letters she sent him after this, the pope refused to receive her in a public audience before his departure from Avignon for Italy. Perhaps he had been shocked by the tough words with which Catherine had reproached him for his indecisiveness and by the nagging advice she had given him about the direction he ought to follow once he returned to Rome. But most of all, the hope she had nourished about playing a role as meditator between the pope and his Italian adversaries revealed itself to lack a real goal; and this severely diminished the importance of the role she could play in the political realm. In addition, she had assured the pope, with a certain innocence, that his arrival in Italy would disarm the rebels. That did not happen and on January 17, 1377, Gregory XI could only enter Rome accompanied by an army of a thousand men led by Raymond of Turenne. A few weeks later, on February 3, 1377, the Breton mercenaries in the service of the Holy See, who were commanded by Cardinal Robert of Geneva, massacred four thousand people in the town of Cesena in the Romagna, whose citizens rose up crying out, "Death to the Bretons! Death to the shepherds of the Church!" thereby stirring up strong feelings and profound indignation against the papacy throughout all of Italy.

The sojourn in Avignon was not, however, a totally negative affair for Catherine. Raymond of Capua was confirmed in his function as spiritual director of Catherine's little group in a letter in which the pope approved the involvement of the saint and her companions in the crusade preparations. Gregory XI likewise bestowed upon Catherine the privilege of having a portable altar on which she could have Mass celebrated, which saved the group from having to ask for hospitality from the local churches during their journeys and especially allowed her to take communion every day. Finally, he attached to her person two other confessors of her choice who had the power to absolve the penitents she would bring to them. By all accounts, the papacy intended to support her apostolate with its aim of converting sinners and mobilizing Christians against the Turks who had invaded Asia Minor at the beginning of the fourteenth century and at that very moment were threatening Constantinople and the Balkans. Moreover, during her stay in Avignon, Catherine had made contact with Louis, duke of Anjou and younger brother of Charles V, who was very interested in her crusading projects. He even gave support to it after a meeting in the chateau of Roquemaure at which she was able to meet with Philippe de Mézières, former chancellor of the Kingdom of Cyprus, who was also trying to revive the crusading spirit within Christianity. The duke suggested to her that she should go to Paris and try to reestablish peace between France and England. Catherine turned down the offer but immediately wrote a letter to Charles V in which she invited him, in very vivid terms, to put an end to this war that was pitting him against Edward III and to join in the crusade being planned by Gregory XI:

> Your quarrels continue to be an obstacle to the mystery of the Holy Passage [= the crusade]. This evil alone must make us dread God's judgment upon us. I beg you: stop causing such harm and impeding the good that would result from the reconquering of the Holy Land and the ransom of these poor souls who do not share in the blood of the Son of God. You should be ashamed of yourself—you and the other Christian princes! To fight with your brother and leave the enemy in peace, to seek to snatch the goods of another and to not recover your own. What shame before the human race and what an abomination before God! Put an end to such ineptitude and blindness. I say it on behalf of Christ Crucified: delay no longer in making peace. Make peace and turn your weapons against the infidels![59]

This letter was probably transmitted to the king of France, although no trace of it has been found in the royal archives; but it certainly would not have pleased him and she never received an answer.

After leaving Avignon, Catherine returned to Italy by way of Genoa. She stayed there for some time with Orietta Scotti, where she wrote her third Oration, trying to dissuade the pope from his intention (which he was toying with at that time) to backpedal. She might even have crossed paths here with the boat that was bringing the pope back to Rome. But, contrary to a legend maintained by certain iconographical representations (especially the great fresco painted in Siena around 1480 by Benvenuto di Giovanni at the hospital of Santa Maria della Scala), she was not present at the entry of the Vicar of Christ into the Eternal City on January 17, 1377, something she had so much wanted to see. From Genoa, she had in fact gone back to Siena, where she spent a lot of energy getting the commune to accept the donation (which had been offered at Belcaro) of the site of an old, abandoned fort located near the city. She wanted to set up a convent of nuns there, placed under the patronage of Saint Mary of the Angels—a name of Franciscan origin, since it was the name given to the church of the Portiuncula outside Assisi and had become rather common in the fourteenth century. Gregory XI approved her project and the convent was founded on April 15, 1377; but its construction could not be realized while she was yet living because of a variety of difficult circumstances, among which was the ultimate refusal of the Sienese authorities, for political reasons, to contribute to it. To find the resources that would enable her to finance this enterprise that was so close to her heart, Catherine went to the Val d'Orcia—a region located to the southeast of the Sienese *contado*, where she tried to reconcile two enemy branches of the Salimbeni family. And she remained for some time in one of their castles: the Rocca de Tentennano. There, in July 1377, she undertook the redaction of her important book, *The Dialogue*, which she would finish in Siena during the first months of 1379. Since the powerful aristocratic lineage of the Salimbeni played an important role in the political life of Siena, the communal government, fearing that the saint was plotting with them and the governors of the Papal States against the regime of the Reformers who were then in power, ordered her to return to the city as quickly as possible. As the letter to the authorities of Siena testifies, this sign of distrust provoked an indignant reaction on her part in which she stated that her only concerns were the salvation of souls and the reconciliation of enemies. And she complained bitterly about their suspicions: "I am really saddened to have to say," she writes to them,

> that my fellow citizens are spending so much time denouncing me that it seems they have nothing better to do with their time than to speak ill of me and of those who accompany me. As to me, they are correct that I have many faults,

> but they are wrong with respect to my companions....What saddens me the most is that the accusations redound to those who hurl them, in such a way that they often inflict on themselves the very punishment which their own faults merit. That's all I am going to say about this.[60]

In fact, Catherine, far from plotting against the Republic, was dividing her time between the writing of *The Dialogue*—what she called in her letters *il Libro* (the Book)—and a veritable mission to the populations of the Val d'Orcia, a rural area that was isolated and only superficially Christianized. "We are in the midst of scoundrels here," she wrote at the time to one of her correspondents. And to use her own words, she lamented, "We are engaged in eating demons," in other words, busy converting sinners.[61] Other than the Dominicans Tommaso dalla Fonte, Bartolomeo Dominici, and Tommaso Caffarini, three or four other priests were giving absolution to all those—several hundred, it would seem—whom she had succeeded in persuading to resume regular religious practices. Caffarini reports how in this way he had heard the confessions of inveterate, hard-core sinners who had not frequented the sacraments for forty years. It would be nice to have more details on this "mission," which lasted four months. Did Catherine preach on these occasions? Her biographers are careful not to allude to this eventuality because that would have risked harming her cause; and so, they limited themselves to noting that she freed the possessed while taking their heads in her hands, ignoring the vermin that these unfortunates were spreading in her lap.[62] But perhaps it is no coincidence that these "subversive activities" had been denounced to the commune of Siena by the archpriest who was responsible for this region.

During this same time, the war between the Holy See and the Tuscan League inspired by Florence continued. Catherine never stopped writing to Gregory XI to recommend that he show kindness toward the rebel towns and to remember that the conquest of souls was more important for the Church than the conquering of cities. But, parallel to this, she also sent stinging reproaches to the Florentine government—"the Eight of War" and "the Eight of Priests"—who, not content with seizing and putting up for sale the possessions of the clergy, were also demanding that the wealthiest citizens buy them up and were purporting to impose taxes on ecclesiastical persons and institutions who had traditionally been exempt from them:

> I have a lot to complain to you about, if it is true, as is being said around here, namely, that you wish to impose taxes on the clergy. This is greatly regrettable for two reasons. First, you offend God, because you cannot do that with a clear conscience. But it seems that you have lost the concept of the good for you to have become attached only to things of the senses and the frivolous, which are as passing as the wind....If you do not stop giving offense to the ministers and priests of the holy Church, you will not conclude peace....I therefore urge you, my dear fathers, to place no obstruction to the grace of the Holy Spirit, especially since, in his clemency, the Holy Father is ready to offer it to you. And what a shame, what an offense this would be for me![63]

If Gregory might have been exasperated by her reproaches and perhaps even by her absence at the time of his entry into Rome, he still asked Catherine, in the spring of 1377, to go back once again to Florence and try to revive the strands of the negotiation in order to arrive at peace. The pope said on this occasion, "I believe that the Florentines will not dare attack Catherine, because she is a woman and they venerate her." Through the involvement of Raymond of Capua (who did not accompany her to Florence but played a very active role secretly in this negotiation), he arranged to have papal bulls sent to her, enabling her to fulfill this delicate mission. Catherine obeyed and, at the end of the year, she returned for the third time to the great Tuscan city, where she was well received by her friends of the *Parte Guelfa*, who judged the moment to be opportune for bringing down the leaders who favored war. But her presence provoked differing reactions among public opinion, as is evident from the account of the Florentine chronicler Marchione di Coppo Stefani, who was hostile to the Guelfs and a member of the commission of "the Eight of Priests" (*Otto dei preti*) that was charged with the seizure and disposition of the goods of the clergy:

> In this year [1377], it happened that there was in Florence a woman named Catherine....Reputed to be very holy, pure, of good and honest life, she began by criticizing the quarrel with the Church. Those who were leading the *Parte* [the Guelf Party] gladly received her and, among the other leaders of the plot, a certain Niccolò Soderini, who had fixed

> up a room in his house for her where she had previously stayed several times. Another was Stoldo di Missere Bindo Altoviti, another still was Pietro Canigiani. These are the ones who praised her the most. And it is true that she knew ecclesiastical affairs by her natural intelligence and also by what she could have learned by chance, and that she spoke and wrote very well....This woman came many times to the *Parte*, either on her own or introduced there through the mischief of such people, to declare that the *ammonire* [that is, the proposal of a kind of motion of censure aiming to exclude from the government certain of its members] was a good thing....This is why those of the *Parte* took her for a prophetess while others for a hypocrite and a suspect woman. Many people were talking about her: some with lies, others because they believed that they were doing good by speaking ill of her.[64]

This mixed portrait—which in fact presents Catherine as a holy woman manipulated by unscrupulous politicians, or even as a phony—really reflects the tensions that were coursing through Florentine society. Ever since Gregory XI had placed an interdict on the city, no religious service could any longer be celebrated in the presence of the faithful. But in 1377, the authorities of the city, confronted with the discontent of a good part of the population who did not take kindly to being deprived of the sacraments, wanted to force the clergy to say public Mass and to absolve penitents. Some clergy and religious left the city in order to not have to disobey the pope, beginning with the bishop of Florence, Angelo Ricasoli, whom Catherine congratulated for his courageous conduct, after having written to him several times previously to reproach his weakness.[65] Others did not pay any attention to the papal sanction, judging it disproportionate to the extent that it was compromising the salvation of the faithful for political reasons. One of Catherine's close friends, Giovanni dalle Celle, a monk of Vallombrosa, approved the attitude of these last individuals, which earned him a scathing letter from the *mamma* in which she accused him of having "violated the blood of Christ" and threatened him with God's judgment. Ever since her return to Florence, Catherine had tried to strengthen those elements that were favorable to peace between the *Signoria* and the papacy. She also made some new disciples there, like the poet Giannozzo Sacchetti and especially Barduccio Canigiani, who became her particular secretary and remained with her until her death.

The death of Gregory XI on March 27, 1378, and the election, on April 8, of an Italian pope, the archbishop of Bari, Bartolomeo Prignano—who took the name of Urban VI and who was assumed to be favorable to reform—now helped to move things forward. At the same time, significant changes affected the Florentine government and the new *Signoria*, which began its rule on April 1 by demanding that the papal interdict be respected. On the entreaties of the Guelf party, which was relying upon popular discontent, the chief supporters of the war against the pope, who were accused of having Ghibelline sympathies, were soon struck with a legal warning (an *ammonire*) and removed from power, which then opened the way to peace.[66] To Catherine's great displeasure, vendettas then proliferated throughout the city in which the most extreme Guelfs were not shy about entering into conflict with the gonfalonier of justice, Salvestro dei Medici, who, though he belonged to their own party, was demonstrating even-handedness. On June 22, a really violent popular uprising erupted that targeted the Guelfs and, on this occasion, the palaces of the principal friends of Catherine were pillaged and set on fire. The rebels—who were crying out "Long live the people!" and "Down with the hypocrite Niccolò and his saint Catherine!"—broke into the home of the Soderini, where Catherine was staying, and she was almost killed. According to the account that Raymond of Capua gives of it, she declared to the one who had lifted his hand to strike her, "Here I am, take me and leave this family in peace!" Her courage in the face of death ultimately made the rioters leave and she was able to take refuge in the house of the tailor Francesco di Pippino, "a pious and decent man" with whom she later exchanged several letters.[67] A few days later, she succeeded in leaving the city and went to the abbey of Vallombrosa, where she waited out the end of the troubles. But these disturbances started up again with even greater force on July 20, 1378, when the riot known as the Revolt of the Ciompi—that is to say, the textile workers who had been reduced to misery—erupted, during which time Florence experienced both fire and bloodshed for three days. These last events accelerated the conclusion of an agreement between belligerents, because Florence was finding itself weakened by these internal crises and because the new pope needed the support of the Italian cities in order to impose his will on the cardinals who were quickly tiring of his authoritarianism. The peace between Florence and Urban VI was concluded at Tivoli on July 28, 1378, to the great delight of Catherine, who could then return to Siena with the sole regret of not having suffered martyrdom during the Florentine troubles. Disappointed in her hope, she complained to Raymond of Capua that her "Eternal Spouse" had made a "great mockery" of her by refusing the gift of her life and her blood.[68]

IN THE TUMULT OF THE GREAT SCHISM: THE CRUSADE AGAINST THE ANTICHRIST

But Catherine was not going to be able to remain in the shadows for long. During the summer of 1378, the rapport between the new pope, Urban VI, a violent and authoritarian person, and the College of Cardinals deteriorated rapidly, to such a degree that, at the conclusion of a new conclave that gathered in September in Fondi, on the border of the Kingdom of Naples under the protection of Onorato Caetani, the cardinals—the very same ones who had elected him just a few months earlier!—chose one of their own as pope: Robert of Geneva, who took the name of Clement VII.[69] Once she was informed of these maneuvers, Catherine wrote a number of strongly worded letters to the cardinals, in particular to Pedro de Luna, whom she had known in Avignon and who appeared to be a virtuous prelate favorable to the reform of the Church. She also tried to impede the three Italian cardinals from making common cause with their colleagues from over the mountains by letting them know that to oppose Urban VI—who had been elected by divine inspiration—was the equivalent of opposing God himself. After this, having received no answer from them, she did not hesitate to treat them as cowards and heretics.

During the same period and up until her own death, she wrote at least eight letters to Urban VI, whom she had also met in Avignon and whom she considered to be a reformer, to support him in his refusal to abdicate and to offer him her advice. Aware of the assistance that she could give him in this battle, the pope asked Catherine to come and join him in Rome. She hesitated for some time, because she feared giving scandal to the respectable levels of Sienese society among whom, it was said, that it was not appropriate for a virgin who wanted to serve

God to run about in the world and that she was all too eager to hit the road once again. Thus, she laid out her perplexities to Raymond of Capua, who was in Rome at that time, in a letter in which she expresses herself like this:

> Although I am personally convinced that I am not at fault on this point and that every time I set out on the road it was to obey God and as his representative and for the salvation of souls, I do not want to be the subject of scandal for anyone, for which reason I have not been able to decide whether to leave. But if the Vicar of Christ absolutely wants me to come, in such a way that his will is done and not mine…if it is thus, then kindly see to it that he notify me in writing what his will might be, so that those who are scandalized might at least clearly see that I do not begin this journey willy-nilly.[70]

We should note in passing the importance that Catherine attaches to the written word, which would confer on the word the power of a proof that she could later use in her own defense, in case of opposition. In this case, her request illustrates above all her concern to protect herself from criticisms directed against her mental stability and motivation. But we can extend this remark to her own writings, which were likely to guarantee her orthodoxy against eventual accusations of heresy.

Catherine received from Rome the order that she was waiting for. On November 20, 1378, she arrived in this city, which she did not know and in which she was going to die a year and a half later on April 29, 1380, surrounded by her *famiglia*. The pope immediately invited her to send a "word of exhortation" to the cardinals in which she strongly urged them to stand firm. He concluded his intervention by saying,

> This little woman (*donnicciuola*) shames us all! We are fearful and alarmed while she, who by nature belongs to the weaker sex, feels no such fear and indeed even encourages *us*. What is the Vicar of Christ to be afraid of when Christ the Almighty is with him? Christ is stronger than the world and it is impossible that he forsake his holy Church![71]

So Catherine, with a little group of disciples and her mother, moved into a house located within the *rione* Colonna, on the Via di Papa (today the Via di Santa Chiara) not far from the Dominican convent of Santa Maria sopra Minerva, whose prior since 1377 was Raymond of Capua, and where there was a sizeable colony of Tuscans, especially of Sienese.[72] She went to Mass every morning at the Dominicans or in other churches or basilicas in order to pray and to ask for indulgences for her protectors, like those she obtained for the Dominican sisters of Saint-Agnese at Montepulciano, shortly before her death. Sometimes she visited Kari (Catherine), the daughter of Birgitta of Sweden, who was living in the Palace of the Papazurri, on the present-day Piazza Farnèse. For a time, there was even a question whether the two women might go together to see Queen Joanna of Naples in order to ask her not to join the party of Clement VII; but, in the end, nothing ever happened. Different from Birgitta, who lived a long time in Rome and ended up discomfiting its inhabitants by having made them feel guilty about the lamentable state into which their city had fallen (in comparison to what it had been at the time of its past grandeur), Catherine probably had developed many relationships with the Romans—if not with the ruling clique of the commune called the *Banderesi*—and with the people of her own neighborhood, for whom she worked several miracles.[73]

In this battle, which she quickly characterized as a crusade against the antichrist (that is, the schismatic pope Clement VII, whom she did not hesitate to refer to also as the "devil"), she came upon Alfonso de Vadaterra, the former spiritual director of Birgitta of Sweden, who had once come to size her up for Gregory XI in 1373; and she was, perhaps along with him, the person behind what is called the first "Urbanist manifesto," that is, favorable to Urban VI. This anonymous text emphasized that, even if from a juridical and formal point of view the election of Clement VII could appear legitimate, it constituted a veritable crime against the spirit of the law, even more so since one associated his rival, Urban VI, with the intention of undertaking the reform of the Church.[74]

During her meeting with Urban VI, Catherine had suggested to the pope that he convene in Rome a "council of saints," a kind of gathering of the great spiritual figures of the Italy of her day, which would give him the weight of their moral authority and affirm that he (Urban) was really the only legitimate pope. In its spirit, this assembly of "the columns of the mystical body" of the Church was going to play the role usually delegated to the cardinals (those whom Urban VI had named did not inspire in Catherine more confidence than did their predecessors who had betrayed it!) and to give advice to the pope about reform. Thus, Catherine's dream, which she had been cherishing for such a long time, could now become a reality: namely, the dream of a Church governed by holy men and freed from the burden of temporal interests, which the Spiritual Franciscans and Dante as well had believed they saw being realized, for a moment, with the coming in 1294 of Celestine V, the "angelic pope." She thus asked the abbot of La Gorgona, the Carthusian Bartolomeo Serafini, to gather together in Rome on January 17, 1379, various men of wisdom and holy life; and she wrote strongly worded letters to several religious personalities, such as the hermits of Monte Luco, near Spoleto, the Carthusian Pietro da Milano, Raymond of Capua, and a few others, in order that they might agree to come to this meeting—about which she had such great expectations.

But her hopes were soon dashed; most of her correspondents did not even bother to respond and even her old friend William Flete refused to leave his hermitage to come to Rome in the middle of winter. Catherine was deeply hurt by this refusal and, since she was not lacking in spirit, she wrote ironically to Antonio da Nizza, who was William's confrère, in Lecceto: "It seems that God is only to be found in the forest and nowhere else!"[75] But she did not let herself get discouraged and, up to her last breath, she was still pressuring the pope to surround himself with a group of virtuous "servants of God," interested in reform and in dedicating themselves to prayer in such a way as to strengthen the bonds between the earthly Church and the spiritual Church. This did not inhibit her from following very closely the evolution of the power relationships between the two popes. She seems to have played some role, with her fiery words, in the mobilization of the Roman militia, which, on April 30, 1379, seized the Castel Sant'Angelo then held by the followers of Clement VII. This then enabled Urban VI to leave Santa Maria Trastevere and reestablish himself once again at Saint Peter's in the Vatican. At this juncture, she wrote to the pope a letter brimming with joy in which she does not hesitate to mention her own role:

> For four weeks ago, we saw that the power of God had accomplished wonderful works by means of a lowly creature

> [= Catherine] in order that we might see clearly that is it He who acts and not the power of men....I rejoice that our very dear mother Mary and the blessed Peter, prince of the Apostles, has put you back in the place which is your own. At the present time, God wishes that you make of your garden the garden of the servants of God![76]

On the same day, April 30, 1379, at the battle of Marino, the Roman militias and the Compagnia di San Giorgio of the condottiere Alberigo da Balbiano had gained the upper hand over the Breton mercenaries in the service of Clement VII, and the pope was forced to leave Italy and to return to Avignon. Catherine then wrote to several sovereigns and heads of state to urge them not to align themselves with the camp of the antipope. Because we do not have the responses that she may have received from any of her correspondents, it is difficult to have a good idea about the impact of her letters. It is very doubtful that the one she sent on May 6, 1379, to Charles V, king of France—asking him to consult with the masters at the University of Paris, "the fountain of learning," before making a decision about the schism—had ever reached him.[77] She seems to have had more success with the king of England, Richard II, who sided with the Roman obedience. However, it is difficult for us to say whether the saint's arguments—which we find word for word in the text of the official decision of the monarch in favor of Urban VI—had had as much weight in this decision than did various other political considerations.

The principal recipient of her letters at this time was the queen of Naples, Joanna I (1326–82), who had first rallied to Clement VII, then returned to the camp of Urban VI, before separating from him again. Exasperated with this frivolous and fickle woman who collected husbands and lovers, Catherine contemplated going to Naples to get her back on the right path; but she had to give up this idea and contented herself with sending one of her favorite disciples, Neri di Landoccio, to transmit her message to her once again. At the same time, she was writing several letters to ladies of the nobility, as well as to Dom Cristofano, a monk of the Carthusians of San Martino, and she ended up making use in Naples of a whole network of pious women among whom she strove to inculcate the principles of a Christian ethic of courtly life and marriage. Since the warnings she had addressed to the queen had had no effect, she then sent her a series of letters full of reproaches to urge her to improve her conduct and to remain faithful to the Roman Church, while simultaneously making an appeal as well to Louis of Hungary and Charles de Durazzo, her enemies, in order that they might exert pressure on Joanna to rally to the camp of Urban VI. Parallel to this, Catherine endeavored to keep Siena, Perugia, and Florence in allegiance to the Roman pope. She encountered fewer difficulties here, since the Italian cities did not want to see a Frenchman once again sit upon the throne of Saint Peter. Not content with practicing an epistolary diplomacy throughout Christianity, she sent her confessor and spiritual director, Raymond of Capua, to France, with the assent of Urban VI, to dissuade Charles V from aligning himself with the Avignon party. But when the Dominican arrived in Genoa, he was warned that an armed group was waiting for him in Ventimiglia to impede him from going further, at which point he preferred to abandon the undertaking. The abandonment of this mission earned him a strongly worded letter from Catherine that aimed to make him feel ashamed for his cowardice and reproached him for not having had the courage to shed his blood for Christ.[78]

But in her relations with the pope himself, Catherine's disappointment was going to be swift and profound. Urban VI devoted all his energies to getting his legitimacy recognized within Christianity and to setting up a College of Cardinals by choosing prelates who could give him political and diplomatic support, rather than being men of God. Yet, his notoriously touchy and capricious character prevented him from involving himself seriously in the reform projects of the Church. Catherine did not hesitate to write him about this: "For the love of Christ, tamp down a little the impulsive movements which human nature stirs up within you and temper this natural inclination with holy virtue."[79] She recommended prudence and moderation to him, especially in his relations with the Roman population and authorities, with whom he tended to be brusque, and urged him to refrain from weighing them down with taxes in order to finance the war and the upkeep of the Curia. Since she was not lacking in humor, she sent him another letter in which she used the image of an orange that, like effort, has a sour taste when it is first eaten but then loses its bitterness and becomes delicious, while at the same time sending him six candied and golden oranges "to sweeten his disposition," as indicated by a note in the manuscript.[80] While yet defending him against his adversaries, she did not hesitate to reproach him for not really wanting to "cleanse the belly of the Holy Church" by combating the abuses within it. And, since he was taking no initiative in this direction, she ended up writing to him, respectfully but firmly: "Christ laments that the Church is not being purified of its sins, and Your Holiness is not buckling down to this task with all the necessary solicitude."[81] From this time forward, refusing to eat or drink, she offered her life in sacrifice for the salvation of the Church and Christians. Exhausted from the privations and sufferings that she had been inflicting upon herself for many years now, she really felt that she no longer had the strength to continue the battle. In a letter from January 1380 addressed to Raymond of Capua, she described for him a long vision that she had just had, during which her soul was separated from her body for a time and was violently assaulted by demons. She then addressed heaven with this moving prayer:

> "Lord, make haste to help me! You have allowed me to be alone in this battle, without the comfort of the father of my soul [Raymond of Capua] whom I am deprived of through my own ingratitude...." Then God imposed on me this obligation to sacrifice the desires of this *famiglia*, all throughout Lent, and to extol before Him this aim alone: the holy Church. He also enjoined on me to hear a Mass every day at dawn—that which, you know, is impossible for me—but in obedience to you, all things are possible....I pray the divine goodness that I may soon see the redemption of his people. At the hour of Terce, I get up from the Mass and you would see a dead woman going to Saint Peter's and there entering to work in the cradle of the Church. I remain there almost until Vespers and from this place I would not want to leave neither day nor night until I see this people at least somewhat refreshed and strengthened around its Father.[82]

Further on, we see her trying, one last time, to put pressure on God, through a kind of blackmail, so that he might grant to her, in exchange for her life, that which was dearest to her in all the world—the reform of the Church:

> It seemed to me that my soul had left my body...but my spirit remained fixed on the abyss of the Trinity. My memory

> was filled with the remembrance of the need of the Church and of the whole Christian people, and I cried out to God's face and asked it [the Trinity = God], with assurance, for divine help, offering up to it [as a sacrifice] the desires and constraining it by the blood of the Lamb and by the pains endured. And the request was so persistent that it seemed to me that it [God] could not refuse it.[83]

Then, at the end of the letter, she gave Raymond of Capua her counsel for the future and dictated to him her wishes, as if she had understood that this message was the last that she would be sending to him: namely, to keep her "Book" (*The Dialogue*) as well as her other writings (her letters and prayers), and do with them "what appears to you to be most useful for the honor of God," that is, to make them known outside the small circle of her disciples; to be "father and governor" of her *famiglia*; and to persevere with even greater ardor in the battle for the reform of the Church.[84] On her deathbed, she also wrote, it seems, to the Dominican general chapter that was going to gather in Bologna in order that it might elect Raymond of Capua as master general—and this actually happened a few days later, on May 12, 1380.

After these last efforts, she fell into such a state of weakness that she could no longer go to Saint Peter's for her daily religious exercises and had to remain in bed for two months, at the mercy of severe suffering due to her water-only diet, which she endured with patience, according to the testimony of her secretary, Barduccio Canegiani. She then indicated to each of her disciples, male and female, the religious order into which she wanted each to enter after her death. Thus, Stefano Maconi learned from her, to his great surprise, that she wanted him to become a Carthusian; and he did not fail to do just that by withdrawing, as soon as he could, into the Carthusian monastery of Pontignano, near Siena.

Feeling her end drawing near, Catherine asked pardon from the Trinity for her faults and for her ingratitude for the great gifts she had received; she then dictated her spiritual testament, just as Francis of Assisi had done. After having received absolution and having reminded the priest who was at her side that she had received the plenary indulgence from two popes, Gregory XI and Urban VI, she offered a special prayer for the latter, "confessing him to be the true pope and encouraging her sons to lay down their lives for this truth." After crying out "The blood! The blood!" and imploring that the divine mercy be granted to her, she gave up her spirit on April 29, 1380, and was buried in the cemetery next to the church of the Dominican convent in Rome, Santa Maria sopra Minerva. Raymond of Capua and many of her disciples were not present. The pope, for whom she had battled so fiercely, did not honor her remains with a visit. He had used her as a supernatural guarantee of his own legitimacy and policies, but she had ended up being an irritant to him with her reproaches and threats. And even in this role, she was not going to be of great use to him for very long since his rival, Clement VII, was soon going to be able to boast that he, too, had received the support of a saint, in the person of the young ascetical and devout cardinal Pierre de Luxembourg († 1387), and even of a prophetess, the penitent Marie Robine, who had settled in Avignon during these same years.[85] Indeed, the death of Catherine occurred virtually unnoticed outside of the little group of her disciples. Only the Florentine chronicler Marchione di Coppo Stefani mentions her in but a few words: "Many things have been said about her and she did many miracles in Rome."[86] But he said nothing about her changing the mind of the pope and leading him to take the initiative on the reforms that she had asked and hoped for during her public life.

As this succession of episodes shows, one cannot separate the spiritual life of Catherine from her involvement in political and religious issues. This is, however, exactly what Robert Fawtier and Louis Canet have done in their book *The Twofold Experience of Catherine Benincasa* (Paris: Galimard, 1948), a work of high quality that remains foundational. But it suffers from a dichotomy attested to by its title and underlined by the fact that the first of its two authors retraced the steps in Catherine's career chronologically, whereas the second reported on her mystical experience in a thematic fashion. Indeed, it is the love of Catherine for Christ that was at the root of her zeal for the reform of the Church and the society of her day; and one cannot separate these two aspects of her personality without the risk of missing what is essential. This kind of view was perfectly in conformity with the Thomistic tradition, which privileged the search for the "common good," as one finds it defined in the sermons and treatises of the great preachers at the start of the fourteenth century, such as the Tuscan Dominicans Giordano da Pisa, Remigio dei Girolami, and Angelo da Porta Sole.[87]

But to resign oneself to seeing the forces of evil victorious in the world is to assure the triumph of injustice in history. For Catherine, the supreme value is justice—an ideal, which political institutions must ensure prevails by way of law, which is the principal instrument of its realization.[88] The reform movement that she advocated is called to reach out into the whole of the Church where justice must reign; but its apostolic action also embraces the life of politics. For her, the spiritual life and life in the world are closely connected because the renewal produced by grace must make itself felt both at the ethical and practical levels among all Christians; the transformation of the soul is the prelude to the transformation of society and indeed leads to it. In the reality of everyday life, it is neither simple nor easy to determine where to put one's finger on exactly what is "right." And the "politics drawn from the gospel" that she was striving to implement provoked not a few misunderstandings and negative reactions toward her, particularly in Florence and even Siena. On the human level, she never stopped amassing failures: the papacy did return to Rome but not under the conditions she had wished, and her role in this matter remained marginal; the crusade that she had tried to generate at the call of Gregory XI never occurred, and the efforts she expended in this regard were completely wasted. Even the resistance she tried to organize against Clement VII and his supporters ended up only hardening the antagonism between the two rival papacies, which was going to last until the end of the Great Schism in 1415. One certainly cannot lay the blame for this generalized failure on her; but the erroneous way in which she approached these problems contributed in a certain measure to it. Indeed, Catherine reasoned solely within the context of the Church—identified with the hierarchy—in a society in which this was no longer an all-embracing structure; and she intervened in politics in the name of morality, without considering the specificity of this domain and the complexity of situations she understood poorly. In this sense, she can be considered a kind of anachronistic figure: she lived effectively within a theocratic perspective that had lost all actuality since the beginning of the fourteenth century with the rise of national monarchies and, in Italy, of city-states, who jealously guarded their autonomy with respect to the papacy and strove to subject the clergy to their power. Even the popes of her time, on behalf of whom she did so much, were not always grateful to her and often limited themselves to using her as a spiritual guarantee of the rectitude of their actions, without pursuing her requests for reform. Catherine probably experienced real suffering when she had the feeling of not having been taken seriously by the leaders of this Church that she loved passionately. But, with respect to Urban VI, she preferred to keep her silence by simply letting him know, in the final message she sent to him through an intermediary (whose identity remains unknown to us), that God had said to her, "I suffer in finding no one who will serve the Church; it even seems as if everyone has abandoned it. But I will be the one to fix that!"[89]

CHAPTER 2

BECOMING SAINT CATHERINE OF SIENA

Catherine's death was followed by an event that would be decisive for the recognition and dissemination of her sanctity. On May 12, 1380, upon the request of Pope Urban VI, Raymond of Capua was elected master general of the Dominicans. To be sure, due to the Great Schism this involved only half of the order, since a parallel and rival structure, with another master general at its helm, was set up in those countries that adhered to the pope in Avignon. But in Italy, Germany, and England, where obedience to the Roman pope held sway, the Dominicans, thanks to Raymond, were going to become the principal proponents of the work—and soon the cult—of Catherine of Siena. This did not happen overnight, since she was not officially recognized as a saint by the Catholic Church—which by this time had been reunited—until 1461.

In any case, in Siena the news of her death did not stir up any particularly strong feelings. She was not very popular there and, as we have seen, the communal authorities looked upon her with some suspicion because of her close relations with the great aristocratic families. She knew this. Indeed, she had written about it one day to her fellow citizens: "I love you more than you love yourselves!" This is confirmed by the poet Giacomo del Pecora, a young nobleman of Montepulciano, who had been converted by her and who lamented that Siena, "the sweet city, had remained so estranged from her" (*Dolce città, che se'fatta de lei tanto aliena*).[1] It is only in 1385 that her head, detached from her body, which remained in Rome in the cemetery of Santa Maria sopra Minerva, was brought to Siena to be placed in the sacristy of the church of San Domenico de Camporeggi, in the presence of her mother, Monna Lapa, and her sister-in-law and confidante, Lisa Colombini. It was not until 1439 that an altar would be dedicated to her in the church of the Dominicans; and not until 1455 did the communal authorities of Siena decide to devote five candles to her every year on her feast day of April 29, the anniversary of her death. Despite the name under which she is known and what Eugene Dupré Theseider has written about her, Catherine was not really the saint of this city, which only adopted her many years later and where her cult was for a long time in competition with that of Bernardine of Siena, who was born in 1380, the year of her death, and canonized before her in 1450. In contrast to Margaret of Cortona († 1297)—a Franciscan tertiary who immediately after her death became the patron saint of her city and whose cult remained particularly local up to the seventeenth century—Catherine is a universal saint whose veritable home was the Church itself and whose cult was quickly promoted by a great religious order, that of the Friars Preacher, throughout the whole of Christendom.

VENICE: THE FIRST CENTER OF CATHERINE'S CULT

From the start, however, she could count only on a small circle of followers, and they were unsparing in their support for her cause. Beginning in 1382, William Flete, in a truly remarkable sermon, presented Catherine as a mediator between God and the human race and as a "holy virgin" who had assisted Christ in his work of salvation.[2] During the same years, her first confessor, Tommaso dalla Fonte, persuaded the artist Andrea Vanni, one of Catherine's early disciples, to produce the first painting of her, in which she is depicted holding in her hand a lily, the symbol of virginity, and, in her other hand, a book. But most especially, beginning in 1385, Raymond of Capua began to write a grand spiritual biography of her known as the *Legenda maior*.[3] However, due to the numerous activities in which the leadership of the "Urbanist" branch of the Dominican order involved him, he did not complete its redaction until 1395; he then died in Nuremberg in 1399. Raymond had had some experience in the genre of hagiography inasmuch as he had composed, between 1363 and 1366, a *Life* of Agnes of Montepulciano († 1317), an abbess who had undertaken with great determination and spiritual rigor to reform the monastery of Dominican nuns located in this same city. After Catherine's death, as soon as his important duties would allow him some time, he threw himself passionately into writing a biography of her, whom he knew quite well, since he had been her spiritual director between 1374 and 1377. During these decisive years, Catherine and Raymond had fought together for the reform of the Church and of the Dominican order, and even afterward, when he was no longer able to be near her, they remained in close contact through letters, of which only those of Catherine have come down to us. The *Legenda maior*, which Raymond composed in Latin between 1385 and 1395, consists of a long and very complex text that contributed to making Catherine and her spirituality known in ecclesiastical circles. In writing it, Raymond was in fact pursuing two objectives. A man of action and of leadership, he was first of all seeking to get Catherine, for whom he had had a deep admiration, canonized in order to facilitate the dissemination of her cult. But he was also endeavoring to champion the great cause that he had pursued until the end of his life: namely, the reform of the Dominican order, for which Catherine herself had been hoping and praying. But progress on this was very slow. When he went to Siena in 1388, Raymond succeeded in reforming neither the local convent of Dominican friars nor the *Mantellate* who were associated with it. From that time on, the success of Catherine's cult would be tied to that of the Dominican Observant movement, which was first successful in Venice through the foundation by John Dominici, Raymond of Capua's vicar, of the female convent of Corpus Domini. This community had taken as its model the example of the convent in Pisa, which had been founded by Tora-Chiara Gambacorta, with Catherine's help and advice.

Beginning in 1394, Raymond was assisted by Tommaso Caffarini († 1434), a Dominican from Siena who had known Catherine well, even if he did not belong to the "inner circle" of her disciples. Along with John Dominici and a few confrères, Caffarini transformed the two Dominican convents in Venice—San Zanipolo (Saints John and Paul) and San Domenico de Castello—into centers of devotion to Catherine. At first, he devoted most of his energy to persuading the Roman papacy to approve the rule of the Third Order of the Friars Preacher, which brought together lay penitents living alone or in community by taking as its model the kind of life lived by Catherine of Siena. He succeeded in his aims in 1405, and thereafter he became the propagator of her cult and depiction. To make the example of her life more accessible to the greatest number of people, he first composed the *Legenda minor*, an abridged version of the *Legenda maior* of Raymond of Capua, and ensured its translation into Italian. Then he composed the *Libellus de supplemento Legende prolixe virginis beate Catherine de Senis* (Supplementary treatise on the long legend of the blessed virgin Catherine of Siena), which he completed in 1417 or 1418, and in which he gathered together all hagiographical materials regarding the saint. This last work is of great interest inasmuch as one finds here the echo of several traditions that Raymond had not included in his own work. At San Zanipolo, Tommaso set up a workshop of copyists who transcribed numerous copies of Catherine's writings (*The Dialogue* and the letters) and disseminated them throughout all of Italy and the rest of Christendom.

It is thus Venice and not Siena that was the point of departure for the process that would lead to the sanctification of the *Mantellata*. This is not all that shocking since beginning in the last decades of the fourteenth century the city of doges had been an intense center of religious life:[4] Philippe de Mézières, chancellor of Cyprus and counselor of the kings of France, Charles V and Charles VI, evocatively mentions, in his *Songe du Vieil Pèlerin* (Dream of the old pilgrim), this town where there lived a devout lay patrician who dreamed of establishing in Venice a "theological society" in which there would be no separation between everyday life and the aspiration to holiness. We know of some attempts at reform in the religious orders in Venice, especially at Sainte-Justine of Padua for the monks, San Giorgio in Alga for the canons regular, and the convent of San Zanipolo for the Dominicans. The efforts of these Dominicans were supported by the former bishop of Castello, Angelo Carraro, who became Pope Gregory XII in 1406. He had personally known Catherine well; she had sent him a warm letter in 1378 at the time of his elevation to the episcopacy and he had a great devotion for her—attested to by the fact that he always carried on his person one of her teeth encased within a small reliquary.[5] Thus he authorized a preliminary inquiry on her sanctity and cult, which took place in Venice in the convent of Castello between 1411 and 1416, thanks to the efforts of Tommaso Caffarini, who was its organizer and tireless promoter.

The Dominicans had really understood that, in the complicated situation in which the Church found itself in being torn apart by the Great Schism and split between two (and soon three) rival loyalties, the chances of having Catherine's sanctity recognized by the papacy were minimal. But they also recognized that the witnesses who had known her while she was still living were becoming fewer and fewer and that it was time to set down their testimonies in writing. Some people, however, were surprised to see that in the churches of the Dominican convents of the Venetian Laguna, images of the saint were being publicly displayed, her head surrounded by rays constituting a kind of diadem, and that commemorative celebrations, accompanied by sermons in which her praises were sung, were being organized here on the anniversary of her death. Pious souls, scandalized, it seems, by such practices normally reserved for saints duly canonized by the Church, went to the bishop of Castello, Francesco Bembo, to express their astonishment. This led to his opening an investigation on the matter.

Indeed, it seems that this action had resulted from a preliminary agreement between the Dominicans, who could not organize such an inquiry on their own, and the bishop, who was favorable to them and who sought less to reestablish rigorous guidelines for the cult of saints—which, at the time, were still quite imprecise—than to give the Friars Preacher the opportunity to put down in writing the testimonies about Catherine's holiness.[6] Strictly speaking, the Venetian process of 1411–16, which was directed from beginning to end by Tommaso Caffarini, was not a canonization process. Over the next five years, only twenty-four witnesses were heard from, without any framework of interrogation having been established. Twenty-two of them were religious, among whom were six Dominicans; but neither Caffarini himself nor a single woman was called or interviewed. But the inquiry was led with such care and, on certain points, in such a detailed manner that, despite its purely masculine and almost exclusively clerical character, the papacy did not have to call another one when, a half-century later, the question of canonizing the *Mantellata* of Siena came up again. Parallel to these efforts, the office of propaganda set up at San Zanipolo by Tommaso Caffarini, within the wider context of his strategy of promoting her renown, created and disseminated visual representations of the saint under the form of low-grade wood engravings, as well as illuminated manuscripts of the hagiographical texts about her, which greatly contributed to making her name and her sanctity known.

HER CANONIZATION AND THE DISSEMINATION OF HER WRITINGS

We would be on the wrong track, however, if we were to reduce the actions taken by Catherine's disciples only to the events at the Venetian center as they worked to prevent her memory from falling into oblivion. After her death, some of them collected her letters and made them known among themselves. In the process, Stefano Maconi, a layman who had been one of her main secretaries as well as her confidant beginning in 1376, played a particularly significant role. Upon her counsel, he had entered the Carthusians and became prior of the Carthusian monastery of Pontignano, near Siena, and then prior general of the order for the Urbanist obedience[7] in 1398. As such, he was in contact with various rulers, such as the duke of Austria, Albert IV, and King Sigismund of Hungary, to whom he gave relics of the saint—something that helped to disseminate her cult within their states. And most importantly, he put together a collection of Catherine's letters that can be considered absolutely authentic (even if the collection of Tommaso Caffarini has recently been reevaluated). Other disciples, such as Neri di Landoccio, did the same, collecting selected letters and making them more accessible. This, likewise, helped to ensure a wide circulation to these letters, which, once stripped of all the elements connecting them to a specific historical and geographical context, were received as purely spiritual writings.

Over the span of the three decades that followed the Venetian process, Catherine's cause remained up in the air, as the Church had more pressing concerns than the promotion of new saints. If the Council of Constance put an end to the Great Schism and ended up in 1417 electing an Italian pope recognized by all in the person of Martin V, the general atmosphere was hardly favorable to Catherine, who had taken the exaltation of the figure of the pope—"true Christ of the earth"—to a degree that could not but displease the partisans of conciliarism. Moreover, some of the conciliar fathers attributed considerable responsibility to Catherine for causing the schism itself, inasmuch as she had pushed the papacy to return to Rome, which was at the root of the double papal election of 1378.[8] In fact, it is necessary to recognize that the return of Gregory XI to Rome at the beginning of 1377 had not been considered by contemporaries to be a success, given the dramatic events that then ensued. And the memory of Catherine of Siena suffered more than benefited from it, at least during these first years.

We have to wait until the 1450s and the end of the conciliar crisis—with the victory of the Roman papacy and the dissolving of the Council of Basel—for the canonization of Catherine of Siena to regain a certain relevance. In the meantime, her reputation for holiness was widely disseminated throughout Christendom thanks to translations of the hagiographical texts, and especially of *The Dialogue*, into the principal vernacular languages of the West.[9] Moreover, within the Dominican order, the current of the Observance, which was aiming to reform it by reestablishing a certain poverty and a more fervent conventual lifestyle therein, had appreciably advanced, especially in the Germanic countries and in Italy, where, in 1459, the Holy See had granted the reformed Congregation of Lombardy the right to its autonomy within the structures of the order.

In Siena itself, once the canonization of Bernardine of Siena had taken place in 1450—whose relics remained in L'Aquila in the Abruzzi and thus could not be made the object of a cult in his native city—the signs of devotion toward Catherine steadily increased. The favorable occasion was furnished by the election in 1458 of a pope belonging to a family of Sienese origin: Cardinal Enea Silvio Piccolomini, who became Pius II—one of whose ancestors had been a member of Catherine's own *famiglia*. The commune of Siena and the Dominican order then joined their efforts. After inquiries on the miracles attributed to the saint in Rome and Florence and after an examination of the Venetian process of 1411–16 by a committee of cardinals presided over by Cardinal d'Estouteville, the pope then proceeded to her canonization in Rome on June 29, 1461. In his sermon, Pius II praised Catherine's charity, which had led her to intervene in the realm of ecclesiastical politics; and he attributed to her the merit of having paved the way for the return of the papacy from Avignon to Rome. After having emphasized her prophetic gifts, he underlined the importance of her engagement on behalf of the crusade—a theme that had great resonance at a time when the Holy See and Emperor Frederick III were trying to organize an expedition against the Turks, who were threatening Western Christendom after having already seized Constantinople.[10]

It should be noted that the pope never presents Catherine in any way as a Dominican saint, nor does he mention her stigmata. This astonishing silence results probably from the fact that he was, at that time, in conflict with the master general of the Dominicans, Martial Auribelli, who was poorly disposed toward the Observance, which the pope wanted to see disseminated throughout the whole order. Pius II himself wrote the office of the saint, whose liturgical feast is celebrated on April 29.

Immediately after the canonization, the conflict between the Friars Preacher and Friars Minor erupted into the open, when the great Franciscan preacher Roberto Caracciolo, in a sermon preached at Santa Maria sopra Minerva (the Dominican church of Rome where the saint's relics were being kept), rejected the possibility that Catherine could have received the stigmata. The quarrel between the two orders only grew more poisonous, to such an extent that in 1471 and again in 1478, the Franciscan pope Sixtus IV forbade the addition of any trace of these wounds on the paintings that hung in the various churches. But this interdict was hardly respected, and the iconographical representations of her stigmatization spread throughout Italy and all of Christendom.[11]

After her canonization, the Dominicans transferred her relics—which in 1430 had been placed into a lovely sarcophagus by Antonino Pierozzi—to a chapel inside Santa Maria sopra Minerva. Finally, in 1473, a general chapter made it obligatory to celebrate the Feast of Saint Catherine in the convents of the order. In Siena, around 1470, the silver reliquary containing her head was moved into a new chapel created in the church of San Domenico, which was decorated by the painter Giovanni Bazzi (known as Il Sodoma). Catherine's native city thus ended up adopting her, and an abundant iconography developed there in the second half of the fifteenth century, in the cathedral (in the Piccolomini chapel) as well as in the communal palace and the hospital Santa Maria della Scala. In some representations, she appears surrounded by a triple crown symbolizing virginity, martyrdom (because Raymond of Capua had presented her as a martyr of asceticism in his *Legenda maior*), and the teaching function that she had exercised in the Church, once again underscored by the fact that she is often holding a book in her right hand.[12] A confraternity of Saint Catherine of Siena *in*

Fontebranda was founded in connection with the neighboring convent of San Domenico; and the house of the saint was transformed into an oratory in 1464. At the beginning of the sixteenth century, Catherine even ended up becoming the symbol of the city and the defender of its liberties, which were increasingly threatened by Florence (which was going to absorb it in 1555). By this time, however, she had attained a renown that made her a saint known throughout Christendom.

Catherine's reputation also resulted from the wide dissemination of her work and the hagiographical writings about her, thanks to Tommaso Caffarini and to many of her disciples who, since the morning after her death, had been endeavoring to make her known throughout Italy and the whole of Christianity. This strategy of communication took the form of translations for the texts that had been written in Latin—such as the *Legenda maior* and *Legenda minor*—but especially in small collections of selected pieces (called *zibaldoni* in Italian) in which we find recopied versions of a few letters of the saint together with other spiritual writings, fragments of the *Legenda aurea*, or the *Revelations* of Saint Birgitta. One of the centers that produced these booklets in the vernacular was the Brigittine convent of Paradise in Florence, founded in 1394 by the humanist merchant Antonio Alberti. Their principal recipients were cloistered nuns or female recluses. But the influence of Catherine of Siena made itself felt also in the *Regola del governo di cura familiare*, written by the Dominican Giovanni Dominici for those who were living in the world and in the married state. Outside of Italy, France was barely touched at all by Catherine's influence, since the Dominican Observance developed there only later; and the passion with which she had supported Urban VI against the Frenchman Clement VII had also left lingering bad memories there. Up until around 1470, stories about her were translated into French only in the regions controlled by the Dukes of Burgundy, particularly in the Low Countries. One had to await the "mystical invasion" of the seventeenth century for her writings to know a broad dissemination in French, with the publication in Paris in 1644 of a translation of the *Epistres de la séraphique vierge saincte Catherine de Sienne* (Letters of the seraphic virgin Saint Catherine) by Jean Balesdens.

Catherine's texts, however, were quickly translated into English in a spiritual treatise by an unknown author titled *Le Verger de Sion* (The orchard of Syon, around 1420), which was written for the Brigittine nuns of Syon, near London, but was also found in the libraries of the English Carthusians, who saw in her a model of the contemplative life.[13] Similarly in Germany, large extracts from the *Legenda maior* of Raymond of Capua—who had died in Nuremberg in 1399—circulated under the title of *Der Geistliche Rosengarten* (Spiritual Rosary) in convents of Dominican nuns. These were profusely illustrated, with a great deal of space devoted to Catherine's visions and her stigmata. The dissemination of her work followed the progress of the Dominican Observance, which was quite rapid in the Germanic countries. Under the influence of the reformer Johannes Meyer, her writings were sent around to the convents of the Preachers and among the members of the Dominican Third Order in the larger cities of southern Germany.[14] Catherine's influence also extended to the old religious orders and ended up reaching a large audience of pious laity of both sexes.

It is, in fact, thanks to the printing press that Catherine of Siena's fame was extended to the whole of Christianity. *The Dialogue* was first printed in 1472 by Baldassare Azzoguidi. Her letters—which had circulated in the fifteenth century in manuscript form in different collections with a certain number of variants—were the object of a handsome humanist edition in 1500, produced in Venice by Alde Manuce. It is from this work that most of the translations made over the course of the sixteenth and seventeenth centuries took their inspiration. The Sienese scholar Girolamo Gigli (1660–1722) produced a second edition of her work and compiled a valuable *Vocabolario cateriniano* in which he defends the characteristics of the language spoken in Siena and used by Catherine in her letters against Florentine pretensions. In 1630, the prohibition against representing her stigmata was lifted by Pope Urban VIII, which gave a new impulsion to the representation of Catherine as a mystic with the stigmata in works of art and especially in Italian painting. Finally, in 1724, Benedict XIII instituted the Feast of the "Holy Stigmata" of Catherine.

Catherine's popularity throughout Latin Christendom is, however, especially associated with the Rosary, the practice that developed especially in the wake of the Council of Trent. In Italy as much as in Germany and France, innumerable paintings and prints from the late sixteenth and seventeenth centuries show her, along with Saint Dominic, in the process of receiving from the Virgin Mary this collection of prayers and meditations, which became one of the most typical forms of Catholic piety.[15] This depiction of the Sienese saint in the iconography is all the more surprising since the Rosary never appears in her writings or the biographies. She certainly had a devotion to Mary, but no text indicates to us that she had ever worked out any specific form of prayer to the Mother of God. In fact, the Rosary was popularized by a Breton Dominican, Alain de La Roche (ca. 1428–75), who, through his preaching, extolled the specific virtues of praying the "Psalter" or "Rosary" of Mary; a collection composed of the recitation, three times, of five Our Fathers and fifty Hail Marys divided into five "decades" (ten Hail Marys preceded by an Our Father). Each group of five decades was devoted to meditations on one group of fifteen mysteries—joyous, sorrowful, and glorious (five each)—of the Virgin. To the recitation of the Rosary were attached several indulgences, or remissions of some or all the time that a soul would have to spend in purgatory to atone for their sins.

Confraternities of the Rosary were created in considerable number starting in the 1560s, often in connection with the Dominican convents, where special chapels were given to them for their devotional exercises. When the chapels came to be decorated, they depicted the Virgin revealing the form of the Rosary to Saint Dominic, but revealing it also—especially in the seventeenth century—to Saint Catherine, who was considered his feminine counterpart and patron of the Dominican Third Order. Even if it had no historical foundation, her presence at the side of the founder of the order made some sense inasmuch as Catherine had emphasized in her personal life the importance of the prayer of the heart—alone and private—and of the role of intercession in the religious life of the faithful.

CATHERINE: FROM ITALIAN NATIONAL HEROINE TO DOCTOR OF THE CHURCH

After a decline in her cult and devotion over the course of the eighteenth century and the first half of the nineteenth century, Catherine of Siena recovered a certain timeliness after 1850 thanks to the Risorgimento. In 1868, Pius IX made her the secondary patroness of Rome, after Saint Peter, at a time when the temporal power of the pope was being threatened by the progress of the Piedmontese monarchy; and then, during the pontificate of Leo XIII, Cardinal Alfonso Capecelatro

(1824–1912) published, in Siena, in 1878, a new biography of the saint that became popular.

But what revived Catherine's memory the most was surely the new edition of her letters, henceforth arranged in a chronological order different from preceding editions, which Niccolò Tommaseo published in 1860 and which remained until our time as the most up-to-date point of reference.[16] The Sienese saint is presented here as a great figure heralding the Renaissance and one of the major manifestations, along with Dante, of the Italian literary genius. Indeed, in the twentieth century, Catherine was considered in Italy above all as a national saint: thus the Sienese writer Pietro Misciatelli, in his work on the Sienese mystics (*Mistici senesi*) published in Siena in 1913, develops a whole rhetoric of the crusade centered on Catherine, at a time when Italy was seeking to create for itself a colonial empire in Libya and in other Muslim countries.[17] During the First World War, the Sienese saint was drafted into the service of Italian militarism and little booklets were distributed to Italian soldiers containing extracts of some of her letters in which she was calling men into combat and to heroism. Fascism, which was trying to develop the cult of the will—and that had chosen as its slogan the formula, very much in the style of Catherine, "Believe, obey, fight!"—pressed her into service in 1925 and soon exalted her, after Saint Francis of Assisi, as "the saint of the Italians" (*la santa degli italiani*): a heroine who had devoted her whole life to the greatness of Rome and of Italy.[18] Ecclesiastical circles followed suit. The Dominican order promoted works about Catherine with Father Taurisano, historian and editor of texts whose political sympathies were close to those of Fascism; and, in 1930, the master general, Father Gillet, did not hold back from presenting her as "the Saint Joan of the country," likewise contributing to making her a saint for Italy. For his part, Archbishop Sciaccia of Siena, who was on very good terms with the regime, organized letter-writing campaigns addressed to Pope Pius XI as well as to Mussolini to have Catherine of Siena acclaimed patroness of Italy. Satisfaction was given to them when Pius XII, in May 1940, proclaimed Saint Francis of Assisi and Saint Catherine of Siena the copatrons of Italy. And ever since 1962, the evocative statue of Catherine, the work of the sculptor Messina, watches over Rome at the base of the Castel Sant'Angelo.

In France, the first great historical biography of Catherine of Siena was published in 1919. It is the work of Johannes Jørgensen, a

Danish man of letters who converted to Catholicism while living in Italy and who had been the author of a *Vie de saint François d'Assise* (Life of Saint Francis of Assisi) ten years earlier. This dense life was written in a style whose lyrical nature (if a little grandiloquent and prolix) is no longer fashionable for us today; but it was not devoid of merit inasmuch as it was based on a thorough knowledge of the writings of the saint and her contemporaries. But it lacked a critical approach to the sources that characterized the work of historian Robert Fawtier between the two wars. Indeed, beginning in the 1920s, Fawtier, who studied at the École Française in Rome, had devoted several important studies to resisting the idealization that the figure of Catherine of Siena had assumed.[19] In particular, he denounced the interpretation of Catherine as found in Raymond of Capua's *Legenda maior*, which he regarded as largely erroneous, and he rejected some of her letters that had appeared in existing editions as falsely attributed to her. Even if he sometimes went too far in some of his critiques and if several of his assertions eventually proved to be inaccurate, Fawtier had the merit of challenging certain misconceptions, such as the idea—widely believed since the mid-nineteenth century but already present in Pius II's bull of canonization—that it was Catherine who had convinced Pope Gregory XI to put an end to his "captivity in Avignon" and to return to Rome. For him, Catherine was, above all else, a saintly woman: a moving figure surely, but lacking in any political capabilities and someone whose works did not have the importance that one often attributed to them, since her theological learning was inadequate and not very original. Fawtier's investigations culminated in 1948 in a work of synthesis titled *La double expérience de Catherine Benincasa* (The twofold experience of Saint Catherine of Siena). He himself wrote the first part, which concerned the saint's life and political engagements, while another former disciple of Louis Duchesne at the École Française de Rome, Louis Canet, laid out with great surety her spiritual journey and the stages of her mystical life. This dichotomous approach to the life of Catherine is not without its problems; but one should be grateful to Robert Fawtier for having snatched the *Mantellata* of Siena away from the hyperbolic enthusiasm of Italian nationalism—she who had once written to Charles V at the beginning of the Great Schism, "May the eye of your intelligence consider God and his truth, rather than the passion of love of country!" Fawtier, indeed, demonstrated that, far from having prophesied Italian unity, she had been concerned above all else with the unity of the Church and that her exaltation of Rome, which is to be placed within a purely spiritual perspective, never pushed her to present Avignon as the cesspool of all vices and in any case had nothing to do with the Fascist cult of *Romanitas*.

Fawtier's works had the great merit to have spurred new research on Catherine of Siena and to have highlighted the need for a deeper knowledge of the sources of her story. Under the direction of a French Dominican scholar, Father Hyacinthe Laurent, a critical edition of these latter sources was published between 1930 and 1942, in particular that of the *Processo Castellano* of 1411–16, which contains so much valuable information on her life and on the origins of her cult.[20] At the same time, the Istituto storico italiano per il Medioevo undertook the publication of a wholly reliable edition of Catherine of Siena's letters, which had been entrusted to the Roman medievalist Eugenio Dupré Theseider; but, due to the outbreak of the Second World War, the publication was unfortunately aborted after the completion of the first volume (Letters 1–88), which appeared in 1940. If we can hope for the eventual completion of this vast undertaking, which has recently been resumed, the complete critical edition of the letters exists for the time being only in the form of a hard-to-access CD-ROM.[21]

After the Second World War and for a period of thirty years, Catherine of Siena disappeared from the realm of secular history, which no longer had any interest in her. On the other hand, the Catholic Church never stopped showering her with new honors, thereby publicly recognizing the importance of her thought and activities. Indeed, in 1970, Pope Paul VI granted her the title of Doctor of the Church, and the discourse he gave on this occasion at Saint Peter's in Rome allows us to understand the meaning of this honor, which is, at first glance, a little surprising:

> We will not find in the writings of the saint the apologetic vigor and theological rigors which distinguish the great luminaries of the ancient Church of the East and West, nor the elevated speculations proper to scholastic theology.... On the contrary, what is striking in her, is the infused knowledge, that is to say the assimilation—brilliant, profound and exhilarating—of the divine truth and of the mysteries of the faith....Catherine was one of the most brilliant models of these charisms of exhortation, of "the word of wisdom" and

> the "word of knowledge" which Saint Paul demonstrated is at work within each member of the faithful in the early Christian communities.... Her letters are like so many sparks of a mysterious flame in the burning heart of Infinite Love which is the Holy Spirit.[22]

Apparently, the figure of Catherine—about whom the pope states "that she anticipated not only the teaching but also the language of the Second Vatican Council"—deserved to be exalted at a time when the Council had emphasized the essential role that the laity were to play within a Church that was conceived of, above all, as a communion, as God's people. To be sure, Catherine had addressed "urgent appeals and severe reproaches" to the prelates of her day. But she did so "in all humility and all respect for their dignity as ministers of the blood of Christ"; and her action on behalf of Church reform had unfolded "in peace and calm, through humble and continual prayer, in the sweat and tears poured out with a desire full of anxiety for the servants of God" (*The Dialogue*, XV)—that which made of her "a saint of a reform which was, first and foremost, of the inner self, then external, but always in communion with and with filial obedience towards the legitimate representatives of Christ." Finally, Paul VI underlined the modernity of this woman who had not hesitated to throw herself into political activity to try to accentuate justice in the world, while at the same time he pointed out that "one feels the need—particularly today—to make a distinction between the things that belong to Caesar and those that belong to God," more so than in Catherine's time. A few years later, the words of John Paul II, who in 1999 made Catherine the patron saint of Europe along with Birgitta of Sweden, follows the same line of thought: "With a certain bearing and fiery language, she entered into the heart of social and political problems that were tearing apart the Europe of her day," he wrote on this occasion. The association of these two fourteenth-century saints was in any case significant, as it appeared to open the door to a reevaluation of the role of prophecy and of women within the Catholic Church.

The renewal of interest in Catherine of Siena in Western culture likewise dates from the 1970s and 1980s. On the occasion of the sixth centenary of her death, an important colloquium was organized in Siena, whose acts, published in 1981, mark the resumption of university studies on the saint within new perspectives, especially that of the history of women and their place in religious and cultural life.[23] Indeed, those years saw the rediscovery of the essential role played during the later Middle Ages by the *mulieres religiosae*—those laywomen, for the most part illiterate and withdrawn—who, from Marie d'Oignies and Marguerite Porete up to Catherine of Siena and Joan of Arc, profoundly influenced the spirituality and history of their times. Important works were then devoted by American historians to "holy anorexia"; and psychoanalysts were not slow to study, in their turn, the case of this woman whose biographers report that, at the end of her life, she was only nourishing herself with a little water and a few consecrated hosts.[24] Parallel to this we witness the development, especially in Anglo-Saxon countries, of a historiography of feminist inspiration that emphasized the charismatic gifts of these women while presenting these gifts as a kind of compensation for—or even as a form of revenge—by these creatures who had been excluded, solely because of their gender, from the spheres of power and culture. Finally, since the last decades of the twentieth century, literary history—which, for a long time, had not at all been interested in Catherine of Siena on the excuse that her spiritual writings arose from the realm of mysticism and theology—has begun to give Catherine her due alongside Petrarch and Boccaccio, who were her contemporaries. We recognize better today what is fascinating in the life and afterlife of this unlearned laywoman who poured herself into the act of writing by composing by herself *The Dialogue*, and who through her letters has given a certain nobility to the epistolary genre in the vernacular. It is especially from this renewal of studies, which is especially notable in Italy and in the United States, that the present work is attempting to renew, on new foundations, the reflection on the life and work of the saint of Siena whose personality remains in many ways problematic for men and women of the twenty-first century.

CHAPTER 3

INTERPRETATIONS AND DEPICTIONS OF CATHERINE OF SIENA IN THE MIDDLE AGES

Before going any further, it would be appropriate to pause for a moment to examine the depiction—or rather, depictions—of Catherine disseminated through the hagiographical texts that had been the sources of her reputation for holiness and of the devotion to her that developed between the end of the fourteenth century and the middle of the fifteenth century.

CATHERINE AS VIEWED BY HER MEDIEVAL BIOGRAPHERS

As we have seen, Catherine's first biographer was the Dominican Raymond of Capua, who had been her confessor beginning in 1374 as well as her main correspondent, because they had exchanged numerous letters in his absence. These letters show a strong connection between them, even though she did not soften her criticism of him at various times and ended up treating him like a son rather than as her spiritual director. The *Legenda maior*, which he wrote between

1385 and 1395, comprises three parts of varying lengths. The first, which consists of twelve chapters, is devoted to Catherine's childhood and adolescence; the second, of the same length, describes the public ministry that she exercised between 1374 and her death in 1380, as well as the revelations and spiritual experiences about which she had spoken to her entourage and to some of her correspondents. In the third part, which contains only six chapters, the author, after having described Catherine's final illness and death, abandons a chronological order and analyzes her virtues, and concludes by affirming that she really deserved to be canonized.[1]

The picture that we get from this text is above all that of an ascetic and mystic endowed with exceptional gifts. The problem that the hagiographer found himself confronted with was indeed complex and delicate. While she was alive, Catherine had been an atypical and unusual personality. She had led an intense religious life without entering a convent and—although she was but a simple woman lacking any kind of authority—she did not hesitate to intervene in the affairs of the Church at its highest levels (something that could appear as an astonishing presumption). Moreover, she never stopped moving around throughout a considerable period of her lifetime—something that was particularly shocking for a young virgin. In the immediate aftermath of her death, her friend and former spiritual director, William Flete, had developed in a sermon the idea that this lack of stability was compensated by the fact that she was forever living "within the wounds of Christ and the crevice of his side wound"; but his response was not entirely convincing. Aware of this problem, Raymond, therefore, tries in his *Legenda* to defang eventual criticisms of his directee by relating her extremely busy life and her public activities to the norms of feminine spirituality of her time. Thus, he presents her as a contemplative forced by circumstances to enter the melee in obedience to God or, if one prefers, as a mystic who wandered off into politics. If she was inspired by Christ to intervene in temporal affairs, she only did it against her will and for the good of the Church, while at the same time remaining distant from the spirit of the world thanks to the familiarity that she maintained with God within her "interior cell." Raymond thus presents her to us as especially engaged—like all the female saints of her day—in acts of charity and consumed by a "zeal for souls" whom she was trying to bring back to God. He also underlines the fact that, even though she had not been cloistered, she almost always lived in close-knit spaces (the family house, her room, her "interior cell") located close to a church, and that she did not wander about just for pleasure. Presenting himself as a priest and a confessor, the hagiographer wants to convince his reader that Catherine's apostolate did not distance her from the world above to which she belonged, inasmuch as she was dead to herself and was totally possessed by God. Discreet on the miracles (among which he mentions especially those that occurred after her death—in Pisa, Genoa, Florence, and Rome—in such a way as to illustrate the extent of her reputation of sanctity), he prefers to put the emphasis on her supernatural gifts, especially on her ability to read into hearts, which she possessed to the highest degree and which she demonstrated in Avignon during her conversation with Pope Gregory XI, to whom she revealed the vow that he had privately made to return to Rome. Raymond is careful to heighten the role that the saint had played in the return of the papacy to the banks of the Tiber and attributes a decisive role to her interventions in the life of the Church. Her success in this regard testifies that she was truly one sent by God and not a clairvoyant or a sorcerer—as some had said about her while she was still living. But he carefully avoids describing her public involvement in the debates and conflicts of her day so as not to give rise to any criticism.

Moreover, Raymond of Capua proposes in his *Legenda maior* a supernatural interpretation of certain gifts that Catherine possessed and that were at odds with the notion of femininity prevalent in the culture of the time. Thus, he is silent about the fact that she knew how to write—which was exceptional for women of her day, except for the high aristocracy—but he emphasizes, rather, that she had miraculously learned how to read Latin, something that allowed her direct access to Sacred Scripture. Moreover, Catherine suffered from the double handicap of being both a woman and a layperson, something that would normally exclude her from intervening in the affairs of the Church. To overcome this difficulty, Raymond adopts the idea—which had already been widely developed by some hagiographers in the thirteenth century and at the beginning of the fourteenth century—according to which a woman merits to be chosen inasmuch as she is a creature lacking power and learning. In other words, her very weakness makes her a perfect "channel" between the human person and his or her Creator—a privileged instrument of divine communication. Thus, he presents Catherine as a person drawn by God who had so completely denied herself so as to have made herself worthy to receive, in return, the gifts of the Holy Spirit. It is God who had inspired all her works, especially *The Dialogue*, which she had dictated to her entourage during her ecstasies. Raymond emphasizes that through this unlearned woman, though she was endowed with virtues and wisdom, God wanted to confound the pride of men—and especially of learned men—who appropriate to themselves the monopoly of knowledge and yet despise the grace that is offered to them.

Note, however, that Raymond's insistence on the supernatural character of Catherine's holiness is not just a rhetorical or hagiographical technique. Among the Dominicans of the Observance, among which he was one of its leading figures, a certain anti-intellectualism of Augustinian inspiration did indeed predominate that, without doubting the importance of knowledge and studies, distanced itself with respect to the excesses of theological abstraction and endeavored to allow a place for spiritual experience and emotional engagement in the sufferings of Christ on the cross. In sum, the *Legenda maior* of Raymond of Capua consists of a long and complex text that rests on a fragile balance between an undoubted requirement of historical truth and a theological and doctrinal interpretation of the lived experience of Catherine of Siena. The hagiographer especially insists upon the transformation of the body of the young girl into a "christic" body at the conclusion of a rite of passage that unfolded in three steps: the initiation, beginning with her childhood; a liminal phase that led her to withdraw into "the interior cell" and a transfiguration of this body that became spiritual at the conclusion of successive renunciations, opening the door to a decisive ontological transformation, illustrated by her stigmata; and finally, now inhabited and transformed by Christ, she assumed another nature and took on the supernatural powers of glorified bodies, which allowed her, through a divine investiture, to become the fruitful mother of numerous disciples and to work for the salvation of all.

From the first years of the fifteenth century, the Sienese Dominican Tommaso di Antonio Caffarini, who had been Raymond of Capua's collaborator until Raymond's death in 1399, totally devoted himself to the promotion of Catherine's sanctity and wrote two hagiographical works: the *Legenda minor*—an abridgement of the *Legenda maior* of Raymond of Capua; and the *Libellus de supplemento*.[2] The first work, which he wrote in Latin but was quickly translated into Italian, was disseminated much more widely than was the *Legenda maior*, which was a long and difficult text of which only about fifteen manuscripts exist today and had only a few translations into the vernacular. Both the *Legenda minor* and the *Libellus* (which was written a little later) offer a rather different picture of Catherine from the one sketched out by her spiritual director. The goal of Tommaso Caffarini—who was the architect of the Process of Venice from 1411 to 1416—was also to bring about the canonization of the saint; but he thought that it would have a much better chance of success if he emphasized her visions, her mystical experiences, and her miracles as well as her writings. More so than Raymond of Capua, he thus privileged the spiritual and prophetic aspect of Catherine's holiness, while at the same time he sought to deepen the meaning of her apostolic activity by placing it within the same line as that of the holy doctors: from the time of Saint John the Evangelist—had she not, like him, written letters and a book?—up to Hugh and Richard of Saint Victor in the twelfth century. Thus, he expended considerable effort gathering her letters into a collection that he then endeavored to disseminate throughout Christendom and having *The Dialogue* copied at the scriptorium of San Zanipolo, a veritable publishing house that operated under his direction in Venice for around thirty years.

In his *Libellus de supplemento*, Tommaso Caffarini added extracts from sources concerning Catherine that Raymond had neglected—in particular, a collection of miracles noted down in Florence in 1374 by an anonymous author and especially the precious notebooks (*Quaderni*) of her first confessor, the Dominican Tommaso dalla Fonte, who had taught her to read and who had helped her to discover the Bible through a translation made in the Tuscan dialect. These reveal another Catherine: one who possessed a real mastery over nature, protecting the family vineyard from the frost and helping her relatives through miraculous healings. They also demonstrate her beneficent influence upon the people who had been sent to her by their confessors or by those devoted to her, as well as the role of mediator that she played within divided families and between rival bloodlines. Moreover, in contrast to Raymond, who was very discreet on this question—fearful of prompting suspicious or hostile reactions regarding Catherine—Tommaso Caffarini emphasizes her stigmata, which, in his eyes, constitutes the proof of the veracity of her message and the divine character of her inspiration. Thus, he devotes to the stigmata a veritable treatise that aims to place her as the culmination of a line of mystics beginning with Francis of Assisi and proceeding by way of stigmatic figures associated with the Friars Preacher, such as the mystic Helen of Hungary and the Dominican Guatier de Strasbourg. After this demonstration, Catherine finds herself assimilated to the "Poverello," of whom she is presented as a feminine and Dominican equivalent, which did not fail to arouse strong reactions on the part of the Friars Minor all throughout the fifteenth and sixteenth centuries.

From these somewhat divergent interpretations, two images of Catherine emerged to coexist throughout the fifteenth century. For Raymond of Capua, Catherine is first and foremost to be viewed through the lens of verbal communication. In the prologue to his *Legenda maior* he presents her as a mediator: a woman, a "fragile vessel," endowed with a burning eloquence whose source was the Holy Spirit, from whom she received wisdom that she was to convey to men and women to help them to salvation. But he does not mention her learning to write (although she had informed him about this in a letter); and he defined his own personal role as that of the writer who knew how to gather this inspired word and give it a theological status by rendering it into Latin—the language of the sacred and of learning.[3] In fact, it is in this language that he wrote his *Life* and translated *The Dialogue* in order to overcome the double handicap of Catherine's female gender and the vernacular language that shaped her action and work. It can be said that, for Raymond of Capua, Catherine is a woman without a body but with a heavenly voice who handed on to men and women the words that God had first addressed to her. In his eyes, she was a saint, not an author; she did not have talent, but inspiration.

For Tommaso Caffarini, however, Catherine is much more than this. Her words are really her own and she is not simply a channel through which the Creator transmitted his wishes to other human beings. The hagiographer hardly presents her conversations with Christ; rather, he reports her questions or her requests without mentioning the answers she received. Finally, he emphasizes that she put down her message in writing—an art that she had mastered—which does, in fact, make her a real author; these were the writings that, in his eyes, constituted the strongest proof of her orthodoxy and which he was endeavoring to disseminate.[4] For him, Catherine was above all a true mystic, comparable to the greatest figures of Christian spirituality. Whereas Raymond of Capua insists on the fact that her stigmata had never been visible and were manifested only through severe pains in her feet, hands, and side, Tommaso Caffarini attests to their physical reality and sees in them the sign of her intense devotion to the Passion of Christ, as had already been the case for Francis and Clare of Assisi, Clare of Montefalco (in whose heart, after her death, were to be found all the instruments of the Passion), and Gertrude the Great (also known as Gertrude of Helfta), who bore the name of Christ inscribed in her heart in golden letters. Finally, and without hesitation, Caffarini compares her to Saint Paul by applying to her the famous phrase from the Letter to the Galatians (Gal 6:17): "For I carry the marks of Jesus [stigmata] branded on my body." In some manuscripts of the *Libellus de supplemento*, which Caffarini had commissioned in Venice, there are even some sketches attributable to the circle of Cristoforo Cortese, one of which illustrates the reception of Christ's stigmata with bleeding marks on her hands; and the other illustrates a vision that she shared with her entourage, in which Christ is in the process of driving a giant nail into her left hand.[5] What primarily interests Tommaso Caffarini is to win over the public to Catherine and, above all, religious women and tertiaries, Dominicans as well as others, living alone or in community. Most of these women did not know Latin but were capable of reading texts in the vernacular; and occasionally they recopied them in order to absorb their message. For them, the most evocative language was that of the body, transmitted by way of images accompanying Catherine's texts or those about her, which were thus becoming a real aid for meditation or contemplation and a means for drawing their communities together in a shared admiration for the saint. For this reason, it is the writings of Tommaso Caffarini, more than the *Legenda maior* of Raymond of Capua, that influenced the depiction of Catherine that was prevalent during the fifteenth century and beyond, as attested to by the abundant iconography that was devoted to her beginning in the 1450s, where representations of her stigmata, her ecstasies, and her visions predominate.

The inquest aiming to prepare Catherine's canonization that unfolded in Venice between 1411 and 1416 did not change this image greatly inasmuch as it was led from beginning to end by Caffarini, whose deposition alone goes on for some 230 pages in the modern edition of the process! The witnesses—twenty-two religious, of which there were six Dominicans and two laypeople—really wanted to underscore the role played by this woman in their lives. Some of these witnesses were priests—since several had been her confessors—and spiritual sons to whom she had spiritually given birth and formed in her divine school by indicating to them the path that they should follow and by taking upon herself their sins. Their depositions emphasize Catherine's conformity to Christ, which became evident at the moment of her death, which she had foreseen and announced. This theme was taken up again by Tommaso Caffarini in a brief work that attempted to draw a parallel between Catherine and Francis of Assisi, in the manner of Bartholomew of Pisa, on Francis's conformity to Christ—a work approved by the Order of Friars Minor in 1390. Several witnesses insisted on the fact that the saint, by her actions and writings, had blessed the Church with spiritual fruits that she had carried within her while she was yet in this life. Her influence was extended in their day through the revival of the Third Order of Penance of Saint Dominic and the progress of the Observance within the Order of Preachers, of which she is presented as its inspiration and guarantor. Finally, to shelter her from all criticism, the promoters of the inquest did not fail to emphasize that her charisms flowed from the *discretio spirituum*—the spiritual discernment that was the primary norm by which theologians assessed supernatural manifestations—and that she had always respected the ministry of the clergy. Catherine had acted according to a "command to teach" (*munus docendi*) that she had exercised in obedience to a divine commandment; and she always remained submissive to the authority of the Church. Her apostolate, which, according to Stefano Maconi, would have involved the conversion of thousands of people during her lifetime whom she sent to confession, had never been presented as an alternative to priestly power but, rather, was being exercised as something complementary to it.

CATHERINE OF SIENA ACCORDING TO HER OWN WRITINGS

Given that Catherine of Siena left behind a rather important body of work, we need not limit ourselves to the hagiographers' portraits of her; rather, we can establish a comparison between their image of her and the one that comes to us from her own writings. These consist of two main collections: on the one hand, the letters she dictated between 1367 and 1380; and, on the other hand, *The Dialogue*, which she simply called "the Book." We should also add her *Prayers*: a collection of twenty-six prayers recited by the saint during the last four years of her life. The status of these prayers is not the same as her other writings because they were noted down and transcribed—sometimes without her knowledge—by her disciples, and were never revised by her.[6]

Within this collection, the letters constitute the most impressive part: 383 of them have come down to us. And the doubts cast on the authenticity of some of them by Robert Fawtier have now been resolved.[7] Written in the vernacular, they form the most important collection of letters by a medieval woman. To be sure, a few letters by Clare of Assisi have been preserved dating from the mid-thirteenth century; but they are in Latin, and one may well wonder about the role that might have been played by the cleric holding the pen and putting her words down into their present form. Catherine herself, like her fellow citizen Giovanni Colombini a few years earlier, wrote in her mother tongue: the Tuscan vernacular that was spoken in Siena. She did not write these letters herself; she dictated them to scribes who took down the words from her lips and then ensured that the message was delivered to their intended recipients through various channels. In this sense, we can say that they are truly authentic writings. By contrast, after her death her entourage took it upon themselves to detach her message from its original contexts to give it a timeless character. They removed as much as possible all references to dates; thanks to this, only 250 of these letters are dated or datable. In addition, any mention of the places and specific circumstances to which they refer have also been removed. In this way, her disciples excised from the letters any superfluous element so as to transform them into a compendium of moral and spiritual teachings independent of the historical context in which they had originally been written.

These letters were addressed to very diverse correspondents who vary over the course of time: devout laywomen of the nobility and female religious of high society in Siena; political authorities of the Tuscan cities and Italian states; Popes Gregory XI and Urban VI, as well as a few cardinals and prelates of the Curia; and eventually the most important rulers of Europe: Charles V, Edward III, Joanna I of Naples, and many others as well. Given the elevated status of these recipients, they are testimonies to the broadening of Catherine's ambitions and renown. The image of her that we get from these texts is rather different from what Raymond of Capua provides in his *Legenda maior*. Catherine is obviously breaking with the previous tradition of the female mystic—grounded in humility, discretion, the rejection of writing and activity in the world. From the first to the last of her letters, she intervenes with authority and, despite her protestations of unworthiness, is believed to be a prophetess sent by God and charged by him with a message for Christianity. In some of her letters she discloses some "revelations" that she had received and that equipped her to intervene in the affairs of the Church. The only woman who could come close to her is her contemporary Birgitta of Sweden († 1373), who, like herself, did not hold back from harshly shaking up her listeners, both ecclesiastical as well as lay, and from denouncing their weaknesses and failings. But one does not find in Catherine's writings the apocalyptic tone and allegorical vocabulary that made some liken the Swedish saint to the biblical prophets. With Catherine, it was more a mixture of familiarity—she did not hesitate to call the pope *papa* (*babbo*, in vernacular Italian) and her correspondents *figliuoli* (little children)!—and toughness, which lends her style a very lively allure, while at the same time constantly referring to her own personal experience of God. She comes across in these letters as a passionate personality strongly engaged in the battles of her day. In addition to her vibrant calls for conversion, we find very firm positions taken on subjects as varied as the return of the papacy to Rome, the necessity of reforming the Church, and the reestablishment of peace between the Holy See and the rebellious Italian cities. And then, after the eruption of the Schism in 1378, we find violent polemics against the cardinals who betrayed Urban VI and elected Clement VII, as well as interventions in the cities and among Christian sovereigns to rally maximum support to the pope in Rome—which did not impede her from reprimanding the latter when she saw that he was surrounding himself with "bad" cardinals and that he was doing nothing to get moving on the reform of the Church. In this sense, it can be said that in her letters Catherine inaugurates a modern model of holiness that, without excluding a life of intense prayer (indeed, quite the contrary), expresses itself as a total engagement in the life of the Church and no longer only in the life of the world and that of men and women, as had also been the case for Francis of Assisi. The hagiographers tried to minimize this aspect of Catherine's holiness by reducing it to an intervention of supernatural inspiration that alone would have prompted the return from Avignon to Rome of Pope Gregory XI and the Curia. Nevertheless, by placing a one-sided emphasis on her asceticism, mystical life, and stigmata, they buried the highly political combat—in the broader and nobler meaning of the term—that she had led for peace among Christians, the reconciliation of adversaries, and the defense of justice. Thus, her message, stripped of its most original aspects, was received primarily by contemplatives or cloistered women—nuns or tertiaries—whereas she had lived especially in the heart of the world and in the midst of its contradictions.

The other major element of Catherine of Siena's work is a volume that she called "the Book" or "my book," whereas Raymond of Capua refers to it as "the Book of Divine Instruction." In the eighteenth century, the Sienese Domenico Gigli gave it the title of *The Dialogue*, which became its official title in twentieth-century editions. Raymond of Capua claims that this book was supernaturally inspired: "She received from God such clarities on the truth whose lights she saw herself obliged to spread externally by entrusting them to writing."[8] Moreover, he adds that she dictated it during her ecstasies, when her bodily senses were blocked, and that this book was not the result of natural forces but of the infusion of the Holy Spirit. To borrow the apt phrase of Odile Redon, Catherine benefitted from "a writing commission" that allowed her to pass on to her readers the mysteries of God.[9] Contrary to what Raymond of Capua states in the *Legenda maior*, *The Dialogue* was not composed in one sitting during the autumn of 1378 but was the object of successive embellishments between the summer of 1377 and the first months of 1378, while Catherine was on a peacemaking mission and apostolate in the Val d'Orcia, then at Belcaro near Siena. It was, in any case, completed before the beginning of the Great Schism, of which there is no mention in the book. One of her disciples, the notary Cristofano Guidini, described precisely how the book came about:

> The aforesaid servant of Christ again completed a work worthy of note: namely, she dictated a book on the importance of a Missal, while she was engulfed in ecstasy, having lost the use of all her senses, except that of speech. God the Father was speaking in her and she was answering him, questioning him and even repeating the words which came to be addressed to her, while simultaneously she was asking questions and all this was done in Italian.... She spoke and another transcribed: sometimes Ser Barduccio Canigiani

> and sometimes Neri di Landoccio. Once someone made a record of such things, it was hard to accept them, but those who heard these things and put them down in writing are of another opinion: I share their perspective.[10]

The Dialogue, which was initially of a piece, was eventually subdivided into 167 chapters to better facilitate its reading. Admittedly, this work is sometimes turgid and unattractive to the modern reader because of an overabundance of allegories and of circuitous thought, which leads to numerous repetitions. But it also includes some beautiful passages, such as the beginning of the prologue:

> A soul rises up, restless with the tremendous desire for God's honor and the salvation of souls. She has for some time exercised herself in virtue and has become accustomed to dwelling in the cell of self-knowledge in order to know better God's goodness toward her, since upon knowledge follows love. And loving, she seeks to pursue truth and clothe herself in it.[11]

The original plan of this work, both theological and spiritual, is composed of a dialogical structure in three parts: a request by Catherine, an answer from God, and then the saint's prayers of thanksgiving to her Creator. The requests addressed to God by Catherine are four in number: for herself, for the reform of the Church, for the world and peace between Christians, and about an individual case that remains unknown. In the first part, the two major themes of her teaching are developed: the first is that of the Christ-as-Bridge, who alone can help men and women to cross over without drowning in the river that separates the world of the living from that of the dead. The theme has biblical roots, since it echoes the Letter to the Hebrews (Heb 9:11–12):

> But when Christ came as a high priest [*pontifex* in the Latin of the Vulgate] of the good things that have come, then through the greater and perfect tent (not made with human hands, that is, not of this creation), he entered once for all into the Holy Place, not with the blood of goats and calves, but with his own blood, thus obtaining eternal redemption.

But the importance that Catherine gave to this passage is perhaps tied to the influence of visionary literature, which is evident in some fourteenth-century frescoes and miniatures in which one sees numerous souls falling off a very narrow bridge that spans a deep gorge while they try to reach the river of paradise. The second theme, which is related to the first and is omnipresent in her works, is that of the cross. In pouring out his blood on Calvary, Christ has opened to all people, through love, a pathway to God and has offered them salvation. In return, the human person must strive to respond to him by seeking to be conformed to the humbled and suffering Christ. But this movement of return toward God can only happen through the intermediary of the Church, which is the Body of Christ and which "administers" and distributes the redeeming blood. Like Joan of Arc a half-century later, Catherine indeed believes that "of Christ and the Church, it is one" and that the first mark of love that the Christian can give to God is to obey the Church and to help reform her. Indeed, as she writes,

> The Bride of Christ is persecuted by its unfaithful and corrupt members. Whoever raises him- or herself up against the Church becomes, from that moment on, her enemy, for she is none other than Christ himself and the one who dispenses to us the sacraments which give life.

The second part is devoted to a long, highly realistic description of the evils from which the Church of her day is suffering.[12] For her, reform must be, primarily, about the clerics who are giving bad example to the laity instead of edifying them, and are thus leading the Christian people to their damnation. For this battle, God promises his help to those who hope in him, whereas most men and women are letting themselves be guided by their own self-interest. The first and chief remedy to these evils resides in obedience. This then gives Catherine the opportunity to launch into a vibrant praise of the Dominican order, even though she sternly criticizes its decadence and calls it to renew itself in obedience to its vocation.

If we limited ourselves to drawing up an inventory of the ideas or spiritual themes that occur within *The Dialogue*, we would have to admit that there is not much here that is original. It has been often discussed whether Catherine might have been more influenced by

Augustinianism or by the Thomism that was prevailing in the ecclesiastical circles that she frequented. These debates do not hold great interest for us here, since she was formed "on the job" and her religious culture was fashioned in a haphazard way: Bible reading, things absorbed from the liturgy, the influence of vernacular hagiographical texts of a strongly ascetical tone, reflections based on lengthy discussions with her Dominican confessors, patristic references remembered from sermons. All of this constitutes an undoubtedly eclectic foundation that she learned to make her own thanks to her keen intelligence and especially to the passion that animated her. For her, Christ constitutes an absolute model of perfection—something that was a rather banal idea at a time when the *Meditations on the Life of Christ* (by a Franciscan, writing at the beginning of the fourteenth century but falsely attributed to Saint Bonaventure) and its translations into the vernacular constituted the bedtime reading of many devout laity.

On the theological level, Catherine's innovations are rare, even if some of them deserve to be mentioned. Thus, as to the thirst experienced by Christ on the cross, she notes in *The Dialogue* that the responsibility for his suffering falls upon all of humanity and not just on the Jews of her time—an idea that will be picked up again by Pascal when he writes in a very "Catherine-like" manner: "Christ is in agony until the end of time. It is urgent that we not fall asleep in the interim." But for Catherine, this thirsting is not only that of someone condemned to death to whom vinegar is given to drink as he approaches his end; it is also the thirsting for the redemption of souls that he is able to accomplish through his sacrifice. And the image of the Christ of the Passion—joyous, smiling, and impatient as a lover going out to meet his beloved—is also original for its time. However, her ecclesiology, which to us is highly questionable, as she makes a distinction between the laity (who form the universal Church) and the clergy (who constitute for her the mystical body of Christ), was rather banal in her own day. If Catherine is an author and an authority, as Tommaso Caffarini and, after him, the Catholic tradition would have it, let's say that her work has value especially because of the ardor that animates it. She lays out a Thomistic theology and makes it concrete; and her purpose is not to innovate but to actualize and make her message accessible by presenting it as something living. More than a treatise of spirituality, it is a cry: a cry of anguish in the face of sin and for sinners whom she sees dashing headlong toward their damnation; a cry of love when she tirelessly recalls the mercy of God and invites men and women to let themselves be moved and converted by it; a cry of indignation before the decrepitude of the Church and its religious orders and, more generally, the cowardice of people who are no longer capable of behaving in a virile manner—a phrase that she repeats frequently as an ideal.

To express this pain and this love, Catherine, who was writing and singing *laude* and had several poets as her disciples, sometimes has recourse to some truly beautiful images: for example, when she writes that "too foolish would be the one who neglects the rose for fear of the thorns"; or when she calls the breviary, with a little humor, "the priest's spouse," since he had the habit of walking around with it under his arm. The human soul is sometimes compared to green wood that the fire of the love of God makes cry out before being consumed, sometimes to a city or a strong fortress at whose gate stands the watchdog of conscience, who barks at the approach of enemies and is nourished by the blood of Christ and the fire of the Holy Spirit. Is this to say that her work is worth more for its style than for its content? Not at all. We can admit that some of the comparisons she uses appear to us today to be in rather poor taste: as when she speaks about the cross as the "skewer on which the Lamb of the new covenant was roasted in the fire of the Passion" (an image perhaps rooted in her domestic experience as a young girl confined to the ovens by her parents); or even her use of the image of flies landing first upon some excrement and then upon some food, when speaking about gossip. Let us note, nevertheless, that this realistic and sometimes even trivial lexicon is not limited only to her—in particular, the image of the pig that rolls around in the mud as a description of the soul mired in sin is borrowed from the patristic tradition—and that many medieval preachers sometimes had used the same images in their sermons. Indeed, her real originality resides in the fact that she knew how to put down in writing the force of the spoken word and how to translate, with vigor and passion, the love and desire that was inspiring them. She did indeed describe herself as "God's gentle town crier." Her style is a matter of eloquence—or rather of harangue—without making any explicit reference to the rhetoric whose rules she had probably never learned. Catherine wrote, as she never stopped saying, "in the blood of Christ" and with her own blood: metaphor, certainly, for the ink with which she wrote, but also for the effort that she expended to convince her reader of the seriousness of what was at stake and of the urgency of conversion, since, in the final analysis, it is the eternal salvation of the human person that was involved.

Our research on the depictions of Catherine transmitted to us by contemporary sources indicates a tension between different "readings" of her personality and work. On the one hand, her hagiographers, moved by the desire to have her holiness recognized by the Church, attempted to diminish whatever might be atypical in her personage. At a time when female sanctity was still having great difficulty in being recognized, Raymond of Capua underscored, in particular, the eminent service that she had given to the Church—especially in persuading the papacy to return from Avignon to Rome—and the fact that, due to her lack of formal learning, she had served as a marvelous channel for communicating to men and women of her time the messages that God wanted to address to them. For his part, Tommaso Caffarini, aware of the danger that existed in emphasizing a prophetic gift that was becoming controversial within the Church, insisted more on the correctness of her spiritual teaching and the extraordinary character of her mystical experience, while he also affirmed that her stigmata authenticated the inspired character of her work. The problem for the historian is that these images only partially coincide with what is found in the works that she herself has left behind for us and that sometimes contradict the first set of sources. Thus, probably out of humility but perhaps also out of prudence, Catherine never mentions the stigmata that she had received in Pisa in 1375 and that has caused so much ink to be spilled throughout the fifteenth century. Without, of course, rejecting the truth that these hagiographical texts contain, we cannot content ourselves with this alone. And so now we must try to determine in what, exactly, her real greatness and historical importance consisted.

CHAPTER 4

IN SEARCH OF CATHERINE

AN UNCONVENTIONAL PERSONALITY

If, in many ways, the life of Catherine of Siena seems to have ended with a series of failures, she does not remain any less a major personality who made her mark upon her time and who later exerted a profound influence on numerous people. It thus remains for us to explore the origin of the reputation she has enjoyed over the centuries, which results less from the historic role attributed to her (often with exaggeration) than from the unconventional character of her experience and the intensity of her mystical life.

"HOLY ANOREXIA": FASHIONING OF A SPIRITUAL BODY

All those who met Catherine while she was alive, whether they appreciated her or not, were struck by her tireless energy and her indomitable character. It suffices just to read her letters to be convinced of this, since any number of them contain the expression *io voglio* ("I want"). Furthermore, even when she addressed the pope or political leaders at the highest levels, she had difficulty hiding (albeit with an expression of profound humility) the passion that fired her and led her to get involved in what were often overwhelming issues. To understand this ever-present attitude in her, we need to study her psyche, and especially her relationship with the things that shaped her, so as to be able to interpret her spiritual experience. It would not be a matter of summarily resolving this problem from a pseudoscientific perspective, as the school of Charcot has done for the mystics and stigmatics from the end of the nineteenth to the beginning of the twentieth century.[1] Even if some of these behaviors might seem strange or frankly aberrant to us today, it is essential to interpret them by placing them in the historical context of their period and by interpreting them in the light of what we can know from psychology today. Let us say right from the start: at first glance, Catherine presents all the symptoms of anorexia nervosa, an illness of a neuropsychiatric character whose primary manifestation is a fierce opposition to the ingesting of an adequate amount of food. During her adolescence, this refusal of nourishment probably constituted for her the expression of some unresolved relationship with the dominating figure of her mother, whom she blamed her whole life for having loved her with a purely carnal love and for not understanding her, as she said in a letter she wrote to her as an adult:

> I have desired with a great desire to see you, truly the mother not only of my body but also of my soul. I think that if you loved my soul more than my body, all disordered tenderness would die in you and you would not suffer so much over being deprived of my bodily presence....You love more that part of me which I have taken from you—your flesh, the flesh with which you have adorned me—than that part of me which comes from God.[2]

This fundamental trauma was probably worsened by the sudden demise of her older sister, Bonaventura, to whom she was very close and who died when she was a teenager after giving birth. The shock she experienced at that time seems to have been at the root of her refusal to marry her brother-in-law, who was now a widower, as her mother would have wanted—and then extended to marriage itself and physical motherhood. Rejecting the code of the family clan, she chose to become a "liminal" creature, stripped of status, property, and rights.

From that time on, she abstained from eating meat and gave up wine at the age of fifteen, and then bread around the time she turned twenty. Afterward, she drew her sustenance from raw herbs and ended up limiting herself to a few drops of water a day as well as the host and a little wine received during communion, until she finally allowed herself to die of hunger and exhaustion. This abstinence, pushed to the extreme of perpetual fasting in her last years, was considered by her contemporaries, as we have seen, as proof of the miraculous character of her life. It justifies the remarkable study that two psychoanalysts, Ginette Raimbault and Caroline Eliacheff, devoted to her in their book titled *Les indomptables: figures de l'anorexie*, which, in regard to Catherine, was inspired by the work of the American historian Rudolph Bell, *Holy Anorexia*.[3] These two writers have indeed brought together in a pertinent manner a series of anorexic figures who have had a real influence upon their eras, from Antigone to Simone Weil (1909–43) by way of Catherine of Siena. For these women, the urgency that inspires their refusal of food is not just a simple psychological phenomenon; rather, it is more of "an urgent need to acknowledge a desire, a hunger of a sort, an entry into the symbolic order necessary to differentiate between animal nature and the material order of the human condition."[4] "To enter into the other world, it is imperative to cease being a social animal," said Simone Weil.[5] According to them, the will trumps all and certainty is the essential characteristic of their way of thinking. The parallel between Catherine of Siena and Simone Weil is wholly convincing in this respect: both demonstrated an unapologetic intransigence that was translated into their life by an absolute refusal of any compromise and by a kind of aggressiveness toward those who resisted or opposed them. Pushing physical effort to ever extreme limits, forever tormented by violent pains, they nonetheless appear oblivious to fatigue up to the moment when they collapse as if "dead" and then go through periods of depression.

For their entourage and those who met them, the most visible symptom of their state consisted in the privation of food—or rather their inability to take nourishment appropriately—in such a way that it became imperative for them, since adolescence, to share the condition of the poor and excluded. But, more profoundly, this rejection of food is rooted in another desire that would lead them to the ultimate sacrifice. Simone Weil let herself die of hunger in England after the authorities of Free France in London had refused her request to be parachuted into France to participate in the fighting of the Resistance. Catherine of Siena offered her life to God to obtain from him the end of the Schism and the reform of the Church that Pope Urban VI did not seem all that eager to undertake. Their ascetical experiences ended up in the search for martyrdom: they both believed that the ills produced by the faults and crimes of human beings could only be eliminated through the suffering of a totally obedient victim, even to the point of death if necessary. This aspect is especially obvious in Catherine of Siena, who, every time she wrote to people to reproach them for their evil deeds or failures, proposed to them that she would expiate for them and in their place their failures that she was denouncing. Such thinking ended up leading her to commit a senseless act, similar at first glance to suicide, to accomplish the healing of a sick world by leading men and women to become conscious of this hunger for an absolute good at the depth of one's heart and of the obligation to attain it. Catherine's contemporaries were not mistaken because the Dominicans, who were the promoters of her sanctity, asked the pope to canonize her specifically as a martyr—which Pius II did not do.

These women, however, who seem to us to be so somber, were not without hope. The mouth that is closed to food speaks *to* God and *about* God to one's fellow human beings. "The desired outcome on the path towards sublimation was the expectation of God: this fleeting Other—never-failing, all-powerful and all loving"—whom they encountered in the Eucharist: the anticipation of their union with Christ in the next life. As Simone Weil wrote about it—though the phrase could have been Catherine's: "In the supernatural world, the soul, by contemplation, feeds on the truth."[6] Catherine, for her part, never ceased yearning to "drink the blood of Christ" and to counsel her correspondents, beginning with her confessor, to do the same. Beyond the differences that do separate them, Catherine and Weil nevertheless have in common that, for their contemporaries, they both were exasperating personalities due to their larger-than-life character and heavy-handed demands, as well as "living reminders" (according to the expression used by a witness who had known Simone Weil well) pitting—at whatever cost—a mystic of charity against violence and idolatry.

And yet, should Catherine be considered—if not a "hysteric," as was said of her during the nineteenth century—at any rate mentally ill? This does not seem to be the case, inasmuch as her erratic alimentary practices, which were considered, in her lifetime, to be a marvel, were more endured than chosen—if we are to believe her own statements on the matter—and she knew how to make this handicap a springboard that allowed her to master her human condition. For her, anorexia is not the expression of the rejection of human nature and the body, but a preliminary step to its assimilation to and fusion with the body of Christ.[7] Catherine is seeking to destroy not her body but her ego; and, despite appearances, she exhibits no trace of any kind of masochism. As she wrote at the end of her life, "The devil is—and will be—conquered, not through the suffering of our bodies but through the virtue of the flame of the divine: the most ardent and priceless charity."[8] Indeed, for Catherine, physical energy had its source in the power of the soul, itself moved by God. Ever since adolescence, she had used all her strength to acquire perfect mastery over her body, allowing her to live without suffering from the cold—she said that Christ had adorned her with an invisible tunic of red, like his blood—and virtually without sleeping. She also sought to hide her femininity: in her youth, she had dreamed of putting on the Dominican habit to cease being the object of masculine desire and to be able to speak about God to other people. In carrying herself like this, it seemed to her that she was merely conforming herself to Saint Paul's assertion that "there is no longer male and female; for all of you are one in Christ Jesus."[9]

None of this was accomplished without struggle. This is evident from her writings, which allow us to read between the lines a constant confrontation between natural givens, such as hunger, exhaustion, and illness, and spiritual influences, for example, the demands of the soul and the virtues founded on the love of God. Her confessor and biographer, Raymond of Capua, claims that her body would not have been able to resist these assaults, were it not that it had been surrounded by God like a protective shield.[10] But Catherine not only resisted the temptations that her senses inspired within her; she also managed to transpose them onto a spiritual level and to make of them the agents of a supernatural relationship. Tamed, the body becomes a privileged instrument of communication with God, especially through tears, whose spiritual value she laid out in one whole section of *The Dialogue* (§88–97): the highest form are the tears of gentleness, the fruit of a union with God, which ends up going beyond language itself, which has now become useless. Catherine could also intuit the presence of carnal people or sinners in a given place: at the papal court, she caught a whiff of the odor of hell, just as she had experienced a kind of purgatory in the baths of Vignoni; she also saw members of the faithful who were in danger a great distance away from her and sensed, just by looking at someone, the temptation that was holding that person in its grasp. At the end of this process, she became identified with Christ and ended up acquiring the power to heal, and especially to convert souls. Once overcome, her body became capable of expressing the impulses and states of the soul through tears, levitations, and ecstasies, during which time she seemed removed from the sensate life and absent from the world. All of this happened as if Catherine had determined to fashion for herself a spiritual body: the earthly anticipation of the "glorious body" with which, according to Saint Paul, the elect will be endowed at the time of the final Resurrection. In the eyes of her followers, Catherine had in any case already assimilated here below its supernatural powers: a superhuman strength, invulnerability to fire, impassability during ecstasy, and the ability to work miracles, especially the healing of people struck with the plague. However, jealous to safeguard her intimacy and to live in the shadows, she only used these powers for her relatives, beginning with her own mother, whom she "resuscitated" when the latter was in danger of death without having received the sacraments, in order to allow her soul to escape the pains of purgatory, if not hell itself.

THE MYSTIC OF LOVE AND THE LANGUAGE OF THE BODY

The body similarly shapes Catherine's whole spiritual life. Whenever she received communion, she felt her union with Christ in a physical way, as a kind of body-to-body experience in which the rise in pleasure was accompanied by an accelerated fluttering of the heart, groaning, and sometimes even cries. These manifestations raised some discomfort within her entourage to such a degree that they sometimes forbade her to receive communion for this very reason. But they attested that she satisfied her desire of losing herself in the consummation of an amorous love with Christ when her very suffering ended up being transformed into pleasure. For Catherine, there were not two lives, that of the spirit and that of the body. The whole lexicon that describes her relationship with God has a strong corporeal dimension, and she is good at translating spiritual ideas into sensual images by using binary opposites such as hard and soft, dry and wet, open and closed. With Catherine, the heart is the hearth of feeling as well as of spiritual knowledge: the place where the fundamental decision of the will for or against God is located. As to blood, omnipresent in her writings, it constitutes both the principle of life and the fruit of an experience of love that reached its culmination in the Passion of Christ, which she likens to the mystical wine press from which drips the precious redeeming drink (according to an image very popular in the art of the fifteenth century, particularly north of the Alps). But the compassion that the sufferings of Christ inspired in her did not culminate in a moving and realistic vision of Calvary, as can be seen in the altarpiece of Unterlinden in Colmar, where the victim no longer bears human characteristics. Along with a sense of measure that—despite certain appearances—was typical of her, Catherine considered less the physical tortures endured by the Crucified than their moralistic meaning and their beneficial effects for humanity.

Given this, should Catherine be considered a mystic? This term has been so debased that the historian hesitates to even use it. Nevertheless, if we restrict ourselves to Michel de Certeau's definition, it really does seem that it might be legitimately applied to her. Indeed, for de Certeau, the male or female mystic is someone who wants "to offer a body to the spirit, to incarnate speech and to provide a place for the truth."[11] Catherine's experience falls fully within this line of thinking, since, during her brief life, she sought to see and to live the dimension of the real, in which the humanity of Christ and the divinity of the human person are discovered, and to make of her body a place for the articulation of his word. Her mouth, closed to nourishment, speaks *of* God and *to* God in the course of extended colloquies, and she even calls herself "the mouthpiece of holy desire." Here, we are rather far from the mystical speculation that had developed in Germany at the start of the fourteenth century around Meister Eckhart. For Catherine, Christ is not the Logos or the second person of the Trinity; he is, above all else, the inner Master whom she strives to know with all the resources of her psychology and keen sensibility. He is himself a book that he has written with his own blood on the wood of the cross: a text that the entire world is capable of reading and understanding. And as the sight of this Crucified God who died for the human race is not enough to lead sinners to change their lives, Catherine set herself the goal of producing a new body according to the order of the spirit, which might become, in its turn, a sign for those who witnessed her lifestyle or who were in relationship with her. Taking upon herself the physical and spiritual abjectness of others, flagellating her flesh to force it into obedience, she returned her body to the sacred and reestablished a symbolic connection between human beings by the reordering of material and spiritual goods. This, in turn, allowed her to become a christic figure and to ground her own authority in God. Raymond of Capua relates in his *Legenda maior* that one day, while he was listening to her with some skepticism as she described to him a vision that she had just had, he asked her, "Do you think that this is true?" Immediately, he saw her face change and he believed that he recognized the face of Christ shining forth from the darkness, after which he exclaimed, "Oh! Who is this that is looking at me?" to which she responded, "It is the One who is!"[12] For Catherine identified herself both with the Crucified—with his crown of thorns and his bloody wounds—and with the glorious body of the Risen One from whom, in ecstasy, she possessed certain privileges, including impassability, strength, and the power to effect miracles.

The christocentrism that characterizes Catherine's piety and spiritual life was nothing exceptional for the time. Since Francis of Assisi († 1226), it had become the keyword and very heart of Western spirituality. Nor was it all that original to speak about Jesus as "our mother"; this follows a tradition that had originated in the twelfth century and that emphasized the nourishing character of his word, which the soul had to drink from his breast.[13] But Catherine is more original when she stresses the union of the two natures—the divine and the human—in the person of Christ, whom she very often calls "God-and-man," as if his proper name counted for less than his role as redeemer of the world through the Incarnation and Passion. Influenced by the theology of Thomas Aquinas, which she had learned from her Dominican circle, she sees in Christ a "man for others": the Son of God who came into this world to save humanity, whose condition he had shared, and to give meaning to its history. Every Christian, whoever he or she might be, is called to become another Christ inasmuch as the human being can "possess God" in him- or herself and act in union with him. Even the experience of sin (that is, of human misery) can be overcome by the love of God present in us through the contemplation of his Passion, which she mentions much more frequently than the Resurrection.

But the most original aspect of Catherine's thought probably rests in the emphasis she placed in her writings upon the primacy of love. For her, it is the strength of the world because it is the nature of God himself, and this God passionately loves the human person, who is, as a creature endowed with reason, God's masterpiece. Creation is a work of love and it constitutes the purpose for which the human person has been created:

> O Ineffable Love, even though in your light you have seen all the iniquities which your creature was going to commit against you, Infinite Goodness, you have acted as if you have not seen; but you have placed your gaze on the beauty of your creature, of whom, as if crazy and drunk with love, you have been enamored, and through love, you have made the human person like yourself and given that person existence in your image and likeness.[14]

God has manifested his love for the human person in the person of Christ, his Son, who has poured out his blood on the cross for the redemption of the human race; and, doing this, he has grafted the tree of Life—the cross—onto the tree of love, which is the human person, which had been transformed into a tree of death by sin. One cannot thus be lifted up to the perfection of love except by taking as a model Christ Crucified and by following him in his sufferings and tribulations.

From this perspective, the redeeming blood has a special place in the work of Catherine, who returns to this theme many times. All her letters begin with a reference to the blood of Christ and, according to the witnesses of her final sufferings, her last words were, "The blood, the blood!" The blood poured out by Christ on the cross is the proof of the ransom from our faults, the sign of the new covenant between human beings and God; and it alone allows us to present ourselves without fear before his justice. It is the true signifier of Christian identity. As she wrote to Niccolò Soderini, "We are not Jews or Saracens, but Christians ransomed and purified in the blood of Christ."[15]

In this regard, allow me to cite a passage from one of her letters devoted to this essential aspect of her spirituality:

> With his blood, he has washed the face of our soul; by his blood which he spilled out with such an ardor of love and true patience, he has made us reborn in the life of grace. The blood covers our nakedness for it adorns us with grace; the warmth of the blood makes the ice melt and warms up once again the lukewarm state of the human race. The darkness disappears in the blood and the light appears once again. Self-love was obliterated in the blood in such a way that it is true how the soul that sees that it is loved up to the point of blood has reason to flee from the wretched love of the self to love the Redeemer who has given his life with such ardor of love on a passionate journey towards the ignominious death of the cross. If we would but desire it, the blood of Christ will be our drink and his flesh our food. The hunger of the human person cannot be satisfied in any other way and his or her thirst cannot be slaked but by the blood.…For the blood is impregnated with the eternal divinity of the Infinite Being whose nature is superior to that of the human person.[16]

In the wonderful exhortation that she addressed to the prisoners who were detained in Siena on Holy Thursday, April 9, 1377, she picks up the same theme in a pastoral manner:

> My very dear sons in Christ, the gentle Jesus, I, Catherine, servant and slave of the servants of Jesus Christ, I write to you in his precious blood, desirous of seeing you bathed in a holy desire in the blood of Christ Crucified. Fix on him the eye of your intelligence; having done this, you will acquire true patience, for the blood of Christ represents both our iniquities and the infinite mercy and charity of God. Thus does this representation [before God] make us hate ourselves and regret our failings, our sins, and it makes us love the virtues.…In rebelling against one's Creator, the human person had become sick and enfeebled; thus it could not take the bitter remedy which its failure required. Thus did God have to give us the Word, his only Son.…Thus did our doctor survive, such a knight.…By his blood he has healed us of our iniquities; he has given us his flesh as food and his blood as precious drink. This blood is so sweet and pleasing,

> its sweetness and power are such that it healed all infirmities and gives back life to those who have died. It clears away the darkness and brings the light.[17]

Catherine's piety, which differed from some of the spiritual currents of her day, is not centered upon the death of Jesus alone and is not reduced to a "religion of Good Friday." She is a trinitarian mystic, and at the center of her mysticism stands "the Godhead" with whom she is in conversation all throughout *The Dialogue*. In the Trinity, the Father is power, the Son is wisdom, and the Spirit is clemency, which is to say, charity. In becoming incarnate, Christ has not "left" the Trinity, but to the human race he offered the possibility of gaining access, after him, to the power of the Father and the mercy of the Spirit. The human person is insatiable; its desire will be sated only if it accepts to be nourished by faith and by hunger, following the example of Christ. He himself thirsts for our souls—for all souls—to whom he offers his salvation; through him, God in some manner places himself at our service. But this love calls for a response on the part of the human person. As she wrote to Beatrice [Regina] della Scala, wife of Bernabò Visconti, who had told her that she did not experience this feeling, "Love is only acquired by love. The one who wants to be loved must first love, that is, must have the will to love."[18] For her, as for Thomas Aquinas, whose ideas on this point have influenced her, the link between love and will is essential. God has created the human person without that person; but—as she often reminds the recipients of her letters—God will not save that person without that person's help. But the love of neighbor is the only means that we have to render to God love for love, because the Creator does not need our services. God has made the human person in his image and likeness. Such is the fundamental reality and the mystery of our existence: God is love and we are made for this love, which draws us into the joy of his being.

In this same line of thinking, the role of the human being is essential, since he or she becomes, if willing, the cooperator with God in the redemption of the world. Indeed, God and the human person do not encounter one another only in an intimate and unitive love; the one transforms the other. Addressing herself to her Creator, Catherine cries out, "And now by making yourself one with us you have become our image, veiling your eternal divinity in the wretched cloud and dung heap of Adam. And why? For love! You, God, became human and we have been made divine."[19]

Thus, it can be said that Catherine did have a veritable mystical theology, founded on an experience of the divine truths that were translated into a discipline of life that passes through asceticism and abnegation, before arriving at contemplation. She believed that the union of hearts had to be sought after, not for the spiritual consolations it brought to her in intimacy and solitude, but as a source of joy that she desired to share with others.

Catherine is, however, rather clear in that she was aware of the distance between this ideal and the reality she saw around her. In her writings and especially in her letters, she assigns a key role to the self-love that in her eyes constituted, along with servile fear, the main obstacle to the love of God and neighbor and from which proceeded all the evils with which Church and society were burdened. To look upon oneself as supreme is a way of substituting oneself for the Creator and of denying him. In giving us being, God has made, through love, a gift that creates for the human person an obligation of reciprocity from which one can shirk—for the human person is indeed free—but not without a lack of gratitude that will make that person lose the grace. For Catherine, this just God is also and above all merciful. By taking on flesh, he placed himself at the disposition of everyone and offered to the soul the possibility of being ransomed by recognizing its nothingness and by giving its consent to the divine action through the practice of the virtues. To believe that our faults can wear down the divine mercy is a veritable sin against the Holy Spirit, as the fate of Judas illustrates, whose principal wrong, she says, is less in having betrayed Jesus than in having despaired of his forgiveness. To remain united to God, there is no means other than the vocal and mental prayer in what Catherine calls "the cell of the knowledge of self"—the inner self.

One of the most characteristic traits of Catherine's spirituality is without a doubt the importance she attaches to desire and to the will, as the frequency of the word *voglio* ("I want") attests in the letters she addressed to her correspondents. The desire for God manifests itself when the creature carries out the praise and glory of his name by freely participating in one's own salvation. For the human person, this consists in wrenching oneself away from self-love and the seductions of the material life to "increase the fire of holy desire"—which is already in oneself but which one has a reflexive tendency to snuff out. All throughout her writings we find a stern condemnation of all sentimentality, of all retrospective nostalgia for a past of sadness and sin that we cannot prevent ourselves from loving, since it was our own. Giving a contemporary voice to familiar passages from the New Testament, she does not cease urging her correspondents to stop behaving like weathervanes (*uomini da vento*): "Let the dead bury their dead!"; "Do not turn back to the plow, stop looking back behind you!" "Run this *palio* [race]; become intoxicated in the blood of Christ." Catherine always propels herself forward, bound by her desire of joining together, in prayer and in action, the "great desire" for Christ—that inextinguishable fire which impels us constantly to get out of ourselves. "To get to heaven," she writes, "there is no other way than this: to lose oneself, to seek the honor of God, the salvation of souls, and the peace of the nations." The soul, detached from the world, is required to help others—whether it be the pope or a simple believer—to develop what is planted in the deepest part of their being, standing before the evils of the day and the crises of the Church. Mystical life and involvement in the affairs of this world are really the two faces of one and the same love.

A WOMAN IN CHURCH AND SOCIETY: WAS CATHERINE A FEMINIST?

For Catherine, the Church—which gathers all those who know the price of the blood poured out by the Lamb—must be the very love of God shed and poured out. Thus, she does not hesitate to write to Pope Gregory XI, "I want you to be a Tree of love grafted onto the Word of love: Christ Crucified!"[20] Like Christ, Catherine—who believes herself to be like a shepherd of the Church charged with watching over the flock—is ready to sacrifice herself for the redemption of the world and the salvation of souls. Her originality rests above all in the fact of having transposed her conception of motherhood from the private sphere and from intimate experience to the public realm and to engagement in the battles of history based on an identification between the suffering body of Christ and his mystical body that is the Church. For her, souls are not separate entities. They form a spiritual communion that is expressed outwardly in the visible body of the Church—a hierarchical society organized under the authority of the pope, whom she characterizes as "the sweet Jesus here on earth." Catherine sees in the successor of Peter not only the leader of the Church but the representative of Christ in this world: outside of the Church there is no salvation and every human person is a subject of the Roman pontiff. Indeed, in 1377, she writes to Gregory XI, "You are the gate keeper of God's storehouse, the guardian of the blood of his only Son whose place on earth you occupy and no one can receive the blood of Christ except from your hands."[21] To obey the pope is thus to obey God himself and to disobey him is to give offense to the Creator. Catherine does not ask herself about the limits of pontifical power, nor of the relationships between the hierarchy and the Christian people. Even if she had probably never read the writings of Pseudo-Dionysius the Areopagite, she is fully imbued with the theocratic conception of the Church that had been developed throughout the Middle Ages, according to which only the hierarchy and the clergy could enjoy any active role therein: "You (the simple faithful) are in the universal body of the Church and they are in the mystical body, placed there to nourish our souls"—she tells God in *The Dialogue*.[22] Like Francis of Assisi, she venerates clerics for their hands, which have the power to consecrate the host and to administer the body and blood of Christ to the faithful; and, however unworthy they may be, it belongs to the pope and not to civil authority to correct them. But, at the same time, she does not cease to remind her listeners how the traditional distinctions between clergy and laity must be relativized, since, for God, the veritable criterion of perfection is obedience, and not the state of life that one has embraced: "And if you asked me," God says to her in *The Dialogue*, "who has the greatest merit: those who are in orders or other people, I would answer that the merit of obedience is not to be measured by the act nor the place, nor one's state—be it secular or religious…—but by the degree that one is obedient: with this measure is each one measured."[23] These solid convictions—about which she never tires of reminding her Florentine interlocutors in her letters during the crisis of 1375–78—do not prevent her from sometimes being highly critical toward the papacy, which had the tendency to engage in political or diplomatic games and to neglect its own vocation, which was first and foremost spiritual. Thus, she does not hesitate to remind Urban VI that no pope, whoever he is, can behave like an absolute monarch and refuse to take counsel from anyone prior to acting:

> As to authority, you can do everything. But as for what there is to see, not more than anyone else. Whence the necessity that your children see and do with a pure heart, without servile fear, everything that contributes to the honor of God, to your honor, and to the honor and salvation of the sheep who are under your sway.[24]

And, since Urban VI was taking no account of her opinion, she came to ask him, speaking as if on behalf of God (whose spokesperson she believed herself to be), to accept sharing his power with the cardinals—whom she characterized, in a very classic manner, as the "pillars of the Church"—and to introduce a real collegiality in their regard:

> Say to my vicar that he be at peace as much as he can be.... Say also to the columns of the Holy Church that, if they want to remedy such ruins [within the Church], they should join together and form a mantle that covers over the behaviors of their Father which appear imperfect to them. Having done this, I who am the Light, I will give them the light that will be necessary to the Holy Church. When they will have seen, together, what is necessary to do, after mature deliberation they will refer the matter as one mind to my Vicar, promptly and firmly. Then he will acquiesce to their good will because their intentions are good and sound.[25]

When her reminders were not acted upon, she did not hesitate to engage in a kind of blackmail with respect to the Sovereign Pontiff, as when she wrote to Gregory XI, whose prevarications ended up exasperating her: "Act in such a way that I will not have to complain about you to Christ Crucified!" All throughout her letters, she does not cease reminding the prelates that the true riches of the Church are souls and that it is imperative that they conquer them again by the means they have acquired—by poverty, humility, and mildness; and she also continues to urge the pope to return to Rome, without troops, "with the cross in his hand, like the sweet Lamb." Like Christ, the successor of Peter is sent by God to the human race and his role is to promote the reform of the Church, not in its beliefs but in its practices and in its personnel, who are behaving in an unworthy and sometimes scandalous manner.

To Urban VI—who ultimately ended up disappointing her—she wrote in December of 1379 these prophetic words:

> God absolutely wants to reform his Bride; he does not want her to be a leper. If your Holiness does not do everything that is in your power—the reason God has chosen you and raised you up to such a high dignity—He will do it Himself in the midst of great tribulations. He will pull up all those twisted planks and set them aright in his own way. Alas, most Holy Father, let us not wait to be humbled![26]

But this pope—whom she had supported with all her strength against the cardinals who had previously betrayed him and against his rival, Clement VII—had many other concerns on his mind other than the reform of the Church. The calls that Catherine addressed to him to involve himself personally in this cause must have appeared to him to be more unseemly or ludicrous since they were originating from a poor laywoman who had no right to speak to him in this tone other than her own claim to being a messenger from God.

For almost forty years, the renewal of studies on Catherine of Siena, especially in the United States, has resulted in her being regarded as one of the most remarkable figures of feminism in the history of medieval Christianity. In fact, her apostolic and political engagement, her frank speaking to the highest dignitaries in Church and society, and the fascination that she held for her circle—lay as well as ecclesiastical—constitute elements that confer on her life and activity an original and innovative character. Had not Christ revealed to her that he made no distinction between the sexes and that his spirit could be poured out upon women as well as men? At first glance, other indications could lead us to slightly nuance this extraordinary assessment. Thus, one of the words that occurs most frequently in her writings is the adjective *virile*—which expresses, it seems, her personal attitude toward life. Even her style is "virile": she does not hesitate to write to Pope Gregory XI several times with numerous interjections and words in the imperative: "Father, stand up and be a man!" But what does *virility* mean for Catherine? This is not, for her, a typically masculine virtue, for she makes this demand of men as well as women. It is, rather, the fear of God—in the biblical sense of the term—that renders the soul virile, that is to say, strong and responsive, through the exercise of the virtues and the gifts of the Spirit.[27] To live in a virile manner is to show toughness in the ascetical and moral life so as to free up in oneself the desire of God in constant tension with the imitation of Christ. For Catherine, the use of the words *virile* and its opposite *feminine* does not, therefore, have a sexual connotation and does not refer to categories tied to gender. In using them she is simply referring to a medieval stereotype that associates masculinity with courage and a firm mindset and femininity to weakness, as demonstrated by the testimony of her own life.[28]

In this area as in many others, Catherine's behavior and reactions are more revelatory than her words. In none of her writings does she challenge the limits to which women of her time were subject; instead, she goes beyond them through the depth of her spiritual life. Indeed, her contemporaries held that women should be sequestered in the private realm, whereas the public sphere was reserved for men. Catherine was not unaware of this fundamental dichotomy, but she turned it around by positioning herself without hesitation as an apostle—in the line of Saint Paul—and as an itinerant and vocal prophetess sent by God. The dangers of such a claim become evident in view of all the effort expended by Raymond of Capua, in his *Legenda maior*, to hide the criticisms that her life could have raised. He proposed that Catherine's ascetical "excesses" were so improbable from a natural point of view that they, in fact, proved the intervention of God in her life and that they conferred on her a kind of charismatic power. Raymond also tried to justify the fact that Catherine—who, as a religious woman (*mulier religiosa*) would have had to live as a recluse or, in any case, not to spend her time out on the roads—had behaved like an itinerant prophetess and probably had not been aware of the prohibition of Saint Paul against women speaking in the Church. She herself, to believe her biographer, would have desired to become a Friar Preacher in order to be able to go out and proclaim the word of God in far-flung lands. In the Church and society of her time, however, the fact that she was a woman was an obstacle to her apostolic vocation, something of which she was fully conscious ever since Christ had said to her, "I want you to take care of certain people and that your life be a rule and example for many people."[29] In fact, Catherine ended up plowing an original path by exercising a spiritual motherhood—legitimized by frequent references to the Virgin Mary—but especially by her intimate relationship with Christ, whom she considered to be her spouse. This belief—that she was chosen and sent out by God—was manifested in her relationship with those clerics and laity who had entered her *famiglia* and who felt themselves orphaned after her death; with her confessor, whom she did not hesitate to correct and accuse of being lukewarm; and even with the pope and the powers of the world to whom she was unsparing with her criticisms. In short: all who possessed an institutional authority but were perhaps not following her counsels—and yet they had, in general, respect and admiration for her.

Nevertheless, the power that was recognized in Catherine was not, for her, an attribute of her gender, for she was not oblivious to women's weaknesses. To be convinced of this, one need only read the scathing letters she sent from 1378 to 1379 to Queen Joanna I of Naples, to persuade her to support the cause of Pope Urban VI. For Catherine, Joanna apparently incarnates a degraded femininity that stirs up in her nothing but disdain and pity:

> Alas, alas, we can mourn over you as if you were dead! You have taken your distance from the life of grace: dead with respect to the soul, dead with respect to the body if you do not get out from underneath such a serious error.... With the greatest of ignorance, moved by your own passions, you have chosen the most wretched and worst possible counsel that there is.... Open the eye of your intelligence and stop sleeping-walking in such wretchedness! Do not wait until the moment of death to admit your wrongdoing and say: "I thought I was doing the right thing!" That will not help you at all, because you know that you have acted wrongly; but being such a sick and frenzied person, you have allowed yourself to be guided by your passions.[30]

Catherine should thus not be considered a feminist, as she never openly criticized the division of functions among the sexes that existed in the Church and society of her day. But she endeavored to go beyond sexual differences by referring in her writings only to human nature, and she subverted from within the traditional categorizations by proving through her own personal example that it was possible for a woman, born—as we said earlier—into a modest environment and lacking in education, to assume the typically masculine functions of peace messenger and even director of souls and consciences. Even though he kept her at a distance, Gregory XI recognized in her a woman inspired by God and capable of touching hearts and souls. By equipping her with a squad of confessors, he endeavored to frame this specific gift as an original conjunction between missionary activity and ministerial priesthood: Catherine effected the conversion of others and the male religious of her circle assigned the penance to those whom she had led back to God. This allowed her to get around the obstacle of the exclusion of women from the priesthood. Here we doubtless run up against a sacerdotal conception of her role in the Church and in the city that, because of her charism, conferred on her a function as intercessor between humanity and its Creator. And up until the time of her death, she never stopped interceding with God on behalf of her contemporaries. But it is important to note that she did not seek to universalize for others her own personal charism.

Catherine did suffer, however, from being distanced, as a woman, from the consecration of the Eucharist and from frequent communion as a layperson. To believe her biographers, the ravishment she experienced during Mass at the time of the elevation constituted for her a substitute for communion when it was denied to her. But, in fact, it was only the reception of the consecrated host that gave her the *direct* contact with Jesus that she sought above all else. Thus, her refusal to take in normal nourishment was but the opposite side or the compensation for her intense desire to receive as often as possible the body of Christ under the species of bread and wine. These examples of "eucharistic famine" collided with the prohibitions of the Church, which was careful to reserve frequent communion only to priests and religious. According to Tommaso Caffarini, when Catherine had not received from her confessor permission to take communion (generally because he was absent), she sent up this prayer to her mystical Spouse: "Lord, have you not said, 'Unless you eat my flesh…'? I, however, want to eat this flesh and they will not give it to me!" After this, Christ himself came to give communion to her, which she received with delight. While consuming the host and drinking at the chalice, she had the impression she was "eating the flesh of Jesus, of having in her mouth drops of his blood" and of "receiving Christ, tiny and bloodied."[31] For her, God on the altar became food and the priest administered the blood of Christ with which it was necessary to become commingled in order to be saved. This conviction sometimes took on paroxysmal forms: did she not, on one occasion, bite down on the chalice that the celebrant was handing to her with such fervor and force that she left behind an impression of her teeth in the metal?[32] Demonstrations of devotion like this offend our sensibilities because of their graphic nature. They probably originated in visions or dreams conveyed through images that ended up becoming tangible realities for her—like that of the Child Jesus asleep in the manger: all the more moving in her eyes since she knew that he had been promised from his cradle a bloody death. In the hagiographical and spiritual texts of the fourteenth and fifteenth centuries, there abound instances of pious women who "saw in spirit" the Virgin Mary giving suck to the Child Jesus, or the latter having lost a drop of blood after having touched the thorn of a rose. Whether such might be an actual event or a dream, eucharistic communion was above all else for them the occasion for expressing their devotion to the redemptive Passion of Christ and for uniting themselves to his suffering. As Christiane Klapisch-Zuber has aptly stated, what these women were seeking was "to experience in their own bodies theological truths and, above all else, that of the Incarnation. Through female bodily metaphors, a spiritual aspiration is always being expressed."[33]

Finally, Catherine of Siena innovates more profoundly inasmuch as, for her, "life in Christ" consists of being physically united to the Crucified Jesus and to his wounds. On numerous occasions, she speaks—or threatens—to hide herself in the side wound of Christ: that "boutique full of fragrances" is the place where she most eagerly places herself, beyond every human authority. For her, it is not merely a matter of an image or a simple metaphor but of a felt truth: in letting himself be reduced to the state of a suffering body, Christ became woman and mother, since he birthed us to a new life by his torments and wounds. Every Christian, therefore, has a vocation to become "another Christ"—and here we once again find the theme of the *alter Christus*, which was so important in the Franciscan interpretation of the stigmata of Francis of Assisi since the time of Bonaventure—provided one reassesses one's wholly spiritual nature to include a bodily component. For Catherine, the flesh of Christ in the Passion has become a feminine flesh, which she speaks about as a vagina that opens to the prick (*spillo*) of desire. This leads to a kind of inversion of the sexes in the mystical union in which the soul becomes the spouse and Christ becomes the Bride who alone can fulfill its desire. The *imitatio Christi* thus constitutes a practice in which women have an advantage or even a privilege, especially in as much as they (are said) to have come from the man's side.[34]

Thus, as Antonio Volpato has noted, Catherine effected "a charismatic transcending" of the three functions traditionally reserved to the clergy: teaching, the spiritual direction of the faithful, and their sanctification.[35] And yet she considered this privilege a grace that God had given to her and not as an object to reclaim for the female gender.

CATHERINE OF SIENA: PROPHETESS OF SPIRITUAL RENEWAL

Catherine's contemporaries, just like today's historians, had some difficulty in trying to precisely name her charism. If everyone, including her political adversaries, agreed even during her lifetime that she was a holy woman, the characterization of her as a prophetess has sometimes been contested in our own day. Indeed, in comparison with some other irrefutably prophetic women such as Birgitta of Sweden, Catherine cuts a poor figure. She is neither openly adversarial nor apocalyptic; and even in her letters, she strives to discourage her correspondents from talk that, in the tragic climate of Italy at the end of the fourteenth century, interpreted the evils of the day as signs announcing the final cataclysm or, at least, as great collective upheavals. Thus, she wrote to a certain Renaud of Capua, "a distinguished person of Naples who ponders the mysteries of God and of Sacred Scripture,"

> Many are those who, devoid of all humility and without taking the time to recognize their own faults, outsmart themselves and, with their eyes clouded over, claim to understand Holy Scripture and to penetrate into its depths, all the while flattering themselves when explaining it and interpreting it in their own fashion. They study the Apocalypse, not with humility and illumined by the light of faith, but with pride and they get all tangled up in their arguments by throwing themselves into difficulties which they cannot resolve.... Whereas their mind ought to be filled with God, it delights instead in chimera; and the fruit which they cull from them is only confusion and darkness.[36]

Catherine's prophetic nature does not allow her to be reduced to "the pursuit of the millennium"—to use the title of the famous book of Norman Cohn—nor even to the public appeals to conversion proclaimed by travelling preachers such as the Franciscan hermit and tertiary Tomasuccio da Foligno, who, during the 1370s, preached in Siena and in most of the towns of Tuscany while stressing that the endtime was near. Catherine does not have an eschatological perception of history, and we do not find in her writings any detailed announcement of the steps that are to precede the Last Judgment. What is most important for her is the fate of each individual and the state in which he or she will be found at the moment of death. A stranger to every form of millenarianism, she does not project into the future the need to bring about the fullness of the Church and the coming of the kingdom. But if she is indifferent to the unfolding of the last days, the expectation of a messianic fulfilment was at the core of her desire. Like Paul, whose letters and apostolic zeal she strove to imitate, she does not stop insisting to her correspondents that they know how to seize "the opportune moment" or favorable time—that is to say, what is happening right now—to turn their lives around and to begin acting appropriately. Catherine is literally obsessed by the urgency of the moment: "There is no time to lose," she wrote several times to Pope Gregory XI, who kept procrastinating about his return to Rome. It is crucial that he engage in the fight against abuses because the crisis the Church was experiencing was so profound that it might even put into doubt his own role as the instrument of salvation, unless one fixes things without delay. The reform she is trying to promote with all her strength is not located in some distant future; its horizon is not the struggle against an antichrist to come. The only thing to which she applied this title was truly present and actual: it was the antipope Clement VII. Her expectation is more like a harkening for a return to the foundational sites of Christianity, Jerusalem and Rome. It would be imperative to return to the Church's past: to a time when it had been bathed by the blood of Christ and the martyrs and not weighted down with goods and possessions. Based on this broadly symbolic though compelling vision of Christian origins, Catherine aspires to reformulate in religious terms the relationship in the Church between exteriority and interiority; and she urges its leaders to free themselves from sociopolitical factors that were weighing on them, especially the taste for temporal power and the excessive influence of family ties.

More broadly, we can include under the word *prophecy* every systematic attempt to interpret historical deeds in the light of a higher plan. This is really Catherine's attitude, which always makes a connection between the events she has been witnessing and the plan of God. Not content simply to guide Christians in the spiritual life, she was also trying to influence them in their everyday activities. Here we see a constant deepening of her vocation, which is, first and foremost, of an apostolic nature. In the beginning, her mission unfolded in Siena and its surroundings in relation to people—the devout of good society or nuns who had been sent to her by their confessors—as well as in families to which she had been called to serve as mediator and peacemaker. But on April 1, 1376, she had had a decisive vision that she reported in a letter addressed to Raymond of Capua and, through him, to the members of her *famiglia* who were then in Avignon. Its text deserves to be cited *in extenso*:

> Rejoice and exult because the time has come! For, on the first of April during the night, God revealed more concretely his secrets, manifesting his wonders, in such a way that my soul seemed to no longer be in my body, receiving such delights and fullness that my tongue is not even able to put it into words. He explained and laid out in detail the persecution which the Holy Church has now been undergoing, its renovation, its exaltation which will occur in the future, saying that the present time is being permitted in order to bring it back to its [proper] state, quoting two phrases from the Holy Gospel: "Occasions for stumbling are bound to come, but woe to the one by whom the stumbling block comes!" [Matt 18:7], as if he was saying: "I am permitting this time of persecution in order to remove the thorns from my Bride, who is completely covered with them; but I am not permitting the evil thoughts of human beings. Do you know what I am doing? I am acting as I did during the time when I was on the earth, when I made a whip of cords to chase those who were buying and selling, not wanting that the house of my Father be made into a den of thieves. Thus, I am telling you that I am making a whip of creatures and that with this whip I am chasing the worldly, greedy and avaricious merchants who sell and buy the graces of the gifts

> of the Holy Spirit. Thus, with the whip of the persecution of creatures, have I chased them, that is to say, through tribulations and persecution, I am making the disordered and dishonest life disappear." With the fire of holy desire growing in me, full of admiration, I saw enter into the side of Christ Crucified the Christian people as well as the infidel; and me, by desire and the effect of love, I passed through their midst, entering with them into Christ, the sweet Jesus, accompanied only by my father Saint Dominic and Saint John. He then put the cross on my shoulder and the olive branch in my hand, as if he wanted me—and he said to me as well—that I am to carry them to both peoples [= to Christians and to the infidels]....Then I celebrated and exulted, and my soul was truly fuller than ever. It was immersed in the Divine Being....I was so confident about the future that it seemed as if I was already possessing it and enjoying it.[37]

After this prophetic investiture, doubt was no longer permitted. Catherine is henceforth convinced that God has charged her with a mission: to draw the pope, the clergy, and the Christian people into a movement of reform whose positive outcome is certain despite the difficulties of the present, since God has assured her of the final triumph of the Church. Her acute awareness of her teaching office of the Bride of Christ is founded on the conformity between the divine word and her own, verified in prayer and recognized by her spiritual fathers and sons. From that point onward, another period of her life opened in which, with the help of her disciples—clerics as well as laymen and -women—she began to send letters of exhortation or reminders to groups of people of greater and greater importance: members of communal governments, the "lords" of certain Italian cities, jurists, and soon sovereigns throughout all of Christendom. Somewhat embarrassed by this behavior, which could appear pretentious or audacious on the part of a simple laywoman, her first biographer, Raymond of Capua, justified it by emphasizing the fact that, in the particular situation of decline in which the Church found itself, God had chosen to rely upon an unlettered woman, a fragile vase filled with virtues, to confound the proud men who were disdaining his grace.[38] Having said this, he placed himself in the line of Thomas Aquinas, who had referred in his *Summa theologica* (IIa, IIIae, 5, qq. 171 and 175) to a figure from the Old

Testament: the prophetess Hulda, who lived in Jerusalem during the reign of Josiah and whom the high priest and king had both recognized as a messenger from God. At their request, she delivered an oracle in which she threatened with severe punishment the people of Judah who, forgetful of the law, had turned toward gods other than the God of Israel, while at the same time announcing that a momentary pause had been given to them in order that they might be converted (2 Kgs 22:12–20). Similarly, in the eyes of Raymond of Capua, the wise, who have become stupid, will be humiliated and the proud will be brought low, while honors will be showered upon the humble who did not lose faith in the word of God, and especially upon Catherine, who in her lifetime had been the channel of divine love for the human race.

The fact that she had begun to act in the manner of a prophetess by intervening in the public sphere earned her the sarcasm of some and the warnings of others. Bianco da Siena (or of Città di Castello), a former companion of Giovanni Colombini, addressed to her a *lauda* in verses in which he appears disturbed by her success, fearing that it might give her a big head:

> Be careful, my sister / of falling into great ruin.
> If you have the divine grace / do something to keep it…
> Watch out that the temptation / of the prophetic discourse
> Not put you in a prison [of your own making] / for sooner or later, it will depart from you!

After this, he sent her a certain number of warnings, with a tone both friendly and threatening, that can be summarized in a few phrases:

> Be on your guard not to give vain speeches.…You are already considered a saint inspired by the Holy Spirit; if you are truly the Bride of Christ, flee the praise of men which is a poison for the soul. If you fall, many others will lose the faith; therefore, be very careful, poor woman, to not involve others in your own fall and try to give an example of humility![39]

Raymond of Capua refused to read these verses to Catherine, but she had some knowledge of them. And against his advice, she thanked their author, Bianco da Siena, in these highly respectful terms, though not without some wry humor:

> As for me, very beloved Father in Christ-the-sweet-Jesus, I heartily thank you for the holy zeal and solicitude you have for my soul. It seems to me that what you have heard about my way of life has made you very skeptical. I am certain that nothing else impels you except the desire for the honor of God and my soul, which prompts you to fear that the devil's deception is at work. And I am not at all surprised that you might think thus…for this often happens to me and then I tremble with fear. But I rely only upon the mercy of God; I do not trust myself, knowing well that I can expect nothing good from that.[40]

Here we should mention certain prophetesses in the Bible, especially in the Acts of the Apostles, which quotes the prophet Joel (2:28):

> In the last days it will be, God declares,
> that I will pour out my Spirit upon all flesh,
>   and your sons and your daughters shall prophesy,
> and your young men shall see visions,
>   and your old men shall dream dreams. (Acts 2:17)

But those who claimed such powers were exposed to criticism based on the prohibition against women speaking publicly in the Church, as we read in 1 Timothy 2:11–13. Thus, Catherine was careful not to claim explicitly a prophetic function. Unlike Birgitta of Sweden, who asserted that she received her revelations from Mary the Mother of God, Catherine did not present herself as an instrument of continuous revelation. She did not claim to know the future in any detail, nor to be the repository of divine secrets with respect to history (other than what was in Sacred Scripture, which she used prudently by avoiding references to apocryphal texts). From her Dominican masters, she had learned to keep the eye of her intellect clear and lucid. Moreover, in his *Summa theologica,* Thomas Aquinas himself had recognized the possibility of a nonlearned prophetic gift and was thus open, if necessary, to women whose criterion of authenticity was to be judged by their usefulness to the salvation of others.[41] Catherine justified her interventions by saying that, if she spoke in the Church as she was doing, it was in obedience to a very specific mandate that had been given to her by God. This would have conferred on her the right to place herself above the normal ecclesiastical hierarchy, inasmuch as she had a specific function to fulfill as a mother to her sons: namely, to help the human race enter into the open wound of the side of Christ in order to lead it to salvation. And her discourse was all the better received because she declared herself always ready to take upon herself the responsibility for the faults committed by other people, whether it was a matter of war or schism. Thus, after the massacre committed in Cesena by the papal troops in 1377, she wrote to Gregory XI:

> Alas, my *babbo*, my soul is sad to see that my own iniquities are the cause of such misfortunes! It seems to me that the devil has taken possession of the world and it is we ourselves who have given it to him—for by himself he can do nothing. Everywhere that I turn, I see that, under the reign of his corrupt will, each one of us gives him the keys of his or her own free will. I see the laity, religious and clerics rushing headlong with pride towards the delights, honors and riches of the world. But above all else, I see that what afflicts God the most are those flowers planted within the mystical body of the Holy Church and which ought to be sweet-smelling flowers. However, even those whose life ought to be the mirror of virtues—those who ought to prize and cherish the love of God and salvation of souls—instead spread around the infected odor of sin![42]

This rather harsh text about the clergy takes on even greater significance when one realizes that, in Catherine, the expression "mystical body of the Holy Church" refers to the papacy and the ecclesiastical hierarchy!

Her prophetic vocation did not only manifest itself in vigorous denunciations of abuses and failings; it showed itself especially in her enduring concern to understand the spiritual meaning of events. For her, the cause of the serious difficulties experienced in contemporary society was rooted in the moral and religious domain, which was at the origin of the numerous misunderstandings and failures of her actions. Thus, she explained the crisis of the communal system, whose catastrophic effects she saw all around her, as rooted in the exaltation of self-love, which made the search for the common good impossible and that of the good of the Church due to the bad conduct of the clergy. Typical in this regard is her analysis of the behavior of prelates in a letter to Pope Gregory XI in 1376:

> The one who loves himself nourishes within himself a perverse pride—the source and origin of every evil—whatever might be his state in life, prelate or subject. If he loves only himself, that is, if he has love only for himself and not for God, he will act badly and all virtue is dead in him. He is like the woman who gives birth to a still-born child. It cannot be otherwise: if he has not received the life of charity, he will aspire only to praise and his own glory, and not to the glory of God. This is why I say: if this man is a prelate, he acts badly because this love of himself—which impels him to not want to displease other creatures and to which he is tied by pleasure and self-love—stifles in himself holy justice. Thus, when he finds fault with his subjects and sees them committing sins, he acts as if nothing has happened and does nothing to correct them. Or, if he does correct them, it is with such insincerity or half-heartedness that it has no effect at all; and what is worse, forever fearing to be displeasing to others and fearing to make enemies of them, he instead encourages their vice.[43]

Thus, she denounced with vehemence the betrayal of gospel values by the clergy—who have been charged to pass on those values—and their disdain for spiritual realities. Catherine did not hesitate to utter stern judgments against—and even condemnations of—unworthy men of the Church, such as sinful rectors of the Papal State whom she called "devils incarnate," or the cardinals who had elected Clement VII in 1378, whom she respectively called minions of Satan and the antichrist. And yet she always maintained an attitude of restraint and devotion toward priests inasmuch as they are ministers of the sacrament of the altar. For Catherine, the criticism of the failures of the clergy is balanced with an unconditional respect for the ecclesiastical hierarchy and their prerogatives. This puts her in the same company as Hildegard of Bingen († 1179). Her attitude had nothing in common with that of a Petrarch who accused Avignon of being "a false and rich Babylon"; and she never bought into the idea—at the time widespread throughout Italy—that the popes had been "in captivity" on the banks of the Rhone. For her, the evils from which the Church was suffering were not to be found outside itself but within. The overall import of her message about the reform of Christianity places it in the line of biblical prophecy, which aims at the betterment of the human person through a return to the centrality of the divine law in their individual and collective lives. However, the immediate causes of the abuses that she denounces, that flowed in large measure from the breakdowns in the system of benefices and the extremes of Roman centralization, completely escaped her, because her tendency to project human acts onto the level of salvation history caused her to lose sight of the influence of structures upon behavior. Moreover, at a time when the states—whether they be monarchical or communal—were claiming an increased autonomy with respect to the Church on the temporal level, Catherine's aspiration to unify Christian society around a crusading project and to make Italy "the garden of the Church" was running at counterpurposes with historical evolution and was doomed to failure. As to her desire to make the papacy the cornerstone of the unity of the Christian world, it could appear somewhat ridiculous on the eve of the Great Schism!

Catherine differs from Birgitta of Sweden and Vincent Ferrer, both of whom likewise denounced the vices and inadequacies of the clergy of their time, in that she placed the emphasis less on the anger of God than on his mercy; and she also granted a real importance to the prayer of "the true servants of God." These last, in the hiddenness of their withdrawal, were for her the supporting columns of the Church, able even to bend the divine will through their continual prayers. Without a doubt, she considered herself to be among these latter individuals since, in one of her letters, she compared herself to Moses, who was praying with arms uplifted while his people were fighting and carrying the day. In her writings, she presented herself both as a humble, sinning creature and as the relief sent by a higher authority: the Holy Spirit who had mandated her to "watch over a multitude of souls," on behalf of whom, in her letters, she employed reserves of persuasion to guide them onto the path of salvation. This highly original epistolary form of prophecy, which at the end of her life replaced the encounters that had become difficult or impossible, was the concrete manifestation of the mission with which she felt herself invested by God—and that she had accepted—thus entering a profound and lasting communion with the Crucified Love who desired to redeem the world.

In the final analysis, what makes Catherine of Siena a prophetess is not her ability to predict the future—even though, according to Raymond of Capua, she had announced the imminence of a schism when she learned of the death of Gregory XI[44]—but rather the authority and freedom of tone with which she addressed her interlocutors, however highly placed in the lay or ecclesiastical hierarchy they may have been. She wrote fifteen letters to Gregory XI between 1370 and 1378—fourteen of which have come down to us—and at least eight to Urban VI between the spring of 1378 and 1380, with the same mix of humility and confidence: testimony to her conviction of having been chosen by God to remind her contemporaries of the necessity and urgency of a reform of the Church. After his return to Italy, Gregory maintained a more distant relationship with her, as if embittered at having been pushed to leave Avignon and blaming her for the political difficulties he encountered in Rome. According to Jean Gerson, shortly before his death, Gregory invited the ecclesiastical dignitaries around him to "be wary of men and women who, under pretext of religiosity, report visions which they have had in their heads"; and he would add that "he himself, having been abused by people of this ilk, had allowed himself to get involved in (and had involved the Church with him) the crisis of the schism that was imminent."[45] Even though she was not explicitly named, Catherine of Siena is obviously implied, since who more than she had exerted such a constant pressure over him that he return to Rome? As the testimony of Gerson is late and comes from one who was an adversary of the Roman obedience, perhaps we should not overemphasize its importance. However, it probably contains some kernel of truth because Catherine herself had written to Gregory XI in 1377 to tell him that she was feeling personally responsible for the loss of respect toward the Church and the pope that was evident all throughout Italy. At the time of the Venetian process of 1411–16, a few witnesses sought to exonerate her of the accusation—which was being made against her in some circles—that she had been at the origin of the schism of 1378 in pushing the papacy to return to Rome. She continued, however, to defend her action while saying that, if it was rejected, she would take refuge "in the side wound of Christ," from which she would continue her fight since, for her, the authority of her words was guaranteed by her spiritual experience. When she sought to justify her role, she often referred to John the Evangelist, whose writings—especially his letters and the Book of Revelation, whose redaction was attributed to him—constituted for her a model of prophetic vision; and she did not hesitate to present herself as a "servant of God speaking with the voice of God and called, for that reason, to suffer unjust attacks."

During the process of Venice from 1411 to 1416—which had as its essential aim the removal of the doubts concerning Catherine's sanctity—a prominent place was devoted to her prophetic charism. But the promoters of her cause understood that the authenticity of her visions and revelations could be problematic, as there was no decisive proof in this area. Thus, they put the emphasis instead on the fruitfulness that these phenomena had conferred upon her apostolic activity. The witnesses underscored her role in the conversion of numerous religious and the fact that most of the lay members of her *famiglia* had entered into monastic orders after her death. They also endeavored to show that there was no contradiction between her charism and the institutional ministry of the Church, inasmuch as her only public preaching took place in front of the cardinals and after having been invited by Pope Urban VI to do so. Finally, they did not fail to mention the positive influence that Catherine continued to exert in the Church through her writings: through them, she was called to fulfill a salvific function until the end of the world. The emphasis on her works and ideas is typical for a Church in which academics enjoyed a prominent role. In their eyes, she had acquired an authentic wisdom founded on an experiential knowledge of God, who had allowed her to understand what was deeply hidden in Sacred Scripture. And Tommaso Caffarini did not hesitate to say on this occasion that she should be honored as a doctor of the Church just like Hugh and Richard of Saint-Victor, who, even though not canonized, were luminaries for the Christian people.[46] In this way, instead of focusing on her prophetic interventions in their historical context and on her struggle for the peace and the reform of the Church, later tradition would seek to detach her revelations from their specific context and to make of Catherine a timeless spiritual author.

THE VIRTUE OF WRITING: CATHERINE AS AUTHOR

Until recently, Catherine was never presented as a writer of the same stature as her contemporaries Petrarch, Boccaccio, and Coluccio Salutati, who, in the history of Italian and European literature, are regarded as the forerunners of fifteenth-century humanism. Because she was difficult to categorize precisely, she was left on the sidelines under the pretext that her writings had a particularly oratorical and "mystical" character and did not, properly speaking, constitute a literary output. Moreover, the first period of Tuscan humanism is traditionally tied to Latin, the language of culture for those who aspired to return to the golden age that had constituted antiquity. But if Catherine was capable of reading and understanding texts written in Latin, she never used the language either orally—as evidenced by Raymond of Capua's role of interpreter at her meeting with Gregory XI in Avignon—or in writing. However, she was in her own way innovative on the cultural level inasmuch as she frequently had recourse to the epistolary genre. In doing this, she was following the example of Giovanni Colombini († 1367), the pious lay founder of the Jesuati (the Apostolic Clerics of Saint Jerome), who had left behind a collection of spiritual letters. But what was normal for a man was not normal for a woman. Catherine is indeed the first woman in Italy—and even in the West—to have created such an important body of work in the vernacular: 383 surviving letters dating from the years 1367 to 1380, of which eight are "original" (none from her own hand, but we have the first redaction, which she dictated), as well as an important theological and spiritual treatise, *The Dialogue*.

With Catherine, public preaching by women moves from the environment of convents toward a more lay context. From the time of Héloise († 1164) at the Paraclete Monastery and Hildegard of Bingen († 1179) up to Umiltà da Faenza († 1310), we have collections of sermons confirming that some abbesses did preach to their nuns. We also know of two wonderful letters of Clare of Assisi († 1253) sent to Agnes of Bohemia, foundress of a convent of Poor Clares in Prague; but these are in Latin and were probably drafted by a Friar Minor. Up to the middle of the fourteenth century, the mystics and prophetesses—as the examples of Angela da Foligno and Birgitta of Sweden demonstrate—did not seek to establish a direct connection to writing and remained dependent on the clerics in their circle, who rendered their visions or their revelations in good Latin. Thus, they can be spoken of as "written" but "nonwriting" mystics.[47] Access to writing remained prohibited to women for a long time because it could have divulged their identity and conferred an authority upon them. Except for a few princesses or great ladies of the aristocracy, it was enough that they knew how to read, even in fourteenth-century Tuscany—one of the most advanced regions of Europe in the realm of literacy. Reading had an undeniable usefulness: it allowed women to manage better the affairs of the house and to be imbued—through missals or works of moral guidance—with the religious values they were charged to inculcate into the family life and to transmit them to their children. But it was not desirable that women should know how to write because, as Philip of Novara wrote in the middle of the thirteenth century, "God has made her for obedience"; whereas Paolo di Certaldo likewise affirmed around 1360 that it was even useless for a young woman to learn how to read, "unless she wants to become a nun."[48] In this context, the practice of writing remained exceptional for a laywoman, especially when she belonged—as was the case with Catherine—to the lower bourgeoisie. Thus, she really did innovate by relying upon writing and the vernacular to express her most intimate spiritual experiences and to address her correspondents by herself and without an intermediary.

The question of Catherine's connection to writing is, however, more complex than it might first appear. One might think that she acquired the rudiments of writing in her youth from her Dominican confessors, without being able to explain how, once she became an adult, she would have become capable of writing, unless she had benefited, as she says, from a miraculous intervention of the Holy Spirit. But it is important to note that she was aware of her vocation as a writer (and even as an author) while at the same time being aware of the importance of the mission that God had entrusted to her.

The postscript to Letter 272, which she sent in October 1377 to her spiritual director, Raymond of Capua, testifies to this, when she was in the Val d'Orcia, on the lands of the Salimbeni family:

> This letter, and another which I sent to you, I wrote myself in Isola della Rocca with many sighs and tears, to such a point that my eyes for seeing could no longer see; but I was full of admiration towards myself and towards the goodness

> of God, believing his mercy towards creatures endowed with reason and his Providence which abounded towards me. For, to comfort myself—I who am deprived of the consolation which through my ignorance I have not known—he gave me this gift and provided for this consolation by giving me the ability to write in order that, descending from the heights, I might be able to console my heart somewhat with someone in order that it not explode....He has miraculously given this ability to my mind, as the master does for the child to whom he gives a model. As soon as he left me, along with Saint John the Evangelist and Saint Thomas Aquinas, I began to learn while still sleeping.[49]

The authenticity of this text has been contested by Robert Fawtier, who, arguing from the silence of Raymond of Capua on this point, saw here the fruit of an intervention by Tommaso Caffarini, wanting to show that Catherine had been an author inspired by God.[50] This interpretation has no foundation. On the contrary, it seems that if Raymond of Capua does not mention this episode in his *Legenda maior*, it is really because it consists of decisive evidence of Catherine's personal access to the use of writing and a turning point in her evolution toward the claim of autonomy. Indeed, giving up the role of the unlearned and unlettered woman that she had played up to then in order to have her charism acknowledged by clerics, she expresses in this text her consolation and her joy in finally being able to write by herself. Having done this, she courageously breaks with the taboo of female inability in this domain, while at the same time reducing what could have been revolutionary in this affirmation by declaring that it was received as a gift by virtue of a supernatural commissioning in spite of her personal unworthiness.[51] In fact, Tommaso Caffarini reports that, finding herself in a room in the Rocca de Tentennano, Catherine one day took a jar of cinnabar—a product vermillion in color that was used to design initials at the beginning of rubrics—as well as a pen and a piece of parchment and then, moved by divine inspiration, she traced out, with readable and neat penmanship, the text of a versified prayer to the Holy Spirit.[52] And the hagiographer then adds,

> And we should not think that this piece of paper was the only one written in her own hand. For the respectable Dom

> Stefano Maconi who, among others, served as her secretary, confided to me that she herself wrote to the aforesaid Dom Stefano a letter in which she tells him that it is the first missive written in her own hand. He also saw that she likewise traced, other than urgent messages, several pages of the *Book* which she had composed in Italian.[53]

Things are thus entirely clear: by the end of her life, Catherine was perfectly capable of writing by herself, but Raymond of Capua did not want that to be known, whereas Tommaso Caffarini, careful to present her as a spiritual author, had no reason to hide this reality.

Such an interpretation is confirmed by the fact that Raymond of Capua claims that *The Dialogue* had been composed in eight days under the inspiration of the Holy Spirit during Catherine's sojourn in Rome in 1378–79. We take this here as an obvious falsehood, because he could not have been unaware that it had been written between October 1377 and the spring of 1378 in Tuscany, and that it had not been written in a single sitting, as the oldest manuscript shows—that from the Biblioteca Casanatense of Rome, which dates from the years 1380 to 1382 and carries several additions and corrections.[54] Apparently, after the vision described in Letter 272, Catherine felt rather sure of herself and of her mission so as to undertake the redaction of a book of a spiritual and doctrinal character illustrating her direct and intimate relationship with God. But, prudently, she underlines that by intervening on the doctrinal and pastoral level she was merely exercising a kind of magisterium by substitution, made necessary by the betrayal of clerics whose inertia as well as moral failings she reproaches. As Angela da Foligno had said several decades previously about the clergy of Foligno, "The disdain which they had for divine things is made even more appalling by the knowledge that they had of the Scriptures."[55] For Catherine, the majority of them are "dogs who know not how to bark"; and even those who have been taught how to preach are incapable of speaking properly about God to the faithful because they trust in "the knowledge that puffs up," whereas one can only find it in a personal experience founded on humility and the knowledge of one's own nothingness. Whence her engagement in writing, from an apostolic and pastoral perspective, justified by the situation of a profound crisis in which the Church found itself as a result.

Regardless, Catherine is not an author like other authors. She presents herself rather as "an unlettered writer" (*scrittrice illiterata*), in the sense that this phrase had during the Middle Ages: that is, a person unfamiliar with Latin culture and thus with the world of learning and theology.[56] Already in the thirteenth century, Francis of Assisi had characterized himself as *illiteratus et idiota* ("unlettered and unlearned"), even though he knew how to read and write and even sent small letters written, in incorrect Latin, to some of his companions. Catherine falls into the same category: like him, she uses a simple language—the *sermo humilis*—enlivened with a few very concrete images whose purpose was to help the reader to interiorize her spiritual message. But she goes even further by having recourse exclusively to the vernacular, which Francis had apparently only utilized in two of his writings, the most famous of which was the *Canticle of Brother Son* (or *of Creation*). She does not intend to expatiate eruditely on God but to talk about the Ineffable to men and women in their own language, by sharing her experience of loving union with him, which constituted in her eyes the foundation of the indisputable truth of her teaching and the legitimacy of her public speaking.

We could, nonetheless, object that we do not possess a single letter of Catherine's that came from her own hand. We indeed know—through the members of her *famiglia*—that she dictated *The Dialogue* during her ecstasies and that Raymond of Capua described this process well in his *Legenda maior*:

> She gave herself diligently to the composition of a book which, inspired by the Holy Spirit, she dictated in her vernacular tongue. She had asked her secretaries, who were skilled in writing the letters which she sent here and there, to be careful to observe everything, when, as she was wont to do, she was caught up outside of her bodily senses; and then to diligently write what she was dictating to them. This they did with zeal and they put together a book filled with great and useful statements revealed to her by God and dictated by her with her own voice in the vernacular. And thus… through the work of God, the holy woman in ecstasy dictated this whole book.[57]

In fact, Catherine dictated her letters and her writings to people within her entourage, especially to Neri di Landoccio Pagliaresi; a member of the Sienese aristocracy, Stefano Maconi; and the Florentine notary, Barduccio di Pietro Canigiani, all who were at her bedside at the moment of her passing. These men have left us very detailed accounts of the functioning of this private little chancery where sometimes these scribes were drafting several letters simultaneously:

> One of us was writing a letter which had to be sent to the now dead Pope Gregory XI; another was writing a letter to Messer Bernabò, at that time Lord of Milan; a third to a noble lord whose name I no longer remember at the moment. She dictated both to one then to another, sometimes hiding her face in her hands, sometimes staring at the ceiling, arms crossed, sometimes entering into ecstasy, without however ever ceasing to speak.[58]

That Catherine may have preferred to employ secretaries is due to several reasons. The first and most obvious is that God inspired his words in her during her ecstasies, and she would not have been able to put them down in writing herself. The second—hypothetical but probable—is that she did not want to take advantage of her acquired ability to write because that could have been regarded as a form of presumption. Indeed, as Sonia Porzi has written, "The relationship of women to the written word was still somewhat problematic in the 14th century."[59] A laywoman of modest background—who, not content just to move around endlessly and to involve herself in political and ecclesiastical affairs at the highest levels, would have put down in writing, herself, her visions and revelations—could not but have incited a defiant reaction. However, that her male secretaries had been involved in the redaction of her texts and that she had been under the supervision of a Dominican confessor constituted a guarantee of her orthodoxy. By their presence they confirmed her status as an unlettered person, a status that had rendered her worthy to receive and transmit to those around her messages sent by God to the human race.

It has sometimes been said that her entourage may have inserted themselves into the redaction of her writings. In fact, the problem of their authenticity was hardly ever raised: Catherine herself surely reread and edited *The Dialogue*. As to her letters, we can assume that she reread them before having them sent out to their recipients. The rapid widening of the spectrum of her correspondents—which illustrates the rise of

Catherine's influence in the Church and in the society of her time—helped to confer upon her an increased authority. The establishment of a correspondence with them allowed her effectively to create a virtual community with them by transcending the existing institutions in which she had no standing. As we only have at our disposal a very small number of responses to her missives, we do not know whether they were welcomed by their recipients. And we are not even sure whether they even ever arrived at their destinations, especially when they were sent to sovereigns like Charles V, king of France, or the king of Hungary, as was the case at the beginning of the Great Schism.

In any case, Catherine seems very early on to have concerned herself with having her letters copied before sending them out; she probably assumed that they could be as useful to others as to those to whom they had originally been sent. In fact, they were recopied and circulated in informal circles that brought together laity and religious of many orders who desired Church reform. Beyond her small circle of disciples, these constituted around her a kind of "textual community"—in the sense given to the term by Brian Stock[60]—which played a critical role after her death in the spread of her reputation of sanctity. The scribes who surrounded her were surely capable of adding to Catherine's words certain stereotypical formulas. She herself always introduced herself at the beginning of her letters as "the servant and slave of the servants of God"—thus imitating Pope Gregory the Great, who called himself "the servant of the servants of God"—and one generally finds there, too, a reference to the blood of Christ as well as the phrase preceding the conclusion and final greeting: "I will say no more." But the ideas and themes are really those of Catherine, for whom the members—clerics as well as laity—of her special little chancery had too much veneration to dare to modify the articulation of her thought. The intervention of her disciples and copyists was, on the other hand, more telling after her death, when they undertook to put together collections of her letters by stripping them of all their chronological and historical references in order to transform them into spiritual writings, without, however, changing their substance.

Catherine's letters do not have a formulaic construction or a linear rationale, but constitute rather an amplification of themes that were at the core of her mystical experience. She was writing, primarily, in order to transmit her vision of the divine mysteries by firmly emphasizing the love of God and the necessity of her correspondents to acquire sufficient self-knowledge so as to be able to recognize their total dependence upon God. She often gives them injunctions in a highly authoritarian tone, using the expression *Io voglio!* ("I want!"), while using forceful language that stresses the values that she wanted to promote or defend. This expression of desire and of will in writing is not at all typical for a woman. Catherine expresses herself with a kind of magisterial authority, without letting any sort of doubt show through. But she gives counsel rather than lessons; and she proposes models of behavior corresponding to the expectation of her interlocutor, to whom she adapts herself with flexibility. Indeed, she manifests a keen attention to the people whom she is addressing and to their concrete situation, even to the point of identifying with them, as we see in the seven furious letters sent between 1379 and 1380 to Queen Joanna I of Naples, to try to exhort her to start living once again a better moral life and to pledge her fidelity, which was then vacillating, to the cause of the Roman pope, Urban VI:

> O dearest Mother—I call you Mother on the condition that you might be the faithful daughter of the Holy Church—it seems to me that you are not in any way taking pity on yourself. Alas, alas, because I love you, I grieve over the sorry state of your soul and body. I would gladly give up my own life to remedy this cruelty....Oh how my soul would be happy if I could come and see you! I would give my life to bring you the goods of heaven and earth, to take from you the knife of cruelty and give you the knife of piety, which puts to death vice, in order to see you clothed once again with the holy fear of God and the love of the truth, united in his sweet will.[61]

Above all, Catherine sought in her letters to bring back each person to his or her true calling by reconnecting it to transcendence or—more precisely—to tap into the desire of the other so as to rekindle it by reorienting him or her toward God. We see expressed here a veritable ethic of the kind of relationship that even led her to believe herself responsible for the salvation of the one whom she is addressing, whom she sees with pain wandering away or falling back into an egotistical self-love. Her manner of expressing herself really reflects her personality; and her style maintains the force of the spoken word, which she was striving to distance from the ephemeral world of speech by putting that word into writing. What makes it moving is the passion which with she sought contact with her correspondents by using a rhetoric of intimacy that did not impede her from using expressions of deep familiarity: *Dolce babbo* ("Sweet Papa"), she wrote without hesitation to Gregory XI! But Catherine was also a literary author and, as such, she did not write with total spontaneity. Thus, while at the same time often lamenting the physical absence of her interlocutor, she took advantage of that absence to deliver to that person—especially to the popes and sovereigns of her day—a message that she probably would not have dared to give them in person had they actually met. The space created within by the acts of writing authorized her, in effect, to go beyond a simple face-to-face conversation and to establish a relationship of connection with her correspondents, even those whom she had never met. Thus, when she wrote in 1375 to the English *condottiere* John Hawkwood to persuade him to depart with his troops and go on crusade, she addressed him as a "very dear and beloved brother in Christ Jesus" and urged him henceforth to march against the infidels rather than to be making war against other Christians, as he had been doing with his company. "It is thus," she says in conclusion, "that you will demonstrate that you are a virile man and a true knight."[62]

The familiarity of her style is, nevertheless, always balanced with a seriousness of tone and purpose. "I am writing to you in the precious blood of Christ!" she often declared at the beginning of her letters, as if the blood of Christ was interchangeable with the ink itself. Catherine frequently developed the metaphor of ink and blood by comparing herself to Saint Peter Martyr († 1252), a Dominican inquisitor assassinated by heretics, who, before surrendering his spirit, wrote with his own blood the phrase *Credo in Deum* ("I believe in God"), on the ground where he died.[63] How else better to convey that writing was, for her, first and foremost a means of suffering for the faith and of disseminating the word of God around her. Thus, shortly before her death, she confided to Raymond of Capua the task of gathering together and disseminating her writings like relics that lose nothing of their "virtue" (power) when they are divided up into small fragments. Impeded from carrying out this task of gathering up—due to his heavy responsibilities as master general of the Dominican order of the Roman obedience, which began in June of 1380—he charged his confrère, Tommaso Caffarini, to collect Catherine's works in such a way as to extend her presence beyond her death. Caffarini acquitted himself well in this task and collected all the letters that he could find, beginning with a collection that the notary Cristofano di Gano Gandini, a former secretary of the saint, had put together for his own personal use. And in the hagiographical texts that he later dedicated to Catherine, Caffarini did not fail to present her as a real author in the medieval sense of the term—a writer whose texts had authority in the Church.

CATHERINE AND THE DOMINICAN OBSERVANT REFORM MOVEMENT AND A NEW RELIGIOUS PROJECT FOR WOMEN

One of the areas in which the impact of Catherine's intervention in the problems of her time is most easily measurable is her contribution to the reform of the Dominican order. As we have seen, she had been associated, from a very early age, with the order through her first confessor, Tommaso dalla Fonte, who quickly put her into contact with several other Dominicans of the Sienese convent of Camporeggio—such as Bartolomeo Dominici—who served as her spiritual directors during the first years of her religious life. Quite naturally, once she had to choose—following her years of domestic enclosure—a state of life recognized by the Church and society, she asked to enter into and was admitted to the *Mantellate* who circulated within the area of the convent of San Domenico in Siena. She was, however, neither a Dominican nun of the "Second Order" (as was said of those female religious who took solemn vows and lived in community in the shelter of the cloister); nor was she even a tertiary, since the Dominican Third Order as such did not yet exist. Rather, she was a simple penitent attached to her Dominican mentors by somewhat loose ties: simple vows that could be undone and the obligation to attend, with her companions, gatherings of the confraternity, in the course of which male religious gave them a spiritual initiation and moral instruction through preaching.

The relationship between Catherine and the Dominicans would be strengthened in 1374. When she began to become known outside of Siena and to attract the attention of ecclesiastical authorities, she was summoned in 1374, as we saw, to the general chapter of the Friars Preacher, which was being held in Florence at the convent of Santa

Maria Novella during the season of Pentecost. It is possible that the order may have been fearing at that time that she might slip away from their influence, because she had just received the visit of Alfonso da Vadaterra, who, after the death of Birgitta of Sweden on July 25, 1373, was looking for a new "inspired woman," capable of reinvigorating the reform of the Church. Be that as it may, Raymond of Capua, who had recently been named lector at the Dominican convent of Siena, found himself entrusted by the master general, Elias of Toulouse, with the mission of henceforth being her confessor and spiritual director. This decision was in conformity with the rule for penitents as it had been drawn up at the end of the thirteenth century by Munio de Zamora, which provided that the master of the order and the prior provincial proceed to the naming of a friar as "master and director" of their confraternities. In Catherine's case, there was one slight exception: the group was then only an amorphous fraternity of uncertain shape, composed of male and female disciples who operated within its neighborhood and who, henceforth, were going to accompany her in her various journeys. This appointment of Raymond to Catherine and her *famiglia* was confirmed on August 17, 1376, by a bull of Gregory XI that specifically designated him "as master to Catherine and her companions whom you and Catherine will choose for the good reputation of the order" and that "all power which the order possesses over them might be entrusted to him in order that he govern and correct them as it will seem appropriate for him to do."[64] This papal approbation seems to have been requested in order to affirm Catherine's position, as much with an eye on the pontifical entourage that she was going to visit in Avignon as to the local ecclesiastical authorities whom the *Caterinati* would encounter during their moving about and who could react negatively to this informal group of a rather special type. Let us note, however, that the bull presented the lay "fraternity" that was gathering around Catherine as being exclusively female, whereas we know that it included many men.

It is not unthinkable that Catherine might have been able to influence the choice of "master" whom Dominican superiors had thus placed at her side in 1374. Indeed, Raymond of Capua was probably not totally unknown to her and she appreciated his reforming zeal. After this and until her death, Catherine was tirelessly involved with him in the reform of the Friars Preacher, whose three great canonized saints she particularly venerated: Dominic, Peter Martyr, and

Thomas Aquinas, whom God had designated as "the glorious Thomas who, through the light of his intelligence so noble, contemplated in my Truth—where he acquired the supernal light and the knowledge infused by grace—the most ardent light which illuminated the order and the Holy Church and extinguished the darkness of heresies."[65] At the same time, Catherine was well aware that this glory belonged to the past: "Our order is greatly debased," she wrote to Gregory XI at the end of 1375 or beginning of 1376, while asking him to place at its head "a good and virtuous vicar," if he would ever have to designate a new master general.[66] If she held the pope to this general sort of advice, she immediately asked two of the pontiff's closest collaborators—Nicholas of Osimo and Jacopo d'Itri, archbishop of Otranto—to recommend to him that he name Étienne de La Combe, former procurator of the province of Toulouse, "an excellent and courageous man," who was capable, in her eyes, of undertaking the indispensable reform of the order.[67] But this request had no follow-up since Elias of Toulouse was not made a cardinal—contrary to the rumors she had been hearing—and he remained as head of the Dominican order until 1380.

Once Raymond of Capua had been designated as Catherine's "master and (spiritual) director," he quickly became convinced of the holiness of his penitent, who inspired within him—as he himself reports in his *Legenda maior*—the repentance of past failings. Previously, he had been cured of the plague through her intercession, and when they had together visited the monastery of Montepulciano, he had seen the foot of Saint Agnes—within the reliquary where it was housed—lift itself up toward the lips of Catherine, who was trying to kiss it. This reference to Agnes of Montepulciano († 1317) is very important because Raymond of Capua, who had presented her in his *Life* as a model for Dominican nuns to follow, had understood well that, given the profound crisis that the Friars Preacher were experiencing, the reform of the order had to begin through its female branch. Thus, Catherine assisted in this when she undertook, with the approval of the pope, to create a female monastery dedicated to Saint Mary of the Angels in Belcaro, three miles from Siena. It was founded on April 17, 1377, but its growth ran into resistance from the commune of Siena, which refused it any financial backing. Eventually, the convent passed under the control of the Salimbeni and was destroyed soon after Catherine's death. Since Catherine remained very discreet about her intentions, we do not know what purpose she had in mind by throwing herself into this venture. Was she simply seeking an oasis of peace in which she could devote herself to contemplation at the end of her peregrinations? Or did she have the ambition of making it a model for the female religious communities of the area, whose often-deplorable situation she knew better than anyone else? In any case, her initiative testifies to her esteem for the conventual and monastic life.

Beginning in 1377, Raymond of Capua, who had been elected prior of the convent of Santa Maria sopra Minerva in Rome, physically moved away from Catherine but remained in contact with her through letters. Afterward, at the beginning of the Great Schism, Pope Urban VI would use him for diplomatic missions to King Charles V to try to dissuade him from rallying to the side of his rival, Clement VII—after which time he was then made provincial of Lombardy. On February 15, 1380, he received two final letters from Catherine, who entrusted to him the care of her disciples and the dissemination of *The Dialogue*. He was in Pisa when she died on April 29, 1380; but on the same day, he claimed to have heard a voice that told him of the sad news. A few weeks later, on May 12, he was elected master general of the Dominican order or, at any rate, of its "Urbanist" branch, now that Christianity had become divided into two obediences. From that time on, the reform of the order—which Catherine had so much hoped for during her lifetime—could now be set in motion. But it only happened in a slow and progressive manner since most of the Italian Friars Preacher were not favorable to it. In 1385, Raymond began to write his great *Life* of Catherine of Siena, the *Legenda maior* (which he finished only in 1395); and, in 1389, the first Observant Dominican convent was founded in Colmar by Conrad of Prussia, one of the principal leaders of the Observance in the Germanic territories. The parallelism between these two dates is not accidental; for to get the Church and the faithful to recognize Catherine's sanctity was going to be the best way to get the reform to triumph. And, henceforth, the authorities of the order fixed as their objectives both the obtaining of her canonization and the development of the Observance. In 1390, the general chapter decreed that it had to have at least one Observant convent per Dominican province; and Raymond of Capua, a little before his death in Nuremberg on October 5, 1399, named John Dominici to be vicar of the Observant reform in Italy—something that would allow the convents that belonged to this movement to acquire a certain autonomy within the order. The Observance appeared as a reform program of the

Dominican way of life, grounded in a return to poverty and humility, as well as in a devotion centered on the person of Christ, which was going to have more importance in the life of these religious than were studies.

The first concrete initiative moving toward the realization of the Observant ideal did not come from a Dominican woman, however, but from Clare (Chiara), daughter of the "Lord" of Pisa, Pietro Gambacorta. Her real first name was Tora, as we see in two letters that Catherine had written to her in 1375 to persuade her not to be content with living the life of a penitent—undignified for a young noble woman—but, rather, to enter into the monastic life.[68] Catherine met her during a sojourn to Pisa that same year; and she had conversations with her that apparently helped the young woman to decide to leave the world to become a nun. Her father opposed this vocation with all his might. Indeed, he had her removed from the convent of Poor Clares in which she had taken refuge in 1380 and in which she also had taken the veil under the name of Clare. Having changed his mind thanks to the influence of his own family and that of Alfonso da Vadaterra, Pietro finally allowed her, in 1385, to create in Pisa—along with three companions—an Observant female monastery, which took the name of San Domenico and soon boasted around twenty religious. With the help of another sister, Maria Mancini, who had also been in contact with Catherine, Chiara Gambacorta sought to establish there a truly fervent community different from the relaxed life that the Dominican nuns were leading in most of their convents (especially in Pisa at the monastery of Santa Croce, where the two women had made their novitiate). For that, Chiara imposed a strict rule on San Domenico. Even the founders and benefactors of the monastery were not allowed to enter there, and the grille in the parlor, which was reserved for families and for priests needed for confession, had to be draped with an opaque veil that did not allow anyone to make out the faces of one's interlocutors. The sisters recommended a strict application of the Constitutions promulgated by Humbert of Romans in 1259 for the nuns of the Dominican movement. Promising to live in chastity and obedience, they placed their goods in common, did not require a dowry from those who wished to enter the community, and worked with their hands by copying manuscripts and decorating them with miniatures. At the same time, they were assisted in their material chores by *conversae* coming from more modest social milieus. Their principal concern was to live apart from the world, sheltered from the gazes of others in order to pray, meditate on spiritual works—such as the *Soliloquies* of Saint Augustine, which had been translated into the vernacular or Catherine's *Dialogue*—and devote time to contemplation. Nevertheless, they maintained close ties with the Dominican friars through the auspices of Domenico di Peccioli, a supporter of the Observance, who served as their "vicar" from 1385 to 1403. He helped to make their experiment known, and it gained a following in Venice and in Florence, where, in 1417, the female Observant monastery of Saint Peter Martyr was created. Despite their strict enclosure, these religious women were not wholly disinterested in the city in which they were living, and they endeavored to revitalize the religious life of their fellow citizens by offering them the example of a perfect practice of the Christian virtues. The "protomonastery" of Pisa—which was soon to become a reference point for all the convents of reformed Dominican nuns—relied upon a network of lay female and male oblates who had become associated with them. The wealthy among them offered their property to the religious community while at the same time retaining the right to enjoy it until their death; while those of more modest means—often people from out in the countryside—immediately gave over the little that they owned, came to live in the town, and made themselves available for work at the monastery, which, in exchange, provided them food and clothing.[69]

During the years 1390 to 1420, it was really the direct or indirect disciples of Catherine—particularly Tommaso Caffarini and John Dominici—who were the leaders of the Dominican Observant movement in Italy. In 1391, with the support of the Roman pope, Benedict IX, these two prominent religious founded in Venice the convent of San Domenico di Castello and reformed the convents of San Zanipolo (Saints John and Paul) and Chiogga to the south of the Laguna. But they did not limit their efforts to the male convents; rather, they involved themselves very early on with the Dominican nuns as well as the laity. As to the nuns, in 1394 John Dominici created in Venice the monastery of Corpus Christi, which was inspired by the example of the monastery in Pisa and characterized by an extremely strict rule. The sisters took solemn vows, wore the black veil and the scapular, and had no contact at all with the outside world. Twenty-seven women, who came especially from patrician families, all entered at the same time, and they increased to fifty-five by the year 1397. Thanks to the families of these religious women and their networks of "spiritual friends," these Observant Dominican nuns—often called "brides of Christ" in contemporary texts—had a wide influence in the city of Doges as well as on the mainland. In 1401, John Dominici also helped the rich Florentine merchant Antonio degli Alberti to found a double monastery in Florence known as Paradiso, which was attached to the order of San Salvatore. San Salvatore had been created thirty years earlier by Birgitta of Sweden, and its abbess had authority over the small community of men that coexisted with that of the women (the latter were appreciably more numerous). Here, the female religious copied and disseminated the *Revelations* of Saint Birgitta as well as the writings of Catherine of Siena. It is here that John Dominici wrote the *Regola del governo di cura familiare*: a spiritual and moral treatise intended for mothers of families, beginning with Bartolomea degli Alberti, who had become head of her family after her husband had been condemned to exile. As Gabriella Zarri points out, the Observant Dominicans, especially John Dominici and Tommaso Caffarini—by relying upon the example of Catherine—had developed a female-oriented project in the religious domain that was not limited to a mere reinforcement of the discipline imposed upon the supposedly "weaker sex" but that explicitly intended to rely upon the women's spiritual abilities and devotional fervor in order to reform the Church and Christian society.[70]

In 1399, the movement of Flagellants—who were urging the laity to give themselves over to spectacular penitential practices to appease God's anger and to reconcile themselves to him as soon as possible—spread like wildfire throughout northern and central Italy. John Dominici subscribed to this "revival" of popular piety and tried to bring the processions of the Flagellants to Venice. But he ran into opposition from the Venetian authorities, who feared that these uncontrolled crowds would sow disorder throughout the city; and so, they banned the Dominican preacher. Therefore he returned to Tuscany and there, sometime later, founded several Observant Dominican convents, including that of the very famous San Domenico de Fiesole (which later counted among its religious Antonino Pierozzi, future archbishop of Florence, and Fra Angelico, who later decorated the convent of San Marco).[71] But the most important personage of this reform movement was, without any doubt, Tommaso Caffarini († 1434), who was not only Catherine's second biographer and the promoter of the canonization process in Castello from 1411 to 1416 on her sanctity, but also the veritable founder of the Dominican Third Order. All of these objectives were interrelated: by getting the Roman pope, Innocent VII, to promulgate the rule of the male and female penitents of Saint Dominic in 1405 and by officially attaching them to the Dominican order, he gave to Catherine, a posteriori, a religious identity recognized by the Church that she had lacked during her lifetime. At the same time, he proposed to lay people a way of life that could lead them to perfection by following in her footsteps. From 1396, Caffarini had created in Venice a community of Dominican penitents, the *Sorores poenitentiae sancti Dominici*, who lived in their own homes or in small *béguinages* and who gathered together once a month at the Dominican convent of San Zanipolo. This initiative was highly successful, especially among certain single women and widows who were mostly of the middle class, who did not wish to be married or to remarry. These women were not necessarily all that old, because in a period in which daughters were married off as soon as they were sexually developed, widows of fifteen or twenty years of age were not uncommon. The promulgation of the rule of the Third Order of Saint Dominic in 1405 strengthened the bonds between these penitents—who were called in Venice "the Ladies of Saint Dominic"—and the Dominicans, who were striving to make these communities a model for the laity. In this same period, groups of male penitents came into existence who seem to have been rather numerous at the beginning; but after 1430, this movement became more particularly female. The spread of the Dominican Third Order throughout Italy in the fifteenth century remains not very well known outside of Venice; but it seems to have been particularly significant in the Germanic lands, especially in the provinces of Teutonia and Saxony, where the Dominican convents of the Observance were numerous and active.

In Venice, the convents of the Observant Dominicans, with the assistance of the lay fraternities that constituted their circle, were the primary centers for Catherine's cult. At the beginning of the fifteenth century, Tommaso Caffarini deposited in San Zanipolo some of her relics and created there a veritable workshop for the dissemination of her writings and the depictions of her. The art of making woodcuts, which was beginning to become more widespread, allowed him to effectively reproduce these latter images at a low cost. And the members of the Dominican Third Order then disseminated them in their neighborhood oratories as well as in their own homes. In the churches of the

Dominican convents, a commemoration of Catherine took place each year on the Sunday following the Feast of Saint Peter Martyr and a preacher discoursed on her life and holiness. On this occasion, the faithful would bring images of her and ask for her intercession.

The movement of the Dominican Observance, which took its cue from Catherine's life and example, had a considerable influence on religious life in the fifteenth century, in Germany as well as in Italy. The influence that was exerted on the nuns of the Second Order is not entirely clear. Strict enclosure—totally in conformity with the spirit of the saint inasmuch as she was creating a world that was free (or almost free) of all masculine presence—favored their independence and their spiritual resonance in the society around them. The authority of the female prioresses, which relied upon the oblates and "spiritual friends" of the community as well as on the support of the papacy, was strengthened by this and often made itself felt beyond the walls of the monasteries. In this sense, one can say that the adherence to the Dominican Observance allowed these religious to live out their vocation according to a specifically feminine spirituality, under the protection of a structure that guaranteed their independence. But, at the same time, the success of the reform movement was largely because it responded to a social demand: rich and noble families saw in this rigorous cloister the means for enclosing the daughters of the lineage who were not destined for marriage as well as young widows whom one did not wish to expose to the risk of leading a suspect life. This often meant that people entered monasteries who did not have any taste for religious life.

It is remarkable, in any case, that the fifteenth-century Dominican reform movement began with women, under the impetus of Catherine of Siena and Chiara Gambacorta, and that it was later extended to the Third Order—which was composed mostly of women, as we have seen—before winning over the male branch. This mirrors the history of the Friars Preacher, whose founder, Dominic Guzman, had first created a monastery in Prouille for women involved in the Cathar heresy whom he had brought back to the Church and, at the request of Pope Honorius III, reformed the female monastery of Saint Sixtus in Rome, even before founding a convent of friars there. Later, the order distanced itself from those female communities that claimed to be followers of the Dominicans, fearing to be distracted from its apostolic calling by the "care of nuns" (*cura monialium*). In the fourteenth century, this misogynistic attitude tended to become less intense, perhaps through competition with the Friars Minor, who could boast of several holy women belonging to the Franciscan family, such as Clare of Assisi († 1253) and Margaret of Cortona († 1297). Thus, in the 1340s, the master general of the Friars Preacher, Garin de Gy-l'évêque, worked for the canonization of the Dominican nun Margaret († 1271), daughter of King Bela IV of Hungary, and wrote her *Life*, emphasizing her mystical states.[72] Influenced by the iconographical model of Catherine of Siena, Marguerite was also depicted as a stigmatic on the walls of several Dominican churches in Italy in the fifteenth century.[73]

Catherine's intersection with the Observant movement that was in the process of emerging in the 1370s–1380s and her close collaboration with Raymond of Capua, set in motion, after her death, a development that can be described without exaggeration as a "second foundation" of the Dominican order. The *Legenda maior* of Raymond of Capua signals a decisive turning point in this process. In this work, the master general of the Friars Preacher was trying both "to speak about the ineffable," according to Claudio Leonardi's apt phrase (that is, to translate into words Catherine's mystical experience), and to show the historical impact of her message in the Church and society of her day. Along with Tommaso Caffarini and John Dominici, who promoted her work, Raymond made a decisive contribution to the elaboration of a new Christian identity, founded on the example of Catherine, who, on the basis of her mystical experience, had tried to reform and reunify the Church. Thus, it is no exaggeration to say, along with Anna Benvenuti, that the life and work of the Sienese *Mantellata* served as the basis for the institutionalization of the penitential life of women, under a form that would henceforth be particularly monastic.[74]

Catherine's message was also widely accepted in the convents in Italy as well as in Germany and even in faraway England. Without questioning the primacy of theology, especially among the friars, and yet underscoring that prayer and affective devotion—that is, expressions of one's love for God—were more important than learning, the Observant movements enabled the foundation of charismatic monastic or lay communities that strove to unite the active and contemplative lives, to influence cities and princes through the practice of Christian virtues and the recourse to prophecy, and to promote the cause of reform, beginning with reform within the religious orders. Thus, in the fifteenth century, Catherine of Siena was the emblematic figure of this reform movement, and thanks to the hagiographical interpretations of her life after her death, she was considered to be the foundress of—and the spiritual justification for—new forms of female religious life that were being established at that time by the Dominican order or had some connection with it.

In the wake of this movement, there appeared in Italy in the second half of the fifteenth century a whole series of women—mostly Dominican tertiaries and nuns—who issued both verbal and written inspired testimonies and who were supported by their confessors. Gabriella Zarri has called them "living saints" (*sante vive*), as they were often recognized and venerated as such by their contemporaries before their deaths: Osanna Andreasi da Mantua (1449–1505); Colomba da Rieti (1467–1501), who, like Catherine, only fed on the Eucharist and whom Pope Alexander VI Borgia visited in Perugia to be present at one of her ecstasies; and Stefana Quinzani, who in 1497 relived in her own flesh Christ's torments during his Passion. We could also add here the stigmatic Lucia Brocadelli da Narni (1476–1544), author of a book of *Revelations*, whose supernatural gifts Duke Ercole I of Este tried to use to his own advantage.[75] Let us also note that Brocadelli was supported against her detractors by the Congregation of Lombardy, which was the Observant branch of the Dominican order in northern Italy. The connection of all of these figures to Catherine is obvious, as we see in the vernacular *Life* of Colomba da Rieti composed around 1506 by the Dominican Sebastiano Angeli, in which he recounts having assured Pope Alexander VI, during his visit to Perugia, that "everything that is said in the legend of Saint Catherine of Siena is found here once again and is fully verified in the behavior and actions of Sister Colomba."[76] All of the efforts of the Dominicans during the violent conflict that was then pitting them against the Franciscans over the stigmata of Catherine of Siena had as their aim to have it acknowledged that several women belonging to their order, near or far, had been graced with this same favor, from Saint Margaret of Hungary († 1270) to Lucia Brocadelli († 1544). In doing this, they were stating their conviction that Christ could be enfleshed in a woman as well as in a man, and that the numerous stigmatics who lived within the orbit of their convents ought to be venerated by the Church as saints.

Catherine's influence likewise made itself felt on another level at the end of the fifteenth century. We can indeed place in this same line the great preacher Girolamo Savonarola, a Dominican of the Observance who strove in his treatises and sermons to realize in Florence the program of moral and religious reforms that Catherine had tried in vain to get accepted throughout the whole of Christianity through the papacy. After his failure and death on the pyre in 1498, numerous religious communities—Dominican or otherwise—remained faithful to this ideal. But they were now playing only a marginal role, since the prophetic and provocative function that these women were providing and that had animated them had now become suspect in the eyes of the papacy. From that time on, there was no longer any place in the Church for a mystic looking to make her mark in history in order to lead all Christians to holiness: the aspiration to reform, incarnated for a time by Catherine of Siena and then by Savonarola, could only be satisfied by resorting to violent rupture and rejection of the institutional Church, as would occur beginning in the 1520s within the context of the Reformation promoted by Luther and Calvin.

CONCLUSION

Catherine of Siena has been the object of rather different assessments, both during and after her lifetime. For many, she is a saint inasmuch as she lived with intensity and in obedience to the Church her vocation of a consecrated laywoman. For others, she is above all else a great mystic whose inner experience and knowledge of divine mysteries puts her on the same level as a Theresa of Avila. And for others still, she was the first woman who dared to get involved at the highest level in the affairs of the Church and in the politics of her time. There is some truth in each one of these assessments and the foregoing pages have allowed us to glimpse the complexity of the figure of Catherine and the characteristics of her personality that made her disagreeable to some of her contemporaries. But if one tries not to *harmonize* (which would be very difficult) but rather to *prioritize* these divergent points of view, it is imperative for us to distinguish the essential from the ancillary and to try to rediscover the internal coherence of the personality.

It is certain that over the course of her brief life Catherine exhibited a sincere but sometimes disorganized zeal on behalf of the Church of her day. Because of her tendency to give a purely moral response to political and religious problems that resulted from many factors other than simply self-love or greed, she does not seem always to have understood the actual stakes in the conflicts in which she found herself involved. For her, to go to war against the pope was equivalent to being confederates of the devil, and to oppose the clergy for political reasons meant placing oneself outside the Church. Catherine never had a concept of the independence of the aims of earthly society. But it is important to emphasize that she had probably been the first person in the Middle Ages—along with Saint Louis in the thirteenth century, though he was a ruler—to try to establish a link between mysticism and politics and connect private revelations to activities by all leaders within the Church and society in order that justice might prevail. Certainly, her idea of the common good, and the means that one could use in order to achieve it, was influenced by the notions of the clergy of her day, especially those of the Dominicans, who had been a part of her life since adolescence. For her, the responsibility and the decision-making power in this domain had to be reserved to the governing elites. Nor does she seem to have been very sensitive to the wretched conditions of life for the poor of her day, other than the sick, as her indifference regarding the revolt of the Ciompi in Florence in 1378 shows. The same thing could be said about her hostility toward the popular movements that appeared one after another in Siena beginning in 1367. However, she did not get involved in politics in order that she might have her ideas prevail in matters of government but in order to affirm the primacy of the spiritual in all situations. Her desire to see the powerful of the world remain faithful to the demands of the gospel in their behavior caused her to be regarded in a negative light by all the parties to a conflict. By urging the leaders of the Italian cities to respect the clergy and to obey the papacy, she alienated almost all of them. And because she reminded Popes Gregory XI and Urban VI that they could not limit themselves to a policy based only on military force and pressure, she succeeded in exasperating them and found herself in a no-man's-land, reduced to powerlessness.

Catherine of Siena has often been presented, especially in our own time, as a model of lay holiness. Here, however, there is a considerable risk of being anachronistic because her spirituality is founded on a total disdain of the world. Her life was built upon a rupture with her own family and with all "carnal" affections. When one of her disciples wrote to ask her whom he ought to marry among three choices he had available, she curtly answered him that she had no advice to give him in this area and that it would be better if he did not marry at all, since he would then be freer to serve God. Not that Catherine was in principle against marriage; but, like Saint Paul, whom she admired a great deal, she reckoned that "in these times which are the last" and in the critical situation in which the Church found itself, there were better things to do. It can be argued that she had not embraced the contemplative life and had preferred to remain in the world to fight the forces of evil. But, in her letters, she does affirm her conviction—several times—that the monastic state is superior to the penitential life that she had chosen, as it is "more certain and more perfect" in its practice of obedience. Thus, she wrote to the *Mantellata* Daniela d'Orvieto, "I regret, miserable poor woman that I am, to never have followed this teaching [= on the monastic life]. I did exactly the opposite and, I admit, I have not infrequently judged my neighbor [= those who have made this choice]."[1] Catherine appears here to be at the crux of those contradictions that make it so difficult to label her—which people have often tried to do. On the one hand, she absorbs the discourse that was traditional and predominant in medieval spirituality about the superiority of the contemplative vis-à-vis the active life, while underlining the inherent contradiction between her choice of a "semi-religious" state of life and the ideal of obedience to a rule, which in her eyes constituted the greater virtue. She acted in the world while at the same time judging it negatively and without taking into consideration the positive values that could be found there. We also know that she expended a great deal of effort to found a monastery in Belcaro, near Siena, thereby following the example of Birgitta of Sweden, who had founded the monastery of Vadstena in Sweden and the order of the Holy Savior, whose rule she had succeeded in getting Pope Urban V to approve. Perhaps Catherine might have had a similar ambition, but the brevity of her life impeded her realizing her intentions in this area.

But, at the same time, as she was waxing eloquent about monasticism, Catherine did persevere until her death in her status as a penitent, living autonomously in the midst of the world and always in motion, which allowed her to act more freely and more efficaciously on behalf of the Church and its reform. She believed herself to be God's messenger charged with warning and counseling humanity about its salvation; but she did not seek to be imitated in this way of life or to insist that this was the only way to accomplish these goals.[2] Moreover, her itinerant prophesying remained an exceptional vocation and, as such, enjoyed no canonical status in the Church, even though its legitimacy was acknowledged by theologians. Catherine wanted to remind her contemporaries—in good times as well as in bad—of the requirements of their divine filiation in all its radicalness, while tempering the acerbic tone that this discourse could have with a great care for "discretion," that is to say, discernment and prudence.[3]

In the last analysis, one can only understand Catherine of Siena by considering what she was and what she did, rather than what she said—because her words often remain germane only to specific situations or are somewhat ambiguous. Through her activity, she inaugurated a new season in the history of the West in which a certain number of women—thanks to a convergence of elements—could make remarkable inroads into many domains. Along with her near-contemporary Birgitta of Sweden, she opened the door to a kind of "female Catholicism," to borrow the expression of Jean Delumeau, which, true enough, belongs to another period of our history. This opportunity would be expanded in the fifteenth century with the female Dominican mystics whom we mentioned previously, but also with the great Poor Clare abbesses such as Caterina Vigri († 1463), foundress of the monastery of Corpus Christi in Bologna, and Colette of Corbie († 1446), who was instrumental—in France and in the Low Countries—in a reform of both female and male Franciscan convents. It is not too far-fetched to add here Joan of Arc († 1431), a simple peasant girl become leader of armies who was considered during her lifetime to be a prophetess and was burned at the stake as a sorceress and fortune-teller. Or, in the realm of writers, we might even mention Christine de Pizan († 1430): an Italian originally from Tuscany who lived in France during the worst moments of the Hundred Years War and was one of the first female writers in the French language, just as Catherine had been a half-century earlier in Italian. This emergence of women in religious and cultural life is connected to the profound crisis over institutions and authority. With the Great Schism and the conciliar crisis, between 1378 and 1450, the Church and the papacy were profoundly shaken. In France as in Italy, the incessant wars, added to the recurring ravages of the plague, had created upheaval in society. After the death of Charles V, the French monarchy, weakened by political crises and military defeats vis-à-vis England, lost its prominence in Europe; and the University of Paris lost its authority within Christianity after its internal conflicts and political compromises. Everything seemed to be happening as if the established powers—both lay as well as ecclesiastical—had become incapable of resolving the problems with which they were being confronted and were no longer managing to cope with uncontrollable outbursts of violence.

Thanks to this generalized crisis and so many conflicts with uncertain outcomes, women at this time succeeded in playing a role that normally had not been recognized as theirs to exercise in the Church and society of the time—and they even, in some cases, replaced the male authorities who were not up to the task. Numerous "inspired" visionaries—who were often mystics as well—called for reforms, inaugurated new forms of religious life, and endeavored to coax the authorities and the people away from their inertia by giving the example—like Catherine of Siena and Joan of Arc—of an indomitable courage and of the most thoroughgoing self-denial. The message of these women had nothing revolutionary about it and it is even hard to characterize it as antiestablishment. The role consisted less in innovating than in reminding their contemporaries of the fundamental truths that had been forgotten: God is love and Christ died for our sins; the pope fully exercises his role only when he resides in Rome (of which he is its bishop) and if he involves himself in the reform of the Church; and France can only be governed by a French king who has received his anointing in Reims, and so forth. These passionately delivered statements—even if they took the form of insistent supplications rather than demands—correspond to the very definition of biblical prophecy: a memory that desires—with the good and the true as its goal—to reestablish an order disrupted by sin and to illuminate truths that had been forgotten or overshadowed. The messages transmitted by these women verbally and in writing—in Catherine's case—are undoubtedly traditional. They were happy to remind each one of his or her calling by asking each one to fully take responsibility for it. But the behavior of these women and their way of intervening in history are innovative, as they did not hesitate to abandon the private sphere to enter the public arena and to turn upside down, to their advantage, the relationship of their dependence upon men—the powers of this world and the learned—that normally had been theirs. Within this brave cohort of women whose influence left its mark upon the last years of the Middle Ages, Catherine is but one figure among many. But she is the only one whose reputation has extended across the centuries and has never stopped exerting an influence upon people.

Around the end of the fifteenth century, after an upheaval that had lasted more than half a century, institutions—and therefore, men—regained the upper hand; and the claim of these women to have found God within their hearts and to speak in his name began to appear suspect. The parenthesis of a Church in which the word of women had been taken into consideration did not take long to be closed once again. We then witness the ecclesiastical hierarchy and theologians—who sought to structure what was a new and disturbing phenomenon for them—once again taking back these private revelations under their own purview. Thus, we see the proliferation of various treatises, such as, those by Pierre d'Ailly and Jean Gerson, that were devoted to the discernment of spirits (*discretio spirituum*) and thus would facilitate the distinction between true and false visionaries.[4] Soon the Inquisition itself became interested in the mystics and, later, in the Spanish *beatas*. Finally, the Fifth Lateran Council (1512–17) condemned wholesale not only the eschatological preaching of "pseudoprophets" who were announcing that numerous evils were imminent, but also the overly vigorous reformers "who were scandalously railing against the bishops, prelates, and other superiors as well as their behaviors."[5] In this sense, it can be said that the canonization of Catherine of Siena by Pius II in 1461 signaled the beginning of the end of an era. The goal of the papacy was to promote an exemplary figure of a Christian in whose life had been harmoniously expressed an intensely lived mysticism, a profound attachment to the sacraments, and a firm ecclesiastical and theological control. This image is not false but, as I have tried to show in this volume, it takes account of only a part of the rich personality and aspirations of the *Mantellata* of Siena.

NOTES

INTRODUCTION

1. Johannes Jørgensen, *Saint Catherine of Siena*, trans. Ingeborg Lund (New York: Longmans, Green & Co., 1938), preface, v (orig. publ. in French: *Sainte Catherine de Sienne*, trans. Marie-Therèse Fourcade [Paris: Beauchesne, 1919], xi).

2. See Robert Fawtier and Louis Canet, *La double expérience de Catherine Benincasa (Sainte Catherine de Sienne)* (Paris: Librairie Gallimard, 1948), 239.

3. The specific references to these works can be found in the bibliography (p. 181).

4. Catherine of Siena, *The Dialogue*, trans. and intro. Suzanne Noffke (New York: Paulist Press, 1980); Catherine of Siena, *The Prayers of Catherine of Siena*, trans. Suzanne Noffke, 2nd ed. (Lincoln, NE: Authors Choice Press, 2001 [orig. publ.: New York: Paulist Press, 1983]); and Catherine of Siena, *The Letters of Catherine of Siena*, trans. Suzanne Noffke, 4 vols. (Tempe, AZ: Arizona Center for Medieval and Renaissance Studies, 2000–2008). English readers are fortunate to have at their disposition the magisterial translation in four volumes of Catherine's letters done by Sr. Suzanne Noffke, OP. However, it should be noted that, for the present translation, I have remained close to Vauchez's own rendering of the Latin into French so as to be faithful to his understanding of Catherine's thought. Nevertheless, every citation of her letters in this volume will also direct the reader to Sr. Noffke's translation.

CHAPTER 1

1. Odile Redon, *L'Espace d'une cité. Sienne et le pay siennois (XIIe–XIVe siècle)* (Rome, 1994).

2. See Rosa Maria Dessì, "L'invention du Bon Gouvernement," *Bibliothèque de l'École des Chartes* 165 (2007): 197–230; Patrick Boucheron, *Conjurer le peur. Sienne, 1338. Essai sur la force politique des images* (Paris, 2013).

3. Agnolo di Tura del Grasso, *Cronaca senese*, ed. Giosue Carducci, 2nd. ed., Rerum Italicarum Scriptores 15/6, fasc. 2, gen. ed. L. A. Muratori (Bologna, 1939), 6.

4. On the political and social life of Siena in the fourteenth century, see Mario Ascheri, *Il Rinascimento a Siena (1355–1555)* (Siena, 1993).

5. See André Vauchez, *Francesco d'Assisi e gli ordini mendicanti*, Medioevo francescano, Saggi 10 (Assisi, 2005), esp. 167–88.

6. Charles-Marie de La Roncière, *Religion paysanne et religion urbaine en Toscane (c. 1250–c.1450)* (Aldershot, 1994).

7. Sonia Porzi, "Giovanni Colombini: un modèle de Catherine de Sienne occulté par ses hagiographes," *Cahiers d'études italiennes* 15 (2012): 37–65 (theme issue: "Héros et modèles"); and Isabella Gagliardi, *I Pauperes Yesuati tra esperienze religiose e compiti internazionali* (Rome, 2004).

8. Donato di Neri, *Cronaca senese*, ed. Giosue Carducci, 2nd ed., Rerum Italicarum Scriptores 15/6, fasc. 2, gen. ed. L. A. Muratori (Bologna, 1939), 569–85.

9. For the account of the childhood and adolescence of Catherine, we are relying upon her first and chief biographer, Raymond of Capua, edited most recently in *Legenda maior*, ed. Silvia Nocentini (Florence, 2013), 132–200. This fundamental text had been translated into English in 1960 by George Lamb, using the Bollandist Latin text of 1860 and the 1934 Italian translation of Giuseppe Tinagli, in *The Life of St. Catherine of Siena* (New York, 1960), and reprinted by Tan Books (Charlotte, NC, 2011).

10. *I Miracoli di Caterina di Jacopo senese* (di anonimo fiorentino), Fontes vitae S. Catherinae Senensis historici 4 (Florence, 1936), 14.

11. Domenico Cavalca, *Vite dei santi Padri*, ed. Carlo Delcorno, vol. 2, Archivio romanzo 15 (Florence, 2009), 1365–83 (for the *Life* of Saint Euphrosyne).

12. See André Duval, "Sainte Catherine de Sienne, dominicaine," *La Vie spirituelle* 640–41 (1980): 828–51.

13. On the esteem given to eremitism in Italy during the last centuries of the Middle Ages, see André Vauchez, ed., *Ermites de France et d'Italie (Xie–XVe siècle)* (Rome, 2003); Cécile Caby, *De l'érémitisme rural au monachisme urbain. Les Camaldules en Italie à la fin du Moyen Age* (Rome, 1999); Alessandra Malquori, *Il giardino dell'anima. Ascesi e propaganda nelle Tebaidi fiorentine del Quattrocento* (Florence, 2012).

14. Raymond of Capua, *Legenda maior*, part III, c. 6, p. 330; but see my more extended discussion below, 102–7.

15. M.-H. Laurent, ed., *Il Processo Castellano*, Fontes vitae S. Catherinae Senensis historici 9 (Milan, 1942), 398–99. An edition in Italian translation is also now available: Tito Centi and Angelo Belloni, eds., *Il Processo Castellano*, Biblioteca di Memorie Domenicane 2 (Florence, 2009).

16. Letter 213, to Daniella da Orvieto, in Catherine of Siena, *Letters*, 3:295–304, at 300 (see intro., n. 4).

17. The text is quoted in Nicole Bériou, "L'épouse du Christ," in *Catherine de Sienne*, Exposition Catalogue, Grande Chapelle du Palais des papes, ed. Marie and Christian Loury (Avignon, 1992), 101–19, at 107.

18. Raymond of Capua, *Legenda maior*, part I, c. 12, p. 82.

19. Letter 165, to Monna Bartolomea di Salvatico of Lucca, in Catherine of Siena, *Letters*, 2:42. But see also Katherine L. Jansen, *The Making of the Magdalen: Preaching and Popular Devotion in the Later Middle Ages* (Princeton, NJ: Princeton University Press, 2000), 254–56.

20. Raymond of Capua, *Legenda maior*, part II, c. 7 (re: Giacomo Tolomei), pp. 185–88; and c. 10 (re: Niccolò Saracini), pp. 226–28; and Jørgensen, *Saint Catherine of Siena*, book II, c. 5, pp. 112–15 (French ed.: *Sainte Catherine de Sienne*, 167–69) (see intro., no. 1).

21. Letter 59, to Pietro, priest of Semingnano, in Catherine of Siena, *Letters*, 1:276–79, at 277–78, passim; and cited also by Jørgensen, *Saint Catherine of Siena*, book II, c. 9, pp. 172–73 (French ed.: *Sainte Catherine de Sienne*, 254).

22. Raymond of Capua, *Legenda maior*, part II, c. 8, pp. 202–5.

23. Raymond of Capua, *Legenda maior*, Part II, c. 4, p. 128; and part III, c. 6, pp. 339–41.

24. Birgitta of Sweden, *The Revelations of Saint Birgitta of Sweden*, trans. Denis Searby, vol. 2 (Oxford: Oxford University Press, 2008), book

IV, c. 77, par. 3, p. 147. The passages where Mary is speaking directly to Birgitta: vol. 3, book VI, cc. 55–62, pp. 116–26.

25. Friedrich Nietzsche, "Thus Spake Zarathustra," in *Ecce Homo: How One Becomes What One Is*, trans. Thomas Wayne (New York, 2004), par. 3, p. 71. [Ed. note: the translation is my own from the French version cited by the author using the edition and translation of Geneviève Blanquis (Paris, 1969).]

26. Raymond of Capua, *Legenda maior*, part II, pp. 90–91, passim.

27. Cristofano di Gano Guidini, *Memorie*, in *I Fioretti di Santa Caterina da Siena*, ed. Innocenzo Taurisano, 2nd ed. (Rome, 1927), 117, 125.

28. Fawtier Canet, *La double expérience*, 76 (see intro., no. 2).

29. Letter 337, to the Priori dell'Arti and the Gonfaloniere of Justice of the People and Commune of Florence, in Catherine of Siena, *Letters*, 4:120–24, at 122. On Catherine's attitude toward the regime of the "Reformers," see Mario Ascheri, "Un intesa impossibile: Caterina e la cultura politico-istituzionale 'popolare' a Siena," in *"Con l'occhio e col lume,"* Atti del corso seminariale di studi su Caterina da Siena (1995), ed. Luigi Trenti and Bente Klange Addabo (Siena, 1999), 81–98.

30. Laurent, *Il Processo Castellano*, 331–34.

31. Raymond of Capua, *Legenda maior*, part I, c. 9, p. 57.

32. On Alfonso Pecha de Vadaterra, see the fundamental article of Eric Colledge, "*Epistola solitarii ad reges*: Alphonse of Pecha as Organizer of the Birgittine and Urbanist Propaganda," *Medieval Studies* 18 (1956): 19–49.

33. *I Miracoli*, cited in Duval, "Sainte Catherine de Sienne, dominicaine," 839.

34. Raymond of Capua, *Legenda maior*, part II, c. 6, p. 153.

35. Raymond of Capua, *Legenda maior*, part II, c. 6, p. 154.

36. Raymond of Capua, *Legenda maior*, part II, c. 6, p. 157.

37. On the debate concerning the iconography of Catherine of Siena, see Alessandra Bartolomei Romagnoli, "La disputa sulle stimmate," in "Virgo digna coelo," *Caterina e la sua eredità*, Pontificio Comitato di scienze storiche, Atti e Documenti 35, ed. Alessandra Bartolomei Romagnoli, Luciano Cinelli, and Pierantonio Piatti (Vatican City, 2013), 407–46.

38. Chiara Frugoni, "Des stigmates," in *Catherine de Sienne*, Exposition Catalogue, 55–76.

39. See the acts of the colloquium: *Santa Brigida profeta dei tempi nuovi*, Rome, 3–7 October 1991 (Rome, 1993).

40. Agostino Paravicini Bagliani, "Caterina da Siena e il papato," in Romagnoli et al., "Virgo digna coelo," 67–76.

41. Jacques Chiffoleau, "La rencontre: Catherine et l'institution," in *Catherine de Sienne*, Exposition Catalogue, 175–87; and Andrea Giardina and André Vauchez, *Rome, l'idée et le mythe* (Paris, 2000).

42. Alphonse Dupront, "Guerre sainte et chrétienté," in *La Paix de Dieu et la guerre sainte en Languedoc au XIIIe siècle*, Cahiers de Fanjeaux 4 (Toulouse, 1969), 45; and Sonia Porzi, "Rome et Jérusalem: les étapes d'un retour aux origines de la chrétienté dans les lettres de Catherine de Sienne," *Revue des études italiennes* 58 (2012): 7–25.

43. Claudio Leonardi, "Caterina e la mistica," in *Agiografia medievale*, ed. Antonella degl'Innocenti and Francesco Santi (Florence, 2011), 632–33.

44. Letters 7 and 11, to Pierre d'Estaing, in Catherine of Siena, *Letters*, 2:262–65 and 521–26, respectively.

45. Letter 109, to Bérenger, abbot of Lezat, Apostolic Nuncio to Tuscany, in Catherine of Siena, *Letters*, 1:264–69. [Ed. note: Noffke (p. 264) places this letter as late as January or February 1376.]

46. Letter 109, *Letters*, 267–68.

47. See Fawtier and Canet, *La double expérience*, 86. This letter (probably written in 1371 or 1372) comes to us in Latin.

48. Letter 28, to Bernabò Visconti of Milan, in Catherine of Siena, *Letters*, 1:132–38.

49. Letter 354, to Pentella of Naples, in Catherine of Siena, *Letters*, 4:243–49, passim; and Letter 201, to Giovanni, Carthusian in Rome, in Catherine of Siena, *Letters*, 3:253–57, at 257.

50. Letter of Gregory XI to Raymond of Capua (August 17, 1376); a French translation of the letter can also be found in Duval, "Sainte Catherine de Sienne, dominicaine."

51. Letter 273, to Raymond of Capua, in Catherine of Siena, *Letters*, 1:85–89, passim; see also the text, as G97, in Fawtier and Canet, *La double expérience*, 125–27.

52. Letter 273, to Raymond of Capua, in Catherine of Siena, *Letters*, 1:85–89, here especially on 88–89.

53. Letter 273, to Raymond of Capua, in Catherine of Siena, *Letters*, 1:88–89.

54. Thomas Luongo, *The Saintly Politics of Catherine of Siena* (Ithaca, NY: Cornell University Press, 2006)—a fundamental and innovative work on the political role played in Italy by Catherine of Siena during the years 1374–80.

55. On the unfolding of the crisis seen from Florence's perspective, see D. S. Peterson, "The War of the Eight Saints in Florentine Memory and Oblivion," in *Society and Individual in Renaissance Florence*, ed. W. J. Connell (Berkeley, CA: University of California Press, 2002), 173–214.

56. Letter 234, to Buonaccorso di Lapo, in Florence, in Catherine of Siena, *Letters*, 2:239–42, at 240.

57. One will find a detailed account of the facts, along with a negative appraisal of the role played by Catherine in the return of the papacy to Rome, in Fawtier and Canet, *Le double expérience*, 144–49.

58. The pope said to her, "I am not asking you to counsel me but to share with me what is God's will concerning this matter"; to which Catherine responded, "Who knows it [the will of God] better than your Holiness—you who have vowed to God to make this journey?" See Fawtier and Canet, *La double expérience*, 149. This testimony has been drawn from Laurent, *Il Processo Castellano*, 295.

59. Letter 235, to Charles V, king of France, in Catherine of Siena, *Letters*, 2:219–24, at 222.

60. Letter 123, to the Defenders of the Commune of Siena, in Catherine of Siena, *Letters*, 2:372–77, at 377.

61. Letter 118, to Caterina dello Spedaluccio and Giovanna di Capo, in Siena, in Catherine of Siena, *Letters*, 2:388–90, at 390. On this campaign, see Jørgensen, *Catherine of Siena*, book III, c. 6, pp. 264–65 (French ed.: *Catherine de Sienne*, 391).

62. Laurent, *Il Processo Castellano*, 49, 392–95, and 425.

63. Letter 230, to the Eight of War, in Florence, in Catherine of Siena, *Letters*, 2:195–97, passim.

64. Marchionne di Coppo Stefani, *Cronaca fiorentina* (1377), Rubrica 773, ed. N. Rodolico, 2nd ed., Rerum Italicarum Scriptores 31 (Città di Castello, 1910), 306. Parts of his testimony have been translated by Suzanne Noffke, in Catherine of Siena, *Letters*, 2:35.

65. Letter 242, to Bishop Angelo Ricasoli, in Catherine of Siena, *Letters*, 2:527–31, at 530. Examples of her irritation with the bishop can be found in ibid, 1:141–42 (Letter 136) and 228–32 (Letter 88).

66. See Peterson, "The War of the Eight Saints."

67. Raymond of Capua, *Legenda maior*, part III, c. 6, pp. 349–51. On the Ciompi, see Alessandra Stella, *La Révolte des Ciompi: les hommes, les lieux, le travail* (Paris, 1993).

68. Letter 295, to Raymond of Capua, in Rome, in Catherine of Siena, *Letters*, 3:148–50, at 149; the text, as G96, is also in Fawtier and Canet, *La double expérience*, 179–80.

69. On the origins and development of the Great Schism in the West, see Hélène Millet, *L'Église du Grand Schisme* (Paris, 2009); and Paul Payan, *Entre Rome et Avignon: une histoire du Grand Schisme (1378–1417)* (Paris, 2009).

70. Jørgensen, *Saint Catherine of Siena*, book III, c. 10, pp. 327–28 (French ed.: *Sainte Catherine de Sienne*, 488–89); and Raymond of Capua, *Legenda maior*, part III, c. 1, p. 276.

71. Raymond of Capua, *Legenda maior*, part III, c. 1, p. 277.

72. On Catherine's time in Rome, see Maria Grazia Bianco, ed., *La Roma di Santa Caterina da Siena* (Rome, 2001).

73. Ludovico Gatto, "La Roma di Caterina," in Bianco, *La Roma di Santa Caterina*, 13–48.

74. G. G. Meersseman, "Gli amici spirituali di Santa Catarina a Roma nel 1378 alla luce del primo manifesto urbaniano," *Bollettino della Società Senese di Storia Patria* 69 (1962): 83–123; and Antonio Volpato, "Le lettere di Santa Caterina sullo scisma," in Bianco, *La Roma di Santa Caterina*, 75–118.

75. Letter 328, to Antonio da Nizza (or Nice), in Catherine of Siena, *Letters*, 4:78–81, at 80; the text, as G130, is also in Fawtier and Canet, *La double expérience*, 204–5.

76. Letter 351, in Catherine of Siena, *Letters*, 4:204–7, at 206.

77. Letter 350, in Catherine of Siena, *Letters*, 4:172–76, at 176 (the phrase, though not explicit, is an allusion to the Parisian Masters).

78. Letter 333, to Raymond of Capua, in Catherine of Siena, *Letters*, 4:88–90, at 89–90; the text is also found, as G100, in Fawtier and Canet, *La double expérience*, 212.

79. Letter 364, to Urban VI, in Catherine of Siena, *Letters*, 4:350–53, at 352.

80. Letter 346, to Urban VI, in Catherine of Siena, *Letters*, 4:56–59, at 58n12.

81. Letter 364, to Urban VI, in Catherine of Siena, *Letters*, 4:350–53, at 351.

82. Letter 373, to Raymond of Capua, in Catherine of Siena, *Letters*, 4:364–70, at 367–68, passim; the text, as G102, is also in Fawtier and Canet, *La double expérience*, 228.

83. Letter 373, 366; the text, as G102, is also in Fawtier and Canet, *La double expérience*, 229.

84. Letter 373, 369–70; the text, as G102, is also in Fawtier and Canet, *La double expérience*, 231–34, passim.

85. See André Vauchez, ed., *Les textes prophétiques et la prophétie en Occident (XIIe–XVIe siècle)* (Rome, 1990); and Alessandra Bartolomei Romagnoli, "Caterina e Robina: profezia e antiprofezia al tempo del Grande Scisma d'Occidente," in *Santità e mistica femminile nel Medioevo* (Spoleto, 2013), 631–56.

86. Stefani, *Cronaca fiorentina*, 378; and translated into French in Fawtier and Canet, *La double expérience*, 235.

87. On Remigio de'Girolami, see Sonia Gentile, "Remigio de'Girolami," in *Dizionario biografico degli Italiani* (Rome, 1999), 51:531–41. On the preaching of the Dominicans on behalf of peace and justice, see R. M. Dessì, ed., *Prêcher la paix et discipliner la société (XIIIe–XVe siècles)* (Turnhout, 2005), 245–78; and Dessì, "*Diligite justitiam vos qui judicatis terram* (Sagesse 1, 1): Sermons et discours sur la justice dans l'Italie urbaine (XIIe–XVe siècle)," *Rivista internazionale di Diritto comune* 18 (2007): 197–230.

88. On the importance of the idea of justice in the thought and work of Catherine, see Charles Lefebvre, "La notion de justice dans les lettres de Ste Catherine de Sienne," in *Atti del simposio internazionale cateriniano-bernardiniano*, ed. Domenico Maffei and Paolo Nardi (Siena, 1982), 149–54.

89. Letter 371, to Urban VI, in Catherine of Siena, *Letters*, 4:359–63, at 359–60.

CHAPTER 2

1. Letter 121, to the Lord Defenders of the City of Siena, in Catherine of Siena, *Letters*, 2:414–17, at 416 (see intro., n. 4). On Giacomo del Pecora, see Jørgensen, *Saint Catherine of Siena*, book III, c. 6, p. 263n4.

2. William Flete, "*Sermo in reverentiam beatae Katharinae de Senis*," ed. Robert Fawtier, in his "Catheriniana," *MEFR* 34 (1914): 3–95, here at 40–75.

3. On this text and its importance, see the introduction of Silvia Nocentini to her critical edition: *Raimondo da Capua. Legenda maior* (Florence, 2013), 3–95, which surpasses all previous editions.

4. Philip de Mézières, chancellor of Cyprus and counselor of Charles V and Charles VI, kings of France, evokes Venice with emotion in his *Songe du Vieil Pèlerin* (Dream of the Old Pilgrim).

5. Letter 341, to Angelo Carraro, newly elected Bishop of Castello, in Catherine of Siena, *Letters*, 4:340–344. [Ed. note: Suzanne Noffke dates this letter to late December, 1379.]

6. See André Vauchez, *Sainthood in the Later Middle Ages*, trans. Jean Birrell (Cambridge, 1997), 376–86, esp. 383–86; and Giorgio Ferzoco, "The *Processo Castellano* and the Canonization of Catherine of Siena," in *A Companion to Catherine of Siena*, ed. Carolyn Muessig (Leiden, 2012), 185–201.

7. "Urbanist obedience" refers to those countries that remained loyal to Pope Urban VI during the Great Schism.

8. Jean Gerson, *De examinatione doctrinarum*, in *Oeuvres complètes*, vol. 9, *L'oeuvre doctrinale*, ed. P. Glorieux (Paris, 1973), 469–70.

9. On the modalities and principal steps of this process, see Jeffrey F. Hamburger and Gabriela Signori, eds., *Catherine of Siena: The Creation of a Cult* (Turnhout, 2013), especially the contributions of Gabriella Zarri ("Catherine of Siena and the Italian Public," 69–79), and Thomas Luongo ("Saintly Authorship in the Italian Renaissance: The Quattrocento Reception of Catherine of Siena's Letter," 135–67).

10. The Bull of Canonization of Saint Catherine of Siena, issued by Pope Pius II (1461), can be found in Laurent, *Il Processo Castellano*, 521–30 (see chap. 1, n. 15).

11. On the stigmata of Catherine of Siena, see David Ganz, "The Dilemma of a Saint's Portrait: Catherine's Stigmata between Invisible Body Trace and Visible Pastoral Sign," in Hamburger and Signori, *Catherine of Siena*, 239–62; and Alessandra Bartolomei Romagnoli, "Un trattatello cinquecentesco in difesa delle stimmate di Caterina da Siena," *Archivio italiano per la storia della pietà* 27 (2013): 177–202.

12. Antonio Volpato, "Corona aurea e corona aureola: ordini e meriti nella ecclesiologia medioevale," *Bullettino dell'Istituto storico italiano per il Medio Evo* 91 (1986): 115–82.

13. Dirk Schulze, "Catherine of Siena in Fifteenth-Century England," in Hamburger and Signori, *Catherine of Siena*, 185–212.

14. Thomas Brackmann, "The Transition of the Upper German Lives of Catherine of Siena," in Hamburger and Signori, *Catherine of Siena*, 83–107; and Kristin Böse, "The Evidence of Visions in Illustrated *Vitae* of Catherine of Siena," in Hamburger and Signori, *Catherine of Siena*, 215–38.

15. Esther Moench and Jacques Chiffoleau, "De la prière perpétuelle. Catherine et le Rosaire," in *Catherine de Sienne*, Exposition Catalogue, Grande Chapelle du Palais des papes (Avignon, 1992), 141–52.

16. Niccolò Tommaseo, *Caterina da Siena. Le Lettere*, 4 vols. (Florence, 1860), text cited by Umberto Meattini, ed., *Santa Caterina da Siena. Le Lettere* (Turin, 1987).

17. Piero Misciatelli, *I mistici senesi*, 2nd ed. (Siena, 1913).

18. See Gerald Parsons, *The Cult of Catherine of Siena: A Study in Civic Religion* (Aldershot, UK, 2008).

19. Robert Fawtier, *Catherine de Sienne. Essai de critique des sources*, vol. 1 (Paris, 1921), and vol. 2 (Paris, 1930).

20. Laurent, *Il Processo Castellano*.

21. Eugène Duprè Theseider, ed., *Epistolario di Santa Catarina da Siena* (Rome, 1940) (which, in fact, contains Letters 1–80). The critical edition of Catherine's letters done by Fausto Sbaffoni and Antonio Volpato is only available on CD-ROM: *Santa Caterina da Siena, Opera omnia. Testi e concordanze* (Pistoia, 2002).

22. Paul VI, discourse of October 4, 1970. One can see the full text in Italian on the Vatican website at https://w2.vatican.va/content/paul-vi/it/homilies/1970/documents/hf_p-vi_hom_19701003.html.

23. Domenico Maffei and Paolo Nardi, *Atti del simposio internazionale cateriniano-bernardiniano* (Siena, 1982). On this historiographical turning point, see Sofia Boesch Gajano, "Caterina nella storiografia," in *Caterina e la sua eredità*, 47–66.

24. Rudolph M. Bell, *Holy Anorexia* (Chicago: University of Chicago Press, 1985); Caroline Walker Bynum, *Holy Feast and Holy Fast* (Berkeley: University of California Press, 1987); and Ginette Raimbault and Caroline Eliacheff, *Les Indomptables. Figures de l'anorexie* (Paris, 1989). On this debate, see also the fine article of Jacques Maître, "Sainte Catherine de Sienne, patronne des anorexiques?" *Clio* 2 (1995), 16 pages (accessible online).

CHAPTER 3

1. Silvia Nocentini, ed., *Raimondo da Capua, Legenda maior*, Edizione Nazionale dei Testi Mediolatini d'Italia 31, Serie 1/19 (Florence, 2013); French translation of the original Latin by R. P. Étienne Hugueny, *Vie de sainte Catherine de Sienne*, 2nd ed. (Paris, 2000; orig. publ. in Paris, 1904). Concerning this *Life*, see Sofia Boesch Gajano and Odile Redon, "La *Legenda maior* di Raimondo da Capua e la costruzione di una santa," in Maffei and Nardi, *Atti del simposio*, 15–35 (see chap. 2, n. 23).

2. Ezio Franchescini, ed., *Tommaso Nacci detto il Caffarini, Legenda minor* (Siena, 1998); and Giuliana Cavallini and Imelda Foralosso, eds., *Libellus de supplemento legende prolixe virginis beate Catherine de Sensis* (Rome, 1974). Henceforth, all citations will be taken from the latter edition. An Italian translation is now available: Tommaso di Antonio da Siena "Caffarini," *Supplemento alla vita di S. Caterina da Siena*, trans. Angelo Belloni and Tito Centi, Biblioteca di Memorie Domenicane 5 (Florence, 2010).

3. The remark is made in Letter 119, to Alessa dei Saraceni, in Catherine of Siena, *Letters*, 2:699–702, at 700 (and Noffke's comments in n6) (see intro., n. 4); the text, as G178, is cited in Fawtier and Canet, *La double expérience*, 186–87 (see intro., n. 2).

4. Jane Tylus, "Writing versus Voice: Tommaso Caffarini and the Production of a Literate Catherine," in Signori, *Catherine of Siena*, 291–312 (see chap. 2, n. 9).

5. On this vision and the iconographical representations that it inspired, see David Ganz, "The Dilemma of a Saint's Portrait," in Hamburger and Signori, *Catherine of Siena*, 252–57 (for the depiction by Cristoforo Cortese).

6. Catherine of Siena, *The Dialogue* and *The Prayers of Catherine of Siena* (see intro., n. 4).

7. For the English translations of her letters, see Catherine of Siena, *Letters*.

8. Raymond of Capua, *Legenda maior*, part III, c. 3, p. 292 (see chap. 1, n. 9).

9. Odile Redon, "Une vie," in *Catherine de Sienne*, Exposition Catalogue, Chapelle du Palais des papes (Avignon, 1992), 25–42, here at 32–33.

10. Cristoforo Guidini, *Memorie*, in *I Fioretti di Santa Caterina da Siena*, ed. Innocenzo Taurisano, 2nd ed. (Rome, 1927).

11. Catherine of Siena, *The Dialogue*, 25.

12. Catherine of Siena, "The Mystical Body of Holy Church," in *The Dialogue*, 205–76, esp. 216–24.

CHAPTER 4

1. Jacques Maître, "De Bourneville à nos jours: interpretations psychiatriques de la mystique," *Évolution psychiatrique* 64 (1999): 765–88.

2. Letter 240, to Monna Lapa, her mother, in Catherine of Siena, *Letters*, 2:249–51, at 249 (see intro., p. 4).

3. Ginette Raimbault and Caroline Eliacheff, *Les Indomptables. Figures de l'anorexie* (Paris, 1989).

4. Raimbault and Eliacheff, *Les Indomptables*, 155.

5. Raimbault and Eliacheff, *Les Indomptables*, 204.

6. Raimbault and Eliacheff, *Les Indomptables*, 203.

7. Alessandra Bartolomei Romagnoli, "Il linguaggio del corpo in Caterina da Siena," in *Santità e mistica femminile del Medioevo* (Spoleto, 2012), 500–523, esp. 519.

8. Letter 371, to Raymond of Capua, in Catherine of Siena, *Letters*, 4:359–63, at 363.

9. Gal 3:28.

10. Cf. Raymond of Capua, *Legenda maior*, part I, c. 11, pp. 72–75, passim.

11. Michel de Certeau, *The Mystic Fable: The Sixteenth and Seventeenth Centuries*, vol. 1 (Chicago: University of Chicago Press, 1992), 80.

12. Raymond of Capua, *Legenda maior*, part I, c. 9, pp. 99–100.

13. Caroline Walker Bynum, *Jesus as Mother: Studies in the Spirituality of the High Middle Ages* (Los Angeles: University of California Press, 1982).

14. "Prayer 13," in *The Prayers of Catherine of Siena*, 129–30 (see intro., n. 4).

15. Letter 171, to Niccolò Soderini, in Catherine of Siena, *Letters*, 2:23–29, at 26.

16. Letter 87, to Giovanna dei Pazzi, in Catherine of Siena, *Letters*, 2:631–34, at 631–32; and also in Jørgensen, *Saint Catherine of Siena*, 457–58 (see intro., n. 1).

17. Letter 260, to the Prisoners in Siena, in Catherine of Siena, *Letters*, 2:316–19, at 316–17, passim.

18. Letter 29, to Regina della Scala, wife of Bernabò Visconti, in Catherine of Siena, *Letters*, 1:204–10, at 204. [Ed. note: Suzanne Noffke identifies this Beatrice as "Regina".]

19. Catherine of Siena, *The Dialogue*, par. 13, p. 50.

20. Letter 252, to Gregory XI, in Catherine of Siena, *Letters*, 2:270–73, at 271.

21. Letter 270, to Gregory XI, in Catherine of Siena, *Letters*, 2:343–46, at 343.

22. Catherine of Siena, *The Dialogue*, par. 23, p. 60.

23. Catherine of Siena, *The Dialogue*, par. 164, p. 355.

24. Letter 302, to Urban VI, in Catherine of Siena, *Letters*, 4:217–18, at 217.

25. Letter 371, to Raymond of Capua, in Catherine of Siena, *Letters*, 4:359–63, at 361. [Ed. note: here, Catherine is channeling a message from God to Pope Urban VI, inserted into a letter to Raymond of Capua.]

26. Letter 364, to Urban VI, in Catherine of Siena, *Letters*, 4:350–53, at 351–52.

27. Vincent de Couesnongle, "Actualité de Catherine de Sienne," *La Vie spirituelle* 640–41 (1980): 683–84.

28. Raymond of Capua, *Legenda maior*, part II, c. 1, pp. 90–91.

29. Tommaso Caffarini, *Libellus de supplemento*, pars I, tract. 2, 8°, p. 21 (see chap. 3, n. 2).

30. Letter 317, to Joanna I, Queen of Naples, in Catherine of Siena, *Letters*, 4:5–11, at 6–7.

31. Caffarini, *Libellus de supplemento*, 78–81.

32. André Vauchez, "Dévotion eucharistique et union mystique chez les saintes de la fin du Moyen Age," in *Les laïcs au Moyen Age. Pratiques et expériences religieuses* (Paris, 1987), 263ff.

33. Christiane Klapisch-Zuber, "L'enfant Jésus. Jeu et dévotion," in *Catherine de Sienne*, Exposition Catalogue, Grande Chapelle du Palais des papes (Avignon, 1992), 121–31.

34. See Luongo, *The Saintly Politics of Catherine of Siena*, 102–3 (see chap. 1, n. 54).

35. Volpato, "Corona aurea e corona aureola" (see chap. 2, n. 12).

36. Letter 343, to Raymond of Capua, in Catherine of Siena, *Letters*, 4:265–70, at 268.

37. Letter 219, to Raymond of Capua and others of his company, in Catherine of Siena, *Letters*, 2:90–93, at 91–93, passim; the text, as G87, is also in Fawtier and Canet, *La double expérience*, 136–38.

38. Raymond of Capua, *Legenda maior*, prologue, 115–31, at 130–31 [= the second *incipit*]; and see also, in the English translation of the *Legenda maior*, part II, c. 10 ("The Prophetess"), 225–41, passim, and esp. 238–39. Unfortunately, the English translation lacks the prologue.

39. Telesforo Bini, ed., *Laudi spirituali del Bianco da Siena, povero gesuato*, strophe 72 (Lucca, 1851), 167: "Or ti guarda, suora mia / Che non caggi in gran ruina; Se hai la grazia divina / Fa che l'abbia conservata"; and strophe 14: "Guardi che la tentazione / Del profetico sermone / Non ti metta in prigione/ Tardi t'avrà lassata."

40. Letter 92, to "B" = a religious person in Florence, probably Bianco da Siena, in Catherine of Siena, *Letters*, 1:160–61, at 160.

41. André Vauchez, *Saints, prophètes et visionnaires. Le pouvoir surnaturel au Moyen Age* (Paris, 1999), 199–207; and Vauchez, ed., *Prophètes et prophétisme* (Paris, 2012), 61–125.

42. Letter 270, to Gregory XI, in Catherine of Siena, *Letters*, 2:343–46, at 344–45.

43. Letter 185, to Gregory XI, in Catherine of Siena, *Letters*, 1:244–50, at 245.

44. Raymond of Capua, *Legenda maior*, part II, c. 10, pp. 232–33.

45. Jean Gerson, *De examinatione doctrinarum*, par. 3, in *Oeuvres complètes*, 9:469–70 (see chap. 2, n. 8).

46. Caffarini, *Libellus de supplemento*, pars III, tract. 4, art. 4, p. 344.

47. Rita Fresu, "La rappresentazione della donna attraverso la lingua dei scritti di S. Caterina," in *La donna negli scritti cateriniani: dagli stereotipi del tempo all'infaticabile cura della vita*, ed. Diega Giunta, (Florence, 2011), 93–132, esp. 95. On the relationship between women and writing in the Middle Ages, see Luisa Miglio, *Governare l'alfabeto. Donne, scrittura e libri nel Medioevo* (Rome, 2008).

48. Philippe de Novare, *Les quatre âges de l'homme*, ed. Marcel de Fréville (Paris, 1888), 14–16; and Paolo da Certaldo, *Libri di buoni costumi*, ed. Alberto Schiaffini (Florence, 1945).

49. Letter 272, to Raymond of Capua, in Catherine of Siena, *Letters*, 2:495–506, at 505.

50. Fawtier and Canet, *La double expérience*, 185–88.

51. See Marina Zancan, "Le lettere di Caterina da Siena," in *Letteratura italiana*, vol. 1, *Dalle origini al Cinquecento*, ed. Alberto Asor Rosa (Turin, 1992), 596–623; and Zancan, *Il doppio itinerario della scrittura. La donna nella tradizione letteraria italiana* (Turin, 1998).

52. "Prayer 25," in Catherine of Siena, *Prayers of Catherine of Siena*, 254–60, passim.

53. Caffarini, *Libellus de supplemento*, pars I, tract. 1, 8 c. 1, par. 8°–9°, here at 9°, p. 18.

54. On the importance of this discovery made by Giuliana Cavallini, see Sofia Boesch Gajano, "Giuliana Cavallini e gli studi cateriniani: il senso di una svolta," in Giunta, *La donna negli scritti cateriniani*, 79–91.

55. Angela of Foligno, *Complete Works: The Memorial*, c. 4 ["Second Supplementary or Twenty-First Step"], ed. and trans. Paul Lachance, The Classics of Western Spirituality (New York: Paulist Press, 1993),148 (French ed.: Angela of Foligno, *Le Livre des visions et révélations*, c. 29 ["Onction"], trans. Ernest Hello [Paris, 1991], 112–13).

56. The expression is Giuliana Cavallini's, cited by Boesch Gajano, "Giuliana Cavallini e gli studi cateriniani," 80.

57. Quoted in Fawtier and Canet, *La double expérience*, 187.

58. Laurent, *Il Processo Castellano*, 403–4.

59. See Sonia Porzi, "Fondement de la persuasion et quête d'autorité chez Catherine de Sienne," *Cahiers d'études italiennes* 2 (2005): 79 (theme issue: "La persuasion").

60. Brian Stock, *The Implications of Literacy: Written Language and Models of Interpretation in the Eleventh and Twelfth Centuries* (Princeton, NJ: Princeton University Press, 1983), chap. 4.

61. Letter 348, to Joanna I, Queen of Naples, in Catherine of Siena, *Letters*, 4:166–70, at 167–68, passim.

62. Letter 140, to John Hawkwood, in Catherine of Siena, *Letters*, 1:80–81, esp. at 81.

63. Catherine of Siena, *The Dialogue*, par. 158, p. 339.

64. See André Duval, "Sainte Catherine de Sienne dominicaine," *La Vie spirituelle* 640–41 (1980): 847.

65. Catherine of Siena, *The Dialogue*, par. 158, p. 339.

66. Letter 185, to Gregory XI, in Catherine of Siena, *Letters*, 1:244–50, at 250.

67. Letter 181, to Nicolas of Osimo, in Catherine of Siena, *Letters*, 1:252–57, at 256.

68. Letters 194 and 262, both to Tora di Piero Gambacorta, in Catherine of Siena, *Letters*, 4:256–58; and 3:323–27, respectively.

69. On this reform movement arising out of the convent in Pisa, see Sylvie Duval, "Chiara Gambacorta et le prime monache del convento al monastero du S. Domenico di Pisa," in *Il velo, la penna e la parola. Le Domenicane: storia, istituzioni e scritture*, ed. Gabriella Zarri and Gianni Festa (Florence, 2009), 93–112; and Duval, *Comme des anges sur terre. Les moniales dominicaines et les débuts de la réforme observante, 1385–1461* (Rome, 2015).

70. See: Gabriella Zarri, "Introduzione," in Zarri and Festa, *Il velo, la penna e la parola*, 11–20; and Maiju Lehmijoki-Gardner, "Le penitenti domenicane tra Duecento e Trecento," in Zarri and Festa, *Il velo, la penna e la parola*, 113–23.

71. On these spiritual associations, see the volume *San Domenico di Fiesole tra storia, arte e spiritualità* (Florence, 2009) (= *Memorie Domenicane*, n.s., 40 [2009]).

72. See Victória Hedwig Deak, *La légende de sainte Marguerite de Hongrie et l'hagiographie dominicaine* (Paris, 2013).

73. Gábor Klaniczay, "Le stimmate di Santa Margerita di Ungheria. Immagini e testi," *Hagiographica* 1 (2002): 16–31.

74. Anna Benvenuti, "Catherine et les autres," in *Catherine de Sienne*, Exposition Catalogue, Chapelle du Palais des papes (Avignon, 1992), 155–67.

75. Gabriella Zarri, *Le sante vive. Profezie di corte e devozione femminile tra '400 e '500* (Turin, 1990); and Tamar Herzig, "Stigmatized Holy Women as Female Christs," *Archivio italiano per la storia della pietà* 26 (2013): 151–75 (special theme issue: Gabor Klaniczay, "Discours sur les stigmates du Moyen Âge à l'époque contemporaine," *Archivio italiano per la storia della pietà*, Roma, 2013, Edizioni di Storia e Letteratura).

76. Sebastiano degli Angeli, *Legenda volgare di Colomba da Rieti*, ed. Giovanna Casagrande (Spoleto, 2002), 155. See also Tamar Herzig, "Le mistiche domenicane nella lotta antiereticale a cavallo tra Quattro e Cinquecento," in Zarri and Festa, *Il velo, la penna e la parola*, 133–49; and Herzig, "Stigmatized Holy Women as Female Christs."

CONCLUSION

1. Letter 65, to Daniella da Orvieto, in Catherine of Siena, *Letters*, 3:233–40, at 240 (see intro., n. 4).

2. Sylvie Duval, "Chiara Gambacorta e le prime monache," 98 (see chap. 4, n. 69).

3. Letter 213, to Daniella da Orvieto, in Catherine of Siena, *Letters*, 3:295–304, passim.

4. André Vauchez, *Saints, prophètes et visionnaires. Le pouvoir surnaturel au Moyen Age* (Paris, 1999), 199–200.

5. See Olivier de La Brosse et al., *Latran V et Trente* (Paris, 1975).

BIBLIOGRAPHY

WORKS OF CATHERINE OF SIENA

Catherine of Siena. *The Dialogue*. Edited and translated by Suzanne Noffke. The Classics of Western Spirituality. New York: Paulist Press, 1980.

———. *The Letters of Catherine of Siena*. Edited and translated by Suzanne Noffke. 4 vols. Medieval and Renaissance Texts and Studies, 202, 203, 329, and 355. Tempe, AZ: Arizona Center for Medieval and Renaissance Studies, 2000–2008.

———. *The Prayers of Catherine of Siena*. Edited and translated by Suzanne Noffke. 2nd ed. Lincoln, NE: Authors Choice Press, 2001.

HAGIOGRAPHICAL SOURCES

Raymond of Capua. *Legenda maior* [*The Life of St. Catherine of Siena*]. Translated by George Lamb. Charlotte, NC: TAN Books, 2011. First published: New York: P. J. Kennedy–Harvill Press, 1960.

Raimondo da Capua. *Legenda maior*. Edited by Silvia Nocentini. Florence: SISMEL-Edizioni del Galluzzo, 2013.

Raymond de Capoue. *Thomas Caffarini, Vie de sainte Catherine de Sienne. Supplément*. Translated by Ernest Cartier. Paris, Poussielgue, 1859.

———. *Vie de sainte Catherine de Sienne*. Translated by R. P. Étienne Hugueny. 2nd ed. Paris: Lethielleux, 1904.

Cavallini, Giuliana, and Imelda Foralosso, eds. *Thomas Antonii de Senis "Caffarini," Libellus de supplemento: Legende prolixe virginis beate Catherine de Senis*. Rome: Edizioni cateriniane, 1974. Reprinted: Florence: Nerbini, 2010.

Franceschini, Ezio, ed. *Sanctae Catharinae Senensis Legenda minor*. Pubblicazioni dell'Università cattolica del Sacro Cuore. Serie 4. Scienze filologiche 38. Milan: Vita e Pensiero, 1942.

Laurent, M.-H., ed. *Il Processo Castellano*. Milan-Siena: Bocca-Università di Siena, 1942 [process laying the groundwork for the canonization of Catherine of Siena that was held in Venice between 1411 and 1416].

STUDIES

Bartolomei Romagnoli, Alessandra. *Santità e mistica femminile nel Medioevo*. Uomini e mondi medievali 37. Spoleto: Centro Italiano di studi sull'Alto Medioevo, 2013.

Bartolomei Romagnoli, Alessandra, Luciano Cinelli, and Pierantonio Piatti, eds. "Virgo digna coeli. Caterina e la sua eredità." Raccolta di studi in occasione dell 550° anniversario della canonizzazione di Santa Caterina da Siena (1461–2011). Pontificio Comitatato di scienze storiche, Atti e documenti 35. Vatican City: Libreria Editrice Vaticana, 2013.

Bell, Rudolph. *Holy Anorexia*. Chicago: University of Chicago Press, 1985.

Bianco, Maria Grazia, ed. *La Roma di Santa Catarina da Siena*. Atti del Convegno, Rome, 2000. Quaderni della Libera università Maria SS. Assunta 18. Rome: Studium, 2001.

Boesch Gajano, Sofia. "Caterina nella storiografia." In "Virgo digna coelo," edited by A. Bartolomei Romagnoli, L. Cinelli, and P. Piatti, 47–76. Vatican City: Pontificio Comitato di scienze storiche, 2013.

Boesch Gajano, Sofia, and Odile Redon. "La *Legenda maior* di Raimondo da Capua: costruzione di una santa." In *Atti del simposio internazionale cateriniano-bernardiniano*, edited by Domenico Maffei and Paolo Nardi, 15–35. Siena: Accademia Senese degli Intronati, 1982.

Cadková, Katarina. *Caterina da Siena e le sue guide spirituali*. Biblioteca dell'Istituto Storico Ceco di Roma 3. Rome–Prague: Historický ústav, Istituto Storico Ceco di Roma, 2014.

Courcelles, Dominique de. *Le "Dialogue" de Catherine de Sienne*. Classiques du christianisme. Paris: Cerf, 1999.

Duval, André. "Sainte Catherine, dominicaine." *La Vie spirituelle* 640–41 (1980): 828–51.

Duval, Sylvie. "*Comme des anges sur la terre.*" *Les moniales dominicaines et les débuts de la réforme observante (1385–1461)*. Bibliothèque des écoles françaises d'Athènes et de Rome 366. Rome: École Française de Rome, 2015.

Fawtier, Robert, and Louis Canet. *La double expérience de Catherine Benincasa (Sainte Catherine de Sienne)*. Bibliothèque des idées. Paris: Gallimard, 1948.

Gagliardi, Isabella. "Caterina madre dell'Osservanza domenicana: nascita e prima diffusione del movimento riformatore." In *Università, teologia e studium domenicano, dal 1360 alla fine del Medioevo*, edited by Roberto Lambertini, 123–35. Atti del Convegno di studi, 21–23 ottobre 2011, Bologna. Florence: Nerbini, 2014 [= *Memorie Domenicane*, n.s., 45 (2014)].

Hamburger, Jeffrey F., and Gabriela Signori, eds. *Catherine of Siena: The Creation of a Cult*. Turnhout: Brepols, 2013.

Jørgensen, Johannes. *Saint Catherine of Siena*. Translated by Ingeborg Lund. New York: Longmans, Green & Co., 1938. French original: *Sainte Catherine de Sienne*. Translated by Marie-Thérèse Fourcade. Paris: Beauchesne, 1919.

Lacelle, Elisabeth J., ed. *Ne dormons plus! Il est l'heure de se lever. Catherine de Sienne (1347–1380)*. Épiphanie. Paris: Cerf, 1999.

Loury, Marie, and Christian Loury, eds. *Catherine de Sienne. Catalogue de l'Exposition de la Chapelle du Palais des papes*. Avignon: Palais des papes, 1992.

Luongo, F. Thomas. *The Saintly Politics of Catherine of Siena*. Ithaca, NY: Cornell University Press, 2006.

Maffei, Domenico, and Paolo Nardi, eds. *Atti del simposio internazionale cateriniano-bernardiniano*. Atti del Convegno di studi, Siena, 17–20 April 1980. Siena: Accademia Senese degli Intronati, 1982.

Mangano Ragazzi, Grazia. *Par obeissance à la vérité. La discrétion comme pivot de la spiritualité de sainte Catherine de Sienne*. Translated by Marilène Raiola. Paris: Cerf, 2013.

Muessig, Carolyn, George Ferzoco, and Beverly Mayne Kienzle, eds. *A Companion to Catherine of Siena*. Brill's Companions to the Christian Tradition 32. Boston: Brill, 2013.

Raimbault, Ginette, and Caroline Eliacheff. *Les Indomptables. Figures de l'anorexie*. Paris: O. Jacob, 1989.

Tylus, June. *Reclaiming Catherine of Siena: Literacy, Literature, and the Signs of the Others.* Chicago: University of Chicago Press, 2009.

Vauchez, André. *Prophètes et prophétisme.* Paris: Seuil, 2012.

———, ed. *La Sainteté en Occident aux derniers siècles du Moyen Age.* Bibliothèques des écoles françaises d'Athènes et de Rome. 2nd ed. Rome: École Française de Rome, 2014. First published in 1981. An English translation of the first edition was published as *Sainthood in the Later Middle Ages.* Translated by Jean Birrell. Cambridge: Cambridge University Press, 1997.

Zancan, M. "Le lettere di Caterina da Siena." In *Storia della letteratura italiana. Le opere.* Volume 1, *Dalle origini al Cinquecento*, edited by Alberto Asor Rosa, 596–623. Turin: Einaudi, 1992.

Zarri, Gabriella, and Gianni Festa, eds. *Il velo, la penna e la parola. Le Domenicane: storia, istituzioni e scritture.* Atti del Convegno internazionale, 11–13 ottobre 2012, Bologna. Biblioteca di memorie domenicane. Florence: Nerbini, 2009.